THE AIA GOLD MEDAL

Richard Guy Wilson

McGraw-Hill Book Company

New York   St. Louis   San Francisco   Auckland   Bogotá
Hamburg   Johannesburg   London   Madrid   Mexico
Montreal   New Delhi   Panama   Paris   São Paulo
Singapore   Sydney   Tokyo   Toronto

To Ellie

_____

1234567890   HAL/HAL   89876543

ISBN 0-07-070810-X

The editors for this book were Joan Zseleczky and Martha Cameron,
the designer was Jan White, and the production
supervisor was Teresa F. Leaden. It was set in Palatino
by Progressive Typographers, Inc.
Printed and bound by Halliday Lithograph.

Library of Congress Cataloging in Publication Data

Wilson, Richard Guy, date.
The AIA Gold Medal.

Includes index.
1. AIA Gold Medal.   2. Architecture—United States—
Awards.   3. American Institute of Architects.   I. American
Institute of Architects.   II. Title.   III. Title: A.I.A.
gold medal.
NA2340.W5 1984   720'.79   83-9429
ISBN 0-07-070810-X

CONTENTS

CONTRIBUTORS

Bruce Abbey
Leslie N. Boney, Jr.
Robert Bruegmann
Kenneth H. Cardwell
Richard Chafee
Elias Cornell
Max Cramer
Gerald Dix
Leonard K. Eaton
James Marston Fitch
John Andrew Gallery
Kevin Harrington
William H. Jordy
Eugene F. Kennedy, Jr.
Henry J. Lagoris
William Lebovich
John Lobell
Travis C. McDonald
William C. Miller
Frederick Doveton Nichols
Richard Oliver
Carlo Pelliccia
Richard Peters
J. MacDougall Pratt
Sidney K. Robinson
Robert A. M. Stern
Sandra L. Tatman
Hans Van Grieken
Winston R. Weisman
Tony P. Wrenn

FOREWORD

My interest in the Gold Medal goes back many years. In 1965 I realized a boyhood dream to visit the Parthenon. As I stood on the windswept hill that dreary October afternoon, I thought that this marvel of proportion and workmanship in marble was really no longer the complete and useful structure that its architect and sculptor and painter had created. We have always revered the golden age of Greece; in fact the figures sculpted on the Gold Medal represent the three Parthenon designers — the architect Ictinus, the sculptor Phidias, and the painter Polygnotus.

My thoughts were refocused 5000 miles from Athens to Washington, where the Lincoln Memorial stands as a complete work of art and is now being visited and admired each day in a different way by thousands of citizens of the world. The Parthenon was a symbol of Greece and that country's contribution of the democratic form of government; our own Lincoln Memorial, designed in the same style, is a symbol of the United States and represents President Lincoln's concern for the unity of our democratic nation and the freedom of humanity. The thought kept coming back to me that the Lincoln Memorial, on a dramatic site comparable to the Acropolis, had not been reduced to a ruin; it was still there for the world to see and enjoy for its intended purpose.

Well, if I was mentally comparing the great Parthenon with the Lincoln Memorial, then who in reality was Henry Bacon, the Memorial's architect? I knew that he and I had attended the same Tileston School in Wilmington, North Carolina, and he had graduated as class salutatorian in 1884. But who was he really, what made him tick, and what other work had he done?

I returned home to find the answers, and therein lay my initial interest in the Gold Medal. I found that Bacon received this honor in 1923 from the hands of President Harding in a spectacular ceremony on the Mall at the Lincoln Memorial. As I learned more about Henry Bacon, I examined the list of other Gold Medalists and wondered who they were and why they had been singled out for this greatest of all honors our profession could bestow.

An opportunity to work on my interest came after I was elected secretary of the AIA College of Fellows in 1977 and became a member of the executive committee. Since its inception as an organization in 1952 the College of Fellows has dealt with elements which are not a part of the day-to-day operation of the professional society and do not relate to the business of architecture. One area of focus has been the creative process and the development of distinguished architecture. Specific reference to preparation of books and other publications to chronicle the lives of the Gold Medalists and other famous architects of the world are found in College minutes of 1961, 1963, 1967, 1968, and 1969; however, none of these starts reached fruition, and the project was dormant until we met as the College's executive committee in Palm Springs, California, in 1978.

Under the leadership of Chancellor George E. Kassabaum, and really without knowledge of the previous attempts, the committee decided to initiate a three-pronged effort related to the AIA Gold Medal. I was designated to coordinate the project, which would include a book of biographies of the Gold Medalists, a videotape of the living Gold Medalists, and personal examples of their talent, such as drawings, photographs, and sketches. Work on this program has been continuous since 1978. Now that the Gold Medal has passed its seventy-fifth anniversary, we can turn to this volume with great pleasure.

During the 1979 term of Chancellor David A. Pugh, videotapes were made at the National AIA Convention in Kansas City, with Gold Medalists Harrison, Belluschi, Johnson, and Pei being interviewed by Paul Goldberger, architecture editor of *The New York Times*. Janet Kutner of *The Dallas Morning News* interviewed the Gold Medalists' wives who were there: Ellen Harrison, Marjorie Belluschi, Eloise Skidmore, Dione Neutra, and Eileen Pei. Discussions were also taped with present members of Gold Medalist firms that had received 1979 honor awards. Walter Gropius's firm, TAC, was represented by Norman Fletcher, FAIA, and John Sheehy, AIA, while David A. Pugh, FAIA, spoke for Skidmore, Owings & Merrill. These videotapes have been made a part of the AIA archives. Interviews with subsequent winners—Sert, Giurgola, and Owings—have been added to the collection. Personal examples of Medalists' work have only been partially assembled to date.

In February 1980, a meeting was arranged in the AIA Washington headquarters to discuss the research, preparation, and writing of the individual biographies. In addition to College Chancellor Robert L. Durham, FAIA, and myself, it was attended by Richard Guy Wilson, Chairman, Architectural History Division, School of Architecture, University of Virginia, Charlottesville, Virginia; J. Norwood Bosserman, FAIA, Dean, UVA School of Architecture; David O. Meeker, Jr., FAIA, Executive Director, AIA;

Don Canty, Editor, *AIA Journal*; Muriel Campaglia, Director, AIA Public Relations; Jean Butler Hodges, President, AIA Foundation; and Susan C. Holton, AIA Librarian. The hope was expressed that the book could be an attractive volume worthy of the men and the esteem accorded to the Gold Medal itself.

As an outgrowth of this meeting, Richard Wilson was selected to write the book. He is a distinguished scholar who is well acquainted with the world of architecture. A frequent reviewer for the *AIA Journal*, he is well known as coauthor of *The American Renaissance*, which covers the period 1876–1917; thus Richard Wilson had a fresh viewpoint on many of the early Gold Medalists. His sabbatical in England and on the continent in 1981 permitted him to do original research on the men and their work. His enthusiasm for the project has been most inspiring. The appealing idea which he had was that the book should be more than a pure biography; it would treat the influence of these distinguished architects on society's taste.

Several potential publishers were contacted, and McGraw-Hill was selected. Their interest in the concept and their ready response has been most encouraging. Now, thanks to the cooperation of the vast McGraw-Hill Book Company and the support of the College of Fellows, not only has Richard Wilson discussed who the Gold Medalists are, but he has also put in perspective their work and its influence on society in the twentieth century.

I would like to acknowledge with gratitude the following College of Fellows Executive Committee members who have also assisted in the project's direction and funding: William R. Jarratt, FAIA, William C. Muchow, FAIA, Bernard B. Rothschild, FAIA, Donald L. Hardison, FAIA, and Vladimir Ossipoff, FAIA.

The College of Fellows hopes this book will satisfy some of your interests in the great Gold Medal.

Leslie N. Boney, Jr., FAIA
Chancellor, College of Fellows 1980–1981
Project Coordinator

ACKNOWLEDGMENTS

A study of this size depends on the assistance and cooperation of many people. First and foremost, I would like to recognize Leslie N. Boney, Jr., FAIA, past Chancellor of the College of Fellows of the American Institute of Architects, who initiated the project and has continued to support it over the past two years. Without his enthusiasm, the book would not be. The College of Fellows has contributed funds for the book. I would also like to acknowledge J. Norwood Bosserman, FAIA, past Dean of the School of Architecture at the University of Virginia, who knew of my interest in American architectural taste and the Gold Medal and brought Leslie Boney and me together.

Other important contributions were made by Tony Wrenn, the AIA Archivist, who sought and found obscure information; Professor Sidney K. Robinson of Iowa State University; Michael Zimny, State Preservation Office, Florida; Barbara Stonehocker and Betty Leake, Secretaries at the University of Virginia; and Joan Zseleczky, Editor at McGraw-Hill. The contributors who supplied the biographical entries for twenty-nine of the forty-four Gold Medalists are gratefully acknowledged. Their names appear at the end of their entries. I am responsible for the remaining unsigned entries. The Gold Medalists and their offices or former offices have often supplied me with information and photographs. In particular I would like to thank: the late Wallace K. Harrison, FAIA; Philip Johnson, FAIA; Hamilton P. Smith, FAIA, of Marcel Breuer Associates; Diane K. Miller of TAC; Nancy Brandenberg of Mitchell/Giurgola Associates; the office of Buckminster Fuller; I. M. Pei, FAIA, and Leicia Black; Janice M. Hoski of Holabird & Root; Roy Slade, John Gerard, and Susan Waller of the Cranbrook Academy of Art; Josep Lluis Sert, FAIA, and Penelope J. Karas; Pietro Belluschi; Mrs. Aliene Stein; Kenzo Tange and Urtec; Joan Capelin and Richard Staub of Haines Lundberg Waehler; Dione Neutra; Elissa Aalto, Hon. FAIA; B. Ann Oliszewicz of Fujikawa, Conterato, Lohan & Associates; Debra Joan Curtin, Sally Draht, and Louis Skidmore, Jr.,

AIA, of Skidmore, Owings & Merrill; Eugene F. Kennedy, Jr., FAIA, of Kennedy & Kennedy.

Thanks also go to the following for photographs: Erika Stoller of ESTO; Rollin R. La France; Mrs. Robert Chalfee; Robert Kincaid of Hedrich-Blessing; Guy Sussman; John Zukousky of the Art Institute of Chicago; Paul Whiting; John Harris of the RIBA Drawings Collection; Stephen Croad of the National Monuments Record, London; Barbara Krulik of the National Academy of Design; William Edmond Barnett; Douglas Kozel, AIA; Mrs. William Norris; Robert B. MacKay and Carol Traynor of the Society for the Preservation of Long Island Antiquities; and Sue Kohler of the Commission of Fine Arts.

Grateful acknowledgement is made for the assistance of: Ruth Kamen and Margaret Stackhouse of the Royal Institute of British Architects Library; Kristiina Nivari of the Museum of Finnish Architecture; Mrs. Lore Mike of the U.S. Office of Foreign Buildings; Mary Ison and Ford Petris of the Library of Congress; Roger Dixon, London; Elaine Evans Dee, Cooper-Hewitt Museum; Janet Parks, Avery Architectural Library, Columbia University; John Maves, Iowa State University; Susan Dart, Lake Forest, Illinois; Ann Sanders, TWA; Bernard B. Rothschild, FAIA; J. Winfield Rankin, Hon. AIA; Alan Powers, London; Richard Peters, AIA, University of California, Berkeley; Kenneth H. Cardwell, FAIA, University of Caifornia, Berkeley; Gerald Dix, The University of Liverpool; Charles Boney, Jr.; Louise Pingusson; Winston R. Weisman; Jean R. St. Clair, the National Academy of Sciences; Elias Cornell, Chalmers Technical Institute, Göteborg, Sweden.

Finally, to my wife, Ellie, and children, Kristina and Abigail, who had the (sometimes) enjoyable task of journeying with me to see some of the buildings herewithin, and living with me as I wrote about them, thank you.

As we went to press, Nathaniel Alexander Owings was awarded the Gold Medal in May 1983. His biography appears in Chapter 8.

GOLD MEDALISTS

The Gold Medal is the highest honor that the American Institute of Architects can bestow. It is awarded by the board of directors in recognition of most distinguished service to the architectural profession or to the AIA.

Sir Aston Webb	1907
Charles Follen McKim	1909
George Browne Post	1911
Jean Louis Pascal	1914
Victor Laloux	1922
Henry Bacon	1923
Sir Edwin Landseer Lutyens	1925
Bertram Grosvenor Goodhue	1925
Howard Van Doren Shaw	1927
Milton Bennett Medary	1929
Ragnar Östberg	1933
Paul Philippe Cret	1938
Louis Henry Sullivan	1944
Eliel Saarinen	1947
Charles Donagh Maginnis	1948
Frank Lloyd Wright	1949
Sir Patrick Abercrombie	1950
Bernard Ralph Maybeck	1951
Auguste Perret	1952
William Adams Delano	1953
Willem Marinus Dudok	1955
Clarence S. Stein	1956

Ralph Walker Centennial Medal of Honor,	1957
Louis Skidmore	1957
John Wellborn Root II	1958
Walter Gropius	1959
Ludwig Mies van der Rohe	1960
Le Corbusier	1961
Eero Saarinen	1962
Alvar Aalto	1963
Pier Luigi Nervi	1964
Kenzo Tange	1966
Wallace K. Harrison	1967
Marcel Breuer	1968
William Wilson Wurster	1969
Richard Buckminster Fuller	1970
Louis I. Kahn	1971
Pietro Belluschi	1972
Richard Joseph Neutra	1977
Philip Cortelyou Johnson	1978
I. M. Pei	1979
Josep Lluis Sert	1981
Romaldo Giurgola	1982
Nathaniel Alexander Owings	1983

THE AIA GOLD MEDAL

THE GOLD MEDAL

THE HIGHEST HONOR THE AMERICAN INSTITUTE OF ARCHITECTS CAN BESTOW
IN RECOGNITION OF DISTINGUISHED SERVICE TO THE PROFESSION

SIR ASTON WEBB 1907   CHARLES FOLLEN McKIM 1909   GEORGE BROWNE POST 1911   JEAN LOUIS PASCAL 1914   VICTOR LALOUX 1922   HENRY BACON 1923
SIR EDWIN LANDSEER LUTYENS 1925   BERTRAM GROSVENOR GOODHUE 1925   HOWARD VAN DOREN SHAW 1927   MILTON BENNETT MEDARY 1929
RAGNAR OSTBERG 1933   PAUL PHILIPPE CRET 1938   LOUIS HENRI SULLIVAN 1944   ELIEL SAARINEN 1947   CHARLES DONAGH MAGINNIS 1948
FRANK LLOYD WRIGHT 1949   SIR PATRICK ABERCROMBIE 1950   BERNARD RALPH MAYBECK 1951   AUGUSTE PERRET 1952   WILLIAM ADAMS DELANO 1953
WILLEM MARINUS DUDOK 1955   CLARENCE S. STEIN 1956   LOUIS SKIDMORE 1957   CENTENNIAL MEDAL OF HONOR RALPH WALKER 1957   JOHN WELLBORN ROOT
WALTER GROPIUS 1959   LUDWIG MIES VAN DER ROHE 1960   LE CORBUSIER 1961   EERO SAARINEN 1962   ALVAR AALTO 1963   PIER LUIGI NERVI 1964
KENZO TANGE 1966   WALLACE KIRKHAM HARRISON 1967   MARCEL BREUER 1968   WILLIAM WILSON WURSTER 1969   RICHARD BUCKMINSTER FULLER 1970
LOUIS I. KAHN 1971   PIETRO BELLUSCHI 1972   RICHARD JOSEPH NEUTRA 1977   PHILIP JOHNSON 1978   IEOH MING PEI 1979   JOSEP LLUIS SERT 1981
ROMALDO GIURGOLA 1982

SEVENTY-FIVE YEARS OF IMAGES AND IDEAS

The Gold Medal is the highest award the American Institute of Architects can bestow upon an individual. It is a great honor and represents a recognition of distinguished achievement and contribution to architecture.

For seventy-five years, from the initial Gold Medal to Sir Aston Webb in 1907 through the special Centennial Medal to Ralph Walker in 1957 and the most recent Gold Medal to Romaldo Giurgola in 1982, the award has gone to some of the most eminent and important architectural figures in the world. The Gold Medal awards represent individual achievement in design, planning, education, engineering, and the practice of architecture. The Gold Medalists have challenged the way the physical environment is seen and changed the way people live for all time. The seminal buildings of the past century have been created by the recipients of the AIA Gold Medal.

The intentions of this book are twofold: to honor and to illuminate. This book is intended to honor the forty-three AIA Gold Medalists, to provide a record of their achievement, and to explain why they were selected for the award. These men and their careers also illuminate changing perceptions and ideas of what has been considered good and important in architecture over the past 100 years.

The Gold Medal provides a historical record of "official architectural taste"—what the professional American architect has admired in the past seventy-five years. From the beginning the medal has been the prerogative

Recipients of the American Institute of Architects Gold Medal: entrance hall, AIA Headquarters Building, Washington, D.C.

of the board of directors of the AIA, whose members are representative of architects from different sections of the country. Thus, one of the distinctive features of the Gold Medal is that it reflects the taste of practicing professional architects, and not of critics, writers, and academics. Yet architecture does not exist in a void. The way in which knowledge of new buildings and ideas is disseminated throughout the world by architects, polemicists, historians, and architectural editors is a crucial issue in the making of reputations and, ultimately, of Gold Medal awards.

The determination of taste — how it is formed and what it means — is a theme of this book. A tension exists between publicly disseminated commentary on buildings and the reality of the practice of architecture. Who writes about architecture and how it is presented, both in the immediate, contemporary sense and as historical perspective, influences architectural perceptions. This study attempts to illuminate some of the shifts that have occurred during the period of the award and the ways that critics, historians, and editors have at times exercised great influence and displaced architects as the arbiters of taste. The role of photography and the discovery of architecture as a fit subject for museum exhibitions has created new avenues for the formation of architectural taste. While polls of most admired buildings must be used with care, the perspective they offer is instructive. Nearly 100 years of polls of American architects' preferences provide a unique record against which to measure the Gold Medal as an indicator of taste.

To claim that the Gold Medal is an accurate representation of the development of world architecture or, more specifically, the preoccupations of American architects is problematical. But the Gold Medal does provide a record of what has appealed to and articulated the professional American architect. Professional architects make a living from architecture, from transferring abstract ideas of form, space, structure, program, and image into designs that can be constructed. They have to deal with clients, and they have to defend and sell their ideas. The consequences of this for the Gold Medal are severalfold. The architects that have received the medal are successes, not simply in producing seminal buildings, but generally also as businessmen. Certainly there are exceptions: architects who have been honored primarily as educators, theoreticians, inventors, and designers. The Gold Medals to Jean Louis Pascal in 1914, Victor Laloux in 1922, Paul Cret in 1938, William Wurster in 1969, and Josep Lluis Sert in 1981 were at least partially because of their contributions to education, while the awards to Louis Sullivan in 1944 and Louis Kahn in 1971 were partially for their role as theoreticians and exponents of new or radical ideas on architecture. In fact, Sullivan and Kahn were never known as astute businessmen. But the Gold Medal list also recognizes men who have been eminently successful in translating abstract and difficult ideas into tangible form: George Browne Post in 1911, Milton Bennett Medary in 1929, Louis Skidmore in 1957, Wallace K. Harrison in 1967, and I. M. Pei in 1979. With few exceptions, all of the Gold Medalists have had large firms and ultimately been occupied with the large building. Walter Gropius, the 1959 Gold Medalist, made a fundamental and crucial change in twentieth-century architectural education — first at the Bauhaus in Germany and later at Harvard University in this country — but he also founded one of the most successful large-scale architectural practices, The Architects' Collaborative. Success in gaining clients and building architecture has been a fundamental key to the Gold Medal.

Because the award is made to individuals whose impact and contributions are long-lasting, the Gold Medal is conservative. It frequently goes to individuals who are at the peak of their careers or beyond. The often-repeated adage "Architecture is not a young person's profession" is nowhere more true than with the Gold Medal. Of those honored while living, the average age has been 70 years. Charles Donagh Maginnis summed up—tongue-in-cheek—his feelings on receiving the medal in 1948: "There is about it . . . such a disconcerting stamp of finality that seems to suggest to a recipient with a feeling for dramatic propriety that nothing is left to him now but to seek out some sylvan shade, there to lie down and peacefully expire. He has exhausted the logic of his career."[1]

One of the results of the age of the medalists is that this study tends to concentrate upon their careers prior to the receipt of the medal. Certainly not all medalists have gone to the "sylvan shade," for many have continued and even increased their prestige subsequent to the award. Pietro Belluschi, Kenzo Tange, Buckminster Fuller, Phillip Johnson, I. M. Pei, Josep Lluis Sert, and Romaldo Giurgola are testimony to continued productivity. Yet their careers were set in motion many years ago, and the reasons they have received the medal are already history.

The Gold Medal has been awarded posthumously on six occasions. Two of the medals, Charles Follen McKim's of 1909 and Howard Van Doren Shaw's of 1927, were actually voted on while they were still alive, but the recipients died before bestowal could take place. The decision to posthumously award Gold Medals to Bertram Goodhue in 1925 and Eero Saarinen in 1962 came within the year of their deaths. These awards were genuine outpourings of sentiment by professional architects to individuals who had already made major impacts upon architecture and whose lives were cut tragically short: Goodhue was 55 years old and Saarinen was 51 years old at death. The two remaining posthumous Gold Medals, those to Louis Sullivan in 1944 and Richard Neutra in 1977, were twenty years and seven years, respectively, after their demise. They represent attempts to make amends for past oversights and, especially in the case of Sullivan, reveal significant shifts in American architectural taste and perceptions of the past.

An aspect of the fundamentally conservative nature of the Gold Medal is that it seldom recognizes new directions in architecture during their infancy. What are "new directions"? When do the critical junctures occur and new ideas, approaches, and styles appear? This is a notoriously difficult question to answer and subject to all types of qualifications and exceptions. Obviously the historical perspective provided by the passage of time is crucial.

One of the revelations of the Gold Medal is that changes in architectural perceptions come slowly. Evolution, and not revolution, is the key, as Eliel Saarinen told the AIA in 1931.[2] In 1981, I. M. Pei echoed this theme at the AIA convention.[3] For many historians and architectural writers, the development of "modern" architecture has been the fundamental concern, the great event of twentieth-century architecture. Modernism does receive

A Monograph of the Works of McKim, Mead & White, Architectural Book Publishing, New York, 1915–1920.

Ausgeführte Bauten und Entwürfe von Frank Lloyd Wright, Ernst Wasmuth, Berlin, 1910

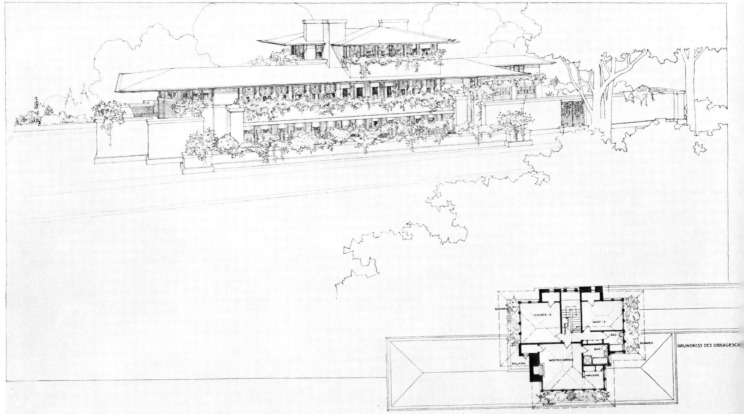

recognition in this book; however, a study of the Gold Medal reveals that modern architecture has been many different things to architects and that modernism was never a monolithic style or movement in terms of such phrases as the International Style, the New Brutalism, or any of the other catch phrases of the recent past. The Gold Medal has recognized the eclectic nature of American architecture, the polymorphous directions of the past 100 years on a worldwide scale.

Architecture, as numerous observers have noted, is the most conservative of the visual arts. The very nature of architecture — the long process of design followed by construction and the level of financial commitment, which is so much greater than in the other arts — of necessity makes it slower to change. Certainly drawings of projects or visionary schemes can make an impact, but violent shifts, where a cataclysmically different building appears, are rare. Rather, change comes through a long period of gestation. Charles F. McKim's Boston Public Library, 1887–1895, Frank Lloyd Wright's Robie House, 1907–1909, Le Corbusier's Villa Stein at Garches, 1927, Pietro Belluschi's Portland Equitable Building, 1943–1948,

McKim, Mead & White: Boston Public Library, Boston, Massachusetts, 1887–1895.

Frank Lloyd Wright: Frederick C. Robie House, Chicago, Illinois, drawing by Frank Lloyd Wright.

Le Corbusier and Pierre Jeanneret: Villa de Monzie-Stein, Garches, 1926–1927, elevation and perspective drawings by Le Corbusier.

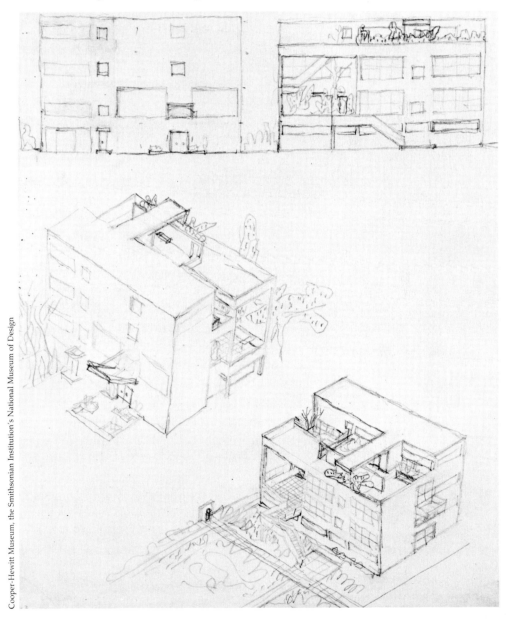

and Louis Kahn's University of Pennsylvania Richards Medical Research Building and Biology Building, 1957–1961, were radical — breakthrough — buildings for their day, yet their origins lay ten to twenty years in the past, and their impact came not so much immediately as ten or twenty years after construction. Obviously the role of the media again raises its head: How do buildings and the ideas they represent become known?

A correlative to architectural conservatism is that architecture is the art of the establishment.[4] "The establishment," for many people, implies homogeneous taste; this is inaccurate. There can be many tastes reflected in the establishment, and there can be many establishments. Chicago, in the years 1900–1920, had several groups of individuals that collectively represented the establishment, and they called upon different architects for their houses: Frank Lloyd Wright and Howard Van Doren Shaw. Wright's and Shaw's clients were all successful businessmen and, in a political, social, and cultural sense, what we would call conservative and establishment. Studies have shown though that the clients of the architects do differ as to group traits in terms of birth, education, methods of monetary success, and personal interests and hobbies.[5] Their houses, of course, differed radically. The Wright clients had low-slung prairie houses oriented to the midwestern land forms, and the Shaw clients lived in houses that recalled English arts-and-crafts and revival styles. Yet in spite of the visual and spatial differences between the two groups of houses, they all served essentially the same purposes. Wright was not the architect of an avant-garde, but of a conservative, establishment group. Wright and Shaw were friends and had respect for each other and their work despite major differences in architectural approach. And they both received the Gold Medal, though at very different times: Shaw in 1927, Wright in 1949. The gap in the awarding of the Gold Medal does reflect the two architects' different career patterns, but, just as significant, it also reflects changes in perception by the professional American architect of what is important.

The AIA Gold Medal provides one index to what has appealed to architects over the past 100 years. There is no single architectural theme as far as style, building type, or philosophy that has dominated the Gold Medal. The Gold Medal has honored the knowledgeable historicism of Charles F. McKim in 1909 and the new historicism of Philip Johnson in 1978. It has honored very different attempts to reject the past, as in the search for the modern by Bertram Goodhue and Josep Lluis Sert, who received the Gold Medal in 1925 and 1981, respectively. Stylistic dogma is not evident, as indicated by the contrast between Charles Donagh Magnnis and Frank Lloyd Wright, the 1948 and 1949 Gold Medalists, or between Marcel Breuer and William Wurster the 1968 and 1969 Gold Medalists. Several of the medalists have had significant careers as city planners, most notably Sir Patrick Abercrombie and Clarence Stein, who received the Gold Medal in 1950 and 1956. Two medalists have not been professional architects in the sense of training and registration: Pier Luigi Nervi, 1964, and Buckminster Fuller, 1970. Both Nervi and Fuller have been much involved with issues of architectural space and structure and have made fundamental contributions to the art.

If there are no overall themes, there are recurring patterns or concerns, such as the American infatuation with classicism. This is classicism, not so much as a style but as an academic tradition that aspires to formal solutions and systematic order. Variations on the theme of classicism can be observed in the earliest medalists, Sir Aston Webb, 1907, and Charles McKim, 1909, the reinterpretations of Sir Edwin Lutyens, 1925, Paul Cret, 1938, and Ralph Walker, 1957, and the modern approach of Mies van der Rohe, 1960, and Wallace K. Harrison, 1967. In recent years classicism has proven to be a theme of the work of Louis Kahn, 1971, Philip Johnson, 1978, and Romaldo Giurgola, 1982. The alternative to classicism is normally seen as romanticism, though in architectural terms this has generally meant an approach that seeks inspiration from vernacular and natural forms, as in some of the work of Bertram Goodhue, 1925, Ragnar Östberg, 1933, Frank Lloyd Wright, 1949, William Wurster, 1969, and Pietro Belluschi, 1972.

Some of the Gold Medalists have made significant contributions to the profession of architecture, serving the AIA in various capacities. Five medalists have been presidents of the AIA: Charles F. McKim, 1909, George B. Post, 1911, Milton Bennett Medary, 1929, Charles Donagh Maginnis, 1948, and Ralph Walker, 1957.

The Gold Medal is international in recognition of architectural achievement, and while no revelations with respect to country of origin are apparent, there are certain patterns to be observed. Those who have practiced in the United States have dominated the list, but the first Gold Medal in 1907 went to the English architect, Sir Aston Webb, and of the forty-three medalists, twenty-five were born abroad. Twelve medalists have had their primary practice outside the United States. For these, four have been from France, including Pascal, 1914, Laloux, 1922, Perret, 1952, and Le Corbusier, 1961 (who was born in Switzerland). Three have been English: Lutyens, 1925, and Abercrombie, 1950, in addition to Webb. The other foreign medalists have been natives and practitioners in Sweden (Ragnar Östberg, 1933), the Netherlands (Willem M. Dudok, 1955), Finland (Alvar Aalto, 1963), Italy (Pier Luigi Nervi, 1964), and Japan (Kenzo Tange, 1966). That so many of the foreign medalists cluster around the 1960s and that there are other medalists from the same period who were born and had significant practices abroad before coming to the United States (Walter Gropius, 1959, Ludwig Mies van der Rohe, 1960, Marcel Breuer, 1968) indicates the European orientation of American architecture in these years. American architecture has always been heavily influenced by foreign developments, and France, followed by Britain and then Germany, has exercised a crucial impact upon the United States.

Of the thirty-one "American" Gold Medalists, thirteen were born abroad. Of the naturalized Gold Medalists, three came as youths: Charles Donagh Maginnis, 1948, Eero Saarinen, 1963, and Louis Kahn, 1971. The other ten naturalized American medalists came later, some for their undergraduate education (I. M. Pei, 1979), and others for their graduate work (Pietro Belluschi, 1972, and Romaldo Giurgola, 1982). Of the remaining seven, with the exception of Richard Neutra, 1977, all had built substantial reputations for themselves. They generally came because of the perceived opportunities for building in the United States and unsettled political conditions at home.

The geographic distribution of the thirty-one American Gold Medalists leans heavily toward the east coast. The principal office of nineteen of the Gold Medalists can be defined as east coast, with twelve of them in New York City. Eight Gold Medalists have come from the midwest, and, not surprisingly, Chicago has been the home of four. Four Gold Medalists (if Pietro Belluschi is included) have come from the west coast. This pattern rather clearly indicates where the centers of architectural activity have been.

Other patterns that emerge from a study of the Gold Medal revolve around the commitment of the medalists to different architectural approaches and the dominance of these approaches at different times. The medal is, of course, given to individuals and not to architectural movements, and there is no evidence that successive boards of directors have attempted to maintain a fidelity and commitment to one specific architectural approach, philosophy, or style. Yet the Gold Medal, in perspective, does reveal certain patterns of belief and the dominance of beaux-arts classicism from 1907 to 1924, romantic imagery from 1925 to 1933, conservative modernism from 1938 to 1958, radical modernism from 1957 to 1977, and, since 1969, the emergence of a new direction still unnamed. There are frequently overlaps between the different groups, both chronologically and individually. At any point in time a wide divergence of opinion exists concerning what architecture should represent. Ragnar Östberg, Frank Lloyd Wright, and Walter Gropius represented fundamentally different architectural approaches, and yet all lived and designed within approximately the same time span. That they were honored with the Gold Medal in 1933, 1949, and 1959 respectively indicates the different appeals of their architecture to the professional American architect. All of the Gold Medalists had long and productive careers and encompassed many architectural expressions and ideas: for example, Charles F. McKim, whose shingle-covered resort cottage contrasts with the Renaissance palazzo form of the Boston Public Library, or Philip Johnson, whose glass house contrasts with the historicist AT&T Building. Yet most of the individuals appear to have formed a core of belief and commitment to certain architectural ideas and approaches, for which they were honored. The architectural approaches by which the individuals have been grouped in this study are not meant to be precise, and they are, in general, nonstylistic, though sometimes there are certain stylistic affinities. However, far more important are the affinities of architectural philosophy: What should be the generator of design? What role does history play? What do the buildings represent?

The question of what the Gold Medal currently represents has inherent difficulties. Many people believe that architecture is undergoing a transition: The modernist imperatives of the 1920s to the 1970s seem to be in question. Philip Johnson in his Gold Medal speech of 1978 said:

> We stand at an enormous watershed. We stand at a place that maybe we haven't stood for 50 years, and that is hard to grasp because we are right in the middle of it. It is the watershed between what we have all been brought up with as the modern, and something new, uncharted, uncertain and absolutely delightful.[6]

Announcement of a period of change or a watershed becomes tiresome, especially if one reads the architectural press; writers and editors proclaim them with increasing frequency — yearly, if not more often. Heedful of this caveat, one can sense the growth in the past ten to fifteen years of a new interest in the architectural past, with both the professional architect and the public. Obvious is a new interest in history — not just antiquity, the colonial period, or the great formers of modern architecture but also "the other side," the traditionalists and eclectics who had been forgotten or ignored. The reasons for this interest include the growth of the historic preservation movement, the bicentennial, the nostalgia craze, and a feeling of disillusionment with the promise of modern architecture. Certain aspects of the architectural watershed are superficial — the young turks challenging an older generation who thought they had all the answers — and the danger exists that whatever was good of the very recent modern will be thrown out with the bad. Yet, beyond the trading of historical allusion for modern structuralism, a more profound implication may be present. Possibly, there will be a more ecumenical acceptance of the past and various approaches to architecture. There is value in understanding the spatial circuits of an Edwin Lutyens plan, the structural dynamics of a Pier Luigi Nervi, and the landscape imagery of a Frank Lloyd Wright.

The award of the Gold Medal has not been all-inclusive. There are certain exclusions and omissions that are puzzling. Many foreign architects and certainly several Americans, such as Daniel Burnham, John Russell Pope, Albert Kahn, and Raymond Hood, might be cited as missing from the list. Yet their absence, and the inclusion of others, reveals the frame of mind of the American architect. An understanding of how the medal is actually awarded and the politics of the award is important. While there might be a certain shortsightedness in the awarding of some of the medals, there has equally been a certain courage. The AIA finally did give the Gold Medal to Frank Lloyd Wright, even though he had always been an outspoken opponent of what he termed "the arbitrary institute of appearances" and never a member. Romaldo Giurgola received the Gold Medal in 1982, even though earlier he and his firm, Mitchell/Giurgola Associates, had to resign the commission for a new AIA headquarters building when a conflict resulted with the Commission of Fine Arts on design review.[7]

The AIA Gold Medal is a great architectural honor. It is an award to individuals for accomplishment. And it is also a revelation of professional architectural taste, what it is and how it is made.

Notes

1 "Charles Donagh Maginnis Accepts the Institute's Gold Medal," *Journal of the AIA*, vol. 10, August 1948, p. 75.

2 "Address of Eliel Saarinen," *The Octagon*, vol. 3, April 1931, p. 8.

3 Pei quoted in Rosalie Merzback, "Gold Medalists Share Insights to Architecture, Cities, Energy," *F. W. Dodge Construction Report*, June 12, 1981, p. 13.

4 Norris Kelley Smith, *Frank Lloyd Wright: A Study in Architectural Content*, Prentice-Hall, Englewood Cliffs, N.J., 1966.

5 Leonard K. Eaton, *Two Chicago Architects and Their Clients: Frank Lloyd Wright and Howard Van Doren Shaw*, MIT Press, Cambridge, 1969.

6 Philip Johnson, "Remarks," *AIA Journal*, vol. 67, July 1978, p. 16.

7 Max O. Urbahn, "Evolution of the Octagon Building," *AIA Journal*, vol. 59, June 1973, p. 50.

Gold Medal presentation to Henry Bacon, Lincoln Memorial, Washington, D.C., May 18, 1923.

HISTORY AND POLITICS

Of the forty-three award ceremonies conducted for the Gold Medal, none have surpassed the May 18, 1923 pageant staged for Henry Bacon. Bacon received the medal on the steps of his most famous work, the recently completed Lincoln Memorial in Washington, D.C. (Plate 1). The ceremony began at nightfall when representatives of the chapters of the AIA and members of learned societies, trade and craft unions, including the National Academy of Design, the American Institute of Arts and Letters, the Brick-layers, Masons, and Plasterer's International Union, the International Hod Carriers, Building, and Common Laborers Union, and others gathered under a pavilion at the east end of the Reflecting Pool. Dressed in brilliantly colored robes and carrying banners and standards, they marched off in twin columns toward the opposite end, accompanying a barge that contained Henry Bacon and his collaborators on the memorial, Daniel Chester French and Jules Guerin, along with the AIA President, William Faville. Three trumpeters of the Marine Corps Band were also in the barge and played a "joyous processional," Walther's "Prize Song" from *Der Meistersinger.* The barge resembled state barges of "olden Time" and a yellow sail at midships contained the seal of the institute.[1] Locomotion was provided by ropes pulled by architecture students along the sides of the pool. Slow-burning torches and pods of incense braziers lined the sides. Heightening the drama was a soft rain that "seemed to flutter down" and recalled to one observer the prints of Hiroshige.[2] Additional Marine Corps bandsmen stationed at

13

the memorial provided accompaniment. At the end on the steps of the memorial, Bacon was greeted by Chief Justice William Howard Taft and presented to President Warren Gamaliel Harding, who gave him the Gold Medal.

An AIA press release described the intentions behind the event:

> In the United States there is little doubt but that a great flood of natural expression lies latent ready to be loosed as an outpouring of admiration for the great works of our time, so many of which are embodied in architectural achievement. It is thus the hope of the American Institute of Architects that this Pageant will serve the purpose of adding one more impulse toward the loosing of this stream.[3]

The ritualistic aspects of the Bacon award gives a clue to the understanding of the Gold Medal. None of the other Gold Medal ceremonies were as spectacular as Bacon's, though all have met Charles McKim's original intention "to make it a somewhat formidable affair."[4] Most have been conducted during a formal dinner, and the presentation has consisted of speeches of introduction, congratulation, and acceptance. The duration of the speeches has varied from lengthy addresses to short pithy remarks, as with Le Corbusier in 1961: "It is Le Corbusier who cleans the toilets of the 35 rue de Sèvres, and that's why I am the boss."[5] Other speeches have not been so admittedly "vulgar" and have concerned themselves with "the existence of eternal values in art," as in the address by Willem Dudok in 1955.[6] Traditionally, architects have admired ritual; their training directs them toward creating buildings that ceremonialize human actions. The origins of the Gold Medal lie in a period of American history when public displays of ceremony were of great importance. The intention of the Gold Medal was to enhance the prestige of American architecture both at home and abroad.

Inaugurated in January 1907, the Gold Medal is an apt indicator of the heady, optimistic, and confident air of Americans at the turn of the century. America had arrived at world-power status, with overseas colonies, and shortly the *White Fleet* would make its world tour. The loudly trumpeted public spirit of nationalism had a cultural implication: Americans would build a civilization containing the best of the old and the new. In many minds the arts flowered as never before and the similarity with the European Renaissance led naturally to naming the new equivalent the American Renaissance.[7]

While the term *American Renaissance* implies in most cases an academically and conservatively oriented expression as regards the visual arts, the entire notion that a comparison could be made between America and the riches of fifteenth-century Florence, sixteenth-century Rome, seventh-century France, or eighteenth-century England indicates the tremendous cultural vigor of America. Existing in the same time frame could be the diverse expressions of Edith Wharton and Frank Norris, John La Farge and Winslow Homer, John Dewey and William Graham Sumner, and George B. Post and Louis Sullivan. Consistency of expression was not the issue; rather, the American experience was unique, and as Prime Minister William Gladstone observed, "Europe may already see in North America an immediate successor in the march of civilization."[8]

Gold Medal presentation ceremony to Auguste Perret, United States Embassy, Paris, October 21, 1952. On left, Wells Bosworth, AIA delegate; center, Perret; right, the Honorable James C. Dunn, American ambassador.

AIA Archives

For architects this turn-of-the-century self-confidence took a number of forms, perhaps most openly in immense projects for the rebuilding of cities, whether Washington, D.C., or San Francisco. There were plans for huge malls, large squares, and long boulevards sprinkled with elaborate civic sculptures and triumphal arches wherein Americans could act out the rituals of citizenship. Another aspect was the world's fair or exposition mania that literally covered the landscape beginning with Chicago in 1893 and progressing through Nashville, Omaha, Buffalo, Saint Louis, Norfolk, and a host of minor sites by 1907. These expositions celebrated the union of art, architecture, and commerce. They were conspicuous-consumption displays of cultural riches and industrial production, and they rewarded quality—whether in liquor, furniture, painting, or architecture—with gold, silver, and bronze medals. In contrast to the attempt to create an ensemble, as in the cities or fairs, there were the tremendous building projects— of skyscrapers, state capitols, libraries, hotels, universities, and country houses— and the architect as never before, and perhaps never since, was a public figure. Architects were viewed as persons who, through their talent and knowledge, could rebuild the United States, providing a new face for cities and housing Americans of all classes in appropriate buildings.

American architecture appeared to have come of age; unique American expressions had been created for nearly all building types. Consensus certainly did not exist on what was the appropriate image or style for

World's Columbian Exposition, Court of Honor, Chicago, Illinois, 1893. From left to right: Agricultural Building, McKim, Mead & White; Machinery Building, Peabody & Stearns; Administration Building, Richard Morris Hunt; Electricity Building, Van Brunt and Howe; Manufacturers and Liberal Arts Building, George B. Post; Statue of Republic, Daniel Chester French.

Cram, Goodhue & Ferguson: Cadet Chapel, The United States Military Academy, West Point, 1903–1910.

American architecture, and one could find at one level the attempt to propose a heroic and monumental national image based upon classicism, as with the firms of McKim, Mead & White of New York or D. H. Burnham of Chicago, and on the other level those that argued for local regional expressions based on vernacular examples, as with Frank Lloyd Wright of Chicago or Bernard Maybeck of Berkeley. And there were other expressions: Bertram Goodhue and Ralph Adams Cram were the leaders of a substantial minority that claimed allegiance to the Gothic, not only for ecclesiastical structures but for universities and schools as well, as with their design of the United States Military Academy at West Point. On a different level there was commercial architecture—high-rise office buildings and hotels or low-rise stores and factories, which also appeared to have evolved unique expressions, whether of structure or ornament. The Chicago school is frequently seen as the leader in commercial architecture, yet great differences existed between the ornamental expressionism of a Sullivan and the structural minimalism of Hollabird & Roche. The historical styles could also play a role. George B. Post headed one of the largest architectural firms in the country, designing extremely pragmatic structures overlaid with a wealth of historical references.

The turn-of-the-century period has been interpreted as a battle between the forces of the new—the originals such as Wright and Sullivan—and the old—the imitators such as McKim, Mead & White and

George B. Post: New York Stock
Exchange, New York City,
1901–1904.

George B. Post, who still looked to European models. The lines of division,
though, were not so firm; beaux-arts classicism could invade even the works
of a Wright or a Maybeck, and on the other hand, McKim, Mead & White
could still design shingle-covered cottages. More importantly, the diversity
of expression was seen as typically American. In a country so large, regionalism — within bounds — was felt to be appropriate. While European images
were obvious in the work of Post or McKim, Mead & White, they were
transformed, and in composition, attention to detail, structure and technology, and execution the buildings were American.

Certainly the topic of whether American architecture should be
unique or derivative was hotly debated. The concern was at least a century
old, for the question of what the character of the American arts should be
had occupied individuals such as Thomas Jefferson, Alexis de Tocqueville,
Ralph Waldo Emerson, Horatio Greenough, and others. Of the many
spokesmen for American architecture at the turn of the century, Charles F.
McKim and Louis Sullivan represent well the opposing viewpoints. Louis
Sullivan wrote:

> When we ask an architect to build a twenty-odd-story office
> building, and he throws up a swaggering mass of Roman rem-
> nants, he is not a scholar but a brute. . . . Roman does not mean
> American, never did mean American, never can mean American.
> Roman was Roman; American is, and is to be, American.[9]

17

Adler & Sullivan: World's Columbian Exposition, Chicago, Illinois, 1893, Transportation Building.

In contrast, there was McKim:

> Architecture is the oldest of the arts. Its principles were developed early in the history of the race; its laws were formulated long before the Christian era; and its most exquisite flowers bloomed under skies that fostered the production of beauty. . . . The architect who would build for the ages to come must have the training of the ages that are past. . . . Purpose and location change with each problem; and happy is he who can satisfy those two requirements without being called upon to also invent the language in which he speaks.[10]

In spite of the debate over the appropriateness of style or image for America, most architects felt that public awareness had arrived at a new plateau. Many Americans still went abroad to the École des Beaux-Arts as a "finishing school," but in most cases they had received their initial training at home. Architectural education in the United States was flourishing; the first architectural school had been founded in 1865, and by 1906 there were thirteen schools that offered degrees in architecture. In addition there were a number of other organizations that supplied training, such as the Architectural League and the Beaux-Arts Society, both of New York, the T-Square Club of Philadelphia, the Chicago Architectural Club, and many others. On the national level, the American Institute of Architects began to achieve some success in convincing states to pass registration laws, with the implication that architecture was a profession on the same level as doctors or lawyers. In 1894 the American School of Architecture in Rome was founded by Charles F. McKim, to be renamed in 1896 the American Academy in Rome. A charter from Congress was received in 1905. The implication of such actions was the belief that American architecture had arrived at a position where it could compete with Europe.

Confirmation of the sense of destiny in American architecture came not only from the American public but, just as important, from abroad. For Europeans, American architecture for much of the nineteenth century had been generally regarded as a wasteland, pale reflections of current English and French movements. In the 1870s foreign opinion began to shift and increasingly laudatory comments on the state of American architecture began to appear. James Fergusson's 1862 edition of *History of the Styles of Modern Architecture* devoted only a few pages to the United States with generally deprecating remarks, but Robert Kerr's 1891 supplement claimed that "the old-fashioned character of the former American building, prosaic and dull even when on the largest scale, has completely changed, so that graceful and picturesque edifices, of all degrees of magnitude, of all classes, of all styles, are to be found everywhere."[11]

Kerr's observations can be paralleled by those of others. In 1888 at the Royal Institute of British Architects (RIBA) during discussion on the award of the Royal Gold Medal to Baron von Hansen of Vienna, past president Alfred Waterhouse noted that the recent death of Henry Hobson Richardson of Boston, "had precluded the placing of his name on the list of those eligible for the distinction of Royal Gold Medalists."[12] The importance of American architecture to Britain is testified to by numerous articles, as well as the decision to award the 1893 Royal Gold Medal to Richard Morris Hunt. The award was viewed by both the Americans and the English not simply as a recognition of Hunt's work, which culminated in that year with the central structure at the World's Columbian Exposition in Chicago, the Administration Building, but additionally as a tribute to the achievements of American architecture.[13]

Others besides Hunt received foreign approbation as a result of Chicago's White City. In 1894, Louis Sullivan was awarded the gold, silver and bronze medals of the French Union Centrale des Arts Décoratifs for his work at the fair. A commissioner for the Union Centrale believed most of the fair to be derivative; only one of the "palaces," Adler & Sullivan's Transportation Building, was "successful and original," and "it has the special merit of recalling no European building."[14] In actuality Sullivan appears to have been more honored for his novel decoration, and he had sent to France models of his ornamental work, including the Golden Door from the Transportation Building. The problem of assessing Sullivan and the Chicago fair would not be unique to the 1890s: His later reputation would vary between being a structuralist and an ornamentalist. The fair was controversial. Young Banister Fletcher, who visited the United States in 1893, questioned upon his return to England the possibility of "the reproduction of these great classic designs all over the country" which would "stay for a prolonged period true progress of art in America." He felt that Sullivan's Transportation Building did not have the answer. It had an interesting color scheme, he thought, but the finest structure was McKim, Mead & White's Agriculture Building.[15] And, of course, the fair in ensuing years has continued to be controversial: It has been seen as the nadir or the zenith of American architecture, depending upon the viewpoint. Not disputable, though, is the fact that the Chicago world's fair brought American architecture to the attention of the world and showed a new scale of accomplishment.

Other expressions of foreign interest in American architecture can be found through the turn-of-the-century years: In Scandinavia, the Low Countries, and Germany there is considerable evidence of American influence and foreign perusal of American periodicals.[16] In 1903 the Royal Institute of British Architects again honored an American: Charles McKim received the Royal Gold Medal. By 1910 the international importance of American architecture was assured. In that year two events are noteworthy: first, in Germany the publication by Wasmuth Verlag of a lavish portfolio and a smaller book on the architecture of Frank Lloyd Wright, and second, in England the publication in the *Journal of the Royal Institute of British Architects* of an assessment of American architecture by Charles Reilly, head of the Liverpool School of Architecture. Reilly had recently visited New York and Washington and claimed:

> America has seized the lead, and as far as I can judge has established an architecture which, while satisfying the most exigent of modern requirements, is yet the conscious heir, as ours, let us hope, is in yet the unconscious, of those forms and thoughts which, born in Greece more than 2,000 years ago, have been for the last four centuries, and must always be, with negligible deviations, the spring and motive of our life and art.[17]

American classicism would heavily influence English and other European Architects well into the 1920s, and yet concurrently the influence of Frank Lloyd Wright can also be felt in the work of the young Walter Gropius at the Fagus Factory office building (1911) and the Cologne Werkbund Exhibition building (1914).

Against this background of artistic and cultural activity and increasing public approbation and foreign interest in American architecture, the American Institute of Architects established the Gold Medal. Charles McKim is certainly the most central figure in its founding. The leading American architect of his day, McKim had long been interested in the AIA, serving in various capacities over the years, including secretary, 1878, and then president, 1902–1903. In its early years, since its founding in 1857, the AIA had been principally a small, elite, east-coast club, with little national impact. In fact, in 1884 midwestern architects, primarily from Chicago, set up a rival organization, the Western Association of Architects, to combat what they saw as eastern snobbishness. In 1889, the AIA and the Western Association amalgamated, with the guarantee that the AIA would be truly national. The passage of the Tarnsley Act of 1893, allowing private architects to compete for government jobs, pushed the AIA more onto a national stage. In 1898, the annual convention voted to move the headquarters from New York to Washington, and in 1899, under the presidency of George B. Post, the AIA rented the Octagon, a venerable building of major historical and architectural significance. Under McKim's direction the AIA later purchased the building. The selection of the Octagon as its headquarters, only two blocks from the White House, indicates the status for architecture and the institute that Post and McKim aspired to. McKim, in spite of a terror of public speaking, was a consummate politician and felt the AIA should strive to secure "the cooperation of influential men . . . and good-will of Government officials." Glen Brown, for years the secretary-treasurer of the AIA, recalled McKim "abhorred devoting the time of conventions to changes in by-laws which did nothing to advance or better the association."[18]

In 1904, just after McKim had stepped down from the presidency, discussion began on suitable ceremonies for the fiftieth anniversary of the AIA, which would be in 1907. McKim sent a letter to a board of directors meeting in St. Louis, noting how impressed he had been with the dinner and award connected with his Royal Gold Medal of the year before and suggesting that the AIA institute an annual dinner to which important public figures would be invited. Also he proposed as a seal for the dinner a copy of the Pope Julius medal of Bramanti's original design for St. Peter's in Rome.[19] The first "formidable" dinner took place in Washington in January 1905. A result was the obtaining of a charter for the American Academy in Rome from Congress. President Theodore Roosevelt attended and spoke about the importance of architecture for the new American empire.[20]

Throughout the remainder of 1905 the idea of the AIA giving a medal on the occasion of the fiftieth anniversary was discussed, and the board of directors obtained a copy of the relevant sections of the RIBA bylaws concerned with the Royal Gold Medal.

Instituted in 1848, many important architectural figures had received the Royal Gold Medal, beginning with Charles Cockerell. The most recent medalist had been Sir Aston Webb, 1905. Awarded annually, the decision on the medal was suggested by the council (board) of the RIBA to the membership for their approval and then forwarded to the monarch for presentation.[21] An "unwritten rule" was that the medal went, in rotation, to an English architect, a foreign architect, and a literary person with architectural instincts.[22] By February 1906, the board of directors of the AIA had decided upon awarding a medal, and they asked McKim "to talk with the President in an informal way, about having this medal presented as the President's Medal, upon the nomination by the American Institute of Architects."[23] McKim was a personal friend of President Roosevelt, having served on the McMillan Commission for Washington, D.C., remodeled the White House, and designed an addition for Sagamore Hill. Both the president and Secretary of State Root replied that it would be inappropriate to name the award the President's Medal, though they left open the possibility that they might attend and participate in the award ceremony.[24] The directors then rethought the award, making it strictly an AIA medal and voted to give it to Sir Aston Webb, in January 1907 "provided he can be present."[25]

Since 1905, McKim had been requesting that the AIA honor Sir Aston.[26] His position in England was analogous to McKim's in America, strongly political; he had designed some very prominent public buildings, such as the Mall and the Admiralty Arch. He had just received the Royal Gold Medal and had been president of the RIBA in 1903 when McKim had

Edwin H. Blashfield: program cover for AIA 50th Annual Anniversary Banquet and Gold Medal presentation, January 9, 1907.

received his medal. The AIA stipulation that Webb "be present" to receive the medal was believed necessary to gain proper public exposure. On June 29, 1906, at the request of the board McKim wrote Webb informing him of the establishment of the AIA Gold Medal, stating: "It is the unanimous desire of the Board that you be invited to become the first recipient."[27]

The actual design of the Gold Medal went through two stages. First, the board of directors asked the chairman of the Fiftieth Anniversary Committee, Edgar B. Seeler, and members, George B. Post and Walter Cook, to work on a design with the specifications that if a portrait was incorporated, it should be that of Washington. However, Post got together with McKim, and they took the design out of the hands of the committee and hired Adolph A. Weinman, a sculptor. Weinman had done extensive work for both men's firms on buildings such as the Wisconsin State Capitol, the Madison Square Presbyterian Church, and Pennsylvania Station. His design is unabashedly American Renaissance. On the obverse are the profiles of Polygnotus, Ictinus, and Phidias and beneath, the symbols of their callings, a brush, a sculptor's modeling tool, and a compass and triangle. The unity of the arts is symbolized on the reverse: A standing eagle with upraised wings plucks a laurel branch rooted to a rock. On the rock "AIA" is inscribed and below, "A. A. Weinman. M.C.M.VII." The name of the recipient and the date were to be placed on the rim.[28]

Webb received the Gold Medal during the annual convention on January 8, 1907, at a night reception at the Corcoran Gallery of Art in Washington, D.C. The presentation was made by AIA President, Frank Miles Day of Philadelphia, who noted in his address that the award was in recognition of the indebtedness of American architecture to British architecture and especially the classic tradition. Webb responded with the usual homilies of appreciation and also a report on the current status of British architecture. The evening closed with an address by the British chargé d'affaires, Esme Howard, and the presentation of the members and guests to Sir Aston Webb.[29] The next evening a formal banquet was held at the New Willard Hotel, toasts were drunk, and Secretary of State Root, Justice E. D. White of the Supreme Court, and others were present. For the dinner, Edwin Blashfield, a prominent mural painter, designed a program cover showing Columbia wrapped in the American flag and holding the Gold Medal. The event met McKim's requirement of "a formal and imposing social function."[30]

In February 1908 the board of directors again took up the subject of the Gold Medal; they decided that it should be awarded every three years and alternate between "a foreigner and an American, subject to modification." The board would make the nomination and notify the recipient, "subject to his attendance to receive the medal in person and subject to the ratification by the Convention." The medal would be conferred at the following convention.[31] This procedure was unofficial, and since it wasn't part of the bylaws, it left an opening for the board not only to modify the sequence of nationality but to forego the convention approval. This they would do at various times until 1930, when the Gold Medal formally became part of the bylaws.

The second Gold Medal to be awarded, Charles McKim's, was the

22

first posthumous award. The decision was made at the December 1908 annual convention, with the award to take place the following year, December 1909.[32] McKim died in September 1909, and the award ceremonies became a memorial meeting in December, with an exhibition of the work of McKim, Mead & White held at the Corcoran Gallery in Washington, D.C. Speakers at the meeting included President William H. Taft, Senator Elihu Root, and the former ambassador to Great Britian, Joseph Choate. The Gold Medal was accepted by his surviving original partner, William R. Mead, and then handed to McKim's daughter Margaret.

The 1911 award to George B. Post and the 1922 award to Laloux subverted the nationalist sequence as well as the triannual rule. The gap between Pascal's medal of 1914 and Laloux's of 1922 was a result of both World War I and the fact that in 1916, before American entry into the war, the board asked for nominations, but the chairman of the committee, C. Grant Lafarge, reported: "The award should be inevitable for very great and conspicious achievement . . . and finding that no person quite meets all of these requirements the Committee reports that it makes no recommendation for this year."[33] Neither Pascal or Laloux received the medal in person. Henry Bacon received the medal in 1923.

The dual medals of 1925, presented to Edwin Landseer Lutyens and Bertram Grosvenor Goodhue, represented an attempt by the board of directors to be international and also to honor the memory of a recently departed American architect of the first rank. In May 1923, Lutyens was proposed to the board as the "outstanding" English architect and deserving of the medal.[34] The board, though, felt the need for an investigation of other possibilities, and in the next year Sir Giles Gilbert Scott and John James Burnet were added to the list. Scott, a member of the famous family of English architects, was well known as the designer of many buildings, including the then-under-construction Liverpool Cathedral. Burnet, slightly older, came from a prominent Glasgow family of architects. His practice in London was large even by American standards. He was known for office buildings and public structures, such as the Edward VII Gallery extension to the British Museum. All would receive the Royal Gold Medal: Lutyens in 1921, Burnet in 1923, and Scott in 1925. One reason for the AIA board's determination to give the Gold Medal to an Englishman was that Thomas Hastings had received the Royal Gold Medal in 1922. In March of 1924, board member Charles Zantzinger of Philadelphia was directed to ask the RIBA in a "confidential letter" who would be best of the three. The RIBA evidently recommended Lutyens, for in November 1924, the board of the AIA voted to award the medal to him.[35]

In the meantime, Bertram Goodhue had died in April 1924, at the relatively young age of 55. An outpouring of sentiment followed. (Coincidently, Louis Sullivan died ten days before Goodhue, and his death was also noted prominently by the AIA.) At the February 1925 meeting of the board it was proposed that Goodhue be awarded the Gold Medal posthumously, and a vote of members was taken through the mail.[36] Only a few members demurred, and at the 1925 annual convention of the AIA in New York City a reception was held at the Metropolitan Museum and both Lutyens and Goodhue received the award. President D. Everett Waid explained the dual award by announcing that "formally . . . in the year 1924 the Institute voted to award" to Lutyens and then "in the year 1925" a vote was taken for Goodhue.[37] Lutyens was present to receive his medal in person; Mrs. Goodhue received the medal for her late husband.

Lutyens's account of his United States visit and the ceremony adds a touch of poignancy. Well-versed in the accomplishments of American architects, he had never before visited the country, and in spite of his terror of public speaking, he welcomed the chance. He arrived in New York by boat and was met by Harvey Wiley Corbett, who was designing Bush House at that time. Lutyens immediately began a round of dinners and sightseeing; McKim's Pennsylvania Station impressed him as "a colossal hall modelled on the baths of Caracalla, 150 feet high, of no use." From New York Lutyens took the train to Washington and observed the landscape: "The countryside is dreadfully untidy. Little white houses of wood stuck down anywhere, no gardens, are squalid and distressingly unhandsome. The dog-wood was in flower, and cherry blossom." In Washington he inspected the site for the new British Embassy he was designing and toured the city. The plan and buildings in general were admirable: "The Lincoln Memorial is a great thing, but placed too close to the Washington Obelisque, which again blocks everything, so big is it" (Plate 3). Back in New York more parties, and then the big event:

> "The whole lot of us went to the Metropolitan Museum where we mustered. . . . They all put on robes, there was a standard-bearer. We were marshalled at the top of a great staircase going down straight into the Great Hall, packed with folk. The band burst out in a blaring march and the standard-bearer goose-stepped down the staircase lined with folk. Then the President in robes, and then me in dinner shift, with Davis who was once Ambassador to us, followed by about 40 robed gentlemen. . . . Everybody standing, and I poor me, before a huge Union Jack. The President spoke a Eulogy and gosh!! called to me and put the medal round my neck — a great and very beautiful golden disc. Then up gets Mr. Davis and he spoke a *most* moving eulogy on what I had done — in the Cenotaph, all very upsetting, and then I was all of a quake and more miserably moved than can be described. I asked the President if I could read my speech, to which he assented. Then I was committed!
>
> "It took ten minutes. I had much better not have read it, but just said thank you as best I could. But off I went, and it got worse. I found myself trembling, but could steady myself by pulling the paper I was reading from hard. Then I was frightened that if I pulled as hard as I was pulling, the paper would burst. . . .
>
> "At last it was over. No one could hear me, which was something. The band played God Save the King and the Star Spangled Banner. . . .
>
> "The Corbetts motored me down to the docks where I got on the steamer about 11:30. . . . My cabin is surrounded with the bottles of whiskey they were always giving me and which I shall bring home as a trophy, of rum-running and my abstinence.
>
> "It was an ordeal.
>
> "Corbett had said that though I had never told him my impressions, he knew what they were . . .
>
> "It is a wonderful place.

"Alive, keen friendly.

"Great achievement and alive only to make achievement.

"The scale they can adopt is splendid.

"The sky-scrapers are growing from monstrosities to emotions of real beauty, and the general character of the work is of a very high standard indeed, far higher than anything on the Continent or England.

"They are all children with gigantic toys, growing, I believe, to equally gigantic manhood.

"But the place does want tidying up and pulling together."[38]

The reputation of the Gold Medal as a tombstone to a career emerged with the 1927 and 1929 awards. Howard Van Doren Shaw's medal was voted on by the membership at the May 1926 annual meeting. Shaw, on his way to the meeting, contracted pernicious anemia in Baltimore and was hospitalized. The board informed his wife of the award just before his death. Reportedly his last words were, "I am pleased." To try to correct the appearance that the medal only went to the departed, the board of directors, in December 1928, voted to give the award to Milton B. Medary, who was 56 years old. At the board meeting it was noted: "The award should be made now to permit its enjoyment by the recipient while in the prime of his professional life, and should not be deferred, as has been the case with others." Also the procedure was changed. "The award should be made by this Board, at this meeting, and the Medal presented at the Convention of 1929."[39] Medary received the medal at ceremonies at the Corcoran Gallery in Washington, D.C., in April 1929. He died unexpectedly in August 1929.

In 1930, the AIA substantially altered the bylaws, and the method of award the board instituted in 1929 became official. Qualifications were stated as "distinguished service to the profession of architecture or to the Institute"; the decision would be made entirely by the board of directors, and not subject to ratification by the members or a convention. The medal could be given only once a year, and the board had to make its decision at least half a year before the convention at which the presentation would take place. As usual, the presence of the recipient was requested, but not required. Posthumous medals were allowed.[40] In 1942 the bylaws were rewritten, and the Gold Medal procedure, which stayed the same, became part of the rules of the board.[41]

The modifications made the Gold Medal decision, which from the beginning had been controlled by the board, now exclusively their duty and hence even more reflective of the professional architect's viewpoint and position. The size of the board has varied over the years: in 1907 there were thirteen directors, in 1930 fourteen, in 1957 seventeen, and in 1982 forty-three. Membership is composed of the officers (president, vice presidents, secretary, treasurer) and regional directors, who are elected on the basis of their region. The number and definition of regions can vary; in 1982 there were eighteen, including Pennsylvania, Texas, California, New England, Western Mountain, and South Atlantic. It is intended that the board represent a broad cross section of the membership.

The first award under the new rules again reflected the institute's attempt to be international. Ragnar Östberg had been proposed as early as

1929. He was joined in nomination the next year by Sir Giles Gilbert Scott of England, previously nominated in 1924, and Horatio Acosta y Lara of Uruguay. Some sentiment was expressed that the medal should go to a member of the Pan American Union. Lara was both a founder and president of the Pan American Congress of Architects. This view did not prevail and Östberg was voted the Gold Medal for 1933. He did not receive it until 1934, when he came to the United States, and a special ceremony was held in the East Room of the White House, with President Franklin D. Roosevelt making the presentation.

The practice that developed initially in 1923, and again in 1930, of nominating several different individuals became firmly established in the later 1930s. Eliel Saarinen was first proposed in 1936 (Paul Cret won), then again in 1939 and 1941, before the decision was reached, in 1946, to award him the medal in 1947. Willem Dudok was first proposed in 1936; he received the Gold Medal in 1955. Long-time consideration has been given to others: Pietro Belluschi was first nominated in 1954, and he received the Medal in 1972; Wallace K. Harrison was proposed at least as early as 1958 and received the award in 1967.[42] Also established was that the supporting information, "portfolios" in a sense, would be submitted and circulated with the nomination. Nominations had to be made by a board member, and while local chapters could submit materials and supporting letters, these had to be introduced by a board member. The result in some people's mind was a campaign for the Gold Medal, and at a 1957 board of directors meeting some members expressed the view "that they were very sorry to see that the membership had instituted a campaign on behalf of a nominee for the Gold Medal, as the award of the medal is a prerogative of the Board and such a campaign could do much to lessen the chances of the nominee in whose behalf it was instigated." Other members of the board, such as Phillip Will, Jr., of Chicago, claimed on the contrary "he did not mind the idea at all.'[43]

The intention of the Gold Medal to honor individual accomplishments was tested in 1935 when the Boston firm of Perry, Shaw & Hepburn was nominated for its work at Colonial Williamsburg. The board decided the medal was for individuals and instead presented "embossed certificates of appreciation" to John D. Rockefeller, Jr., Dr. W. A. R. Goodwin, Arthur A. Shurcliff, and Perry, Shaw & Hepburn "in recognition for their accomplishment in restoring Williamsburg."[44]

The problem of recognizing architectural firms would continue for many years. The Gold Medal was intended to recognize individual accomplishment, and yet the changes that were occurring in the practice of architecture could not be ignored. The rise of the large corporate office, the increased scope and complication of services, and the subordination of the individual to the group was a reality. In 1957, Louis Skidmore, the head of the New York office of Skidmore, Owings & Merrill, received the Gold Medal. Cited in support of his medal were the seminal structures, Lever House and Connecticut General Life Insurance, yet they were designed by an office team headed by Gordon Bunshaft. Skidmore's contribution was as a businessman, salesman, and organizer of the full-service comprehensive architectural office, and the firm led the way in making the International

Style the image of American business. The Skidmore medal was in a sense an office award; as a consequence, in 1961 the AIA established the Architectural Firm Award, which Skidmore, Owings & Merrill received in 1962. Over the years, the Architectural Firm Award has provided an instructive parallel with the Gold Medal; in 1964 the firm was The Architects' Collaborative, in 1965, Wurster, Bernardi & Emmons, and in succeeding years, 1968, I. M. Pei & Partners, in 1976, Mitchell/Giurgola Associates, and in 1977, Sert, Jackson & Associates. The award is given to a firm "which has consistently produced distinguished architecture for a period of at least ten years." Clearly the award goes both to firms that produce distinctive designs and to those that frequently have designers that stand out as individuals in their own right.

Gold Medal presentation ceremony to I.M. Pei, Convention Center, Kansas City, Missouri, June 6, 1979. On left, I. M. Pei; right, Ehrman B. Mitchell, AIA president.

The rise of critics and historians to the position of tastemaker and their influence upon the Gold Medal becomes evident in the 1940s, particularly in the award to Louis Sullivan. Sullivan had died in poverty in 1924, though he was not so completely forgotten as some critics have asserted: As noted earlier, Sullivan's death was mentioned prominently by the AIA.[45] In his later years his *Autobiography of an Idea* was published both serially in the *Journal of the AIA* and then as a book under the AIA imprint. Also the AIA published his *A System of Architectural Ornament According with a Philosophy of Man's Powers.* How much of Louis Sullivan's fall from grace can be attributed to his buildings and ideas, and how much to his personality and drinking habits will be a subject of endless debate. Certainly he was not completely forgotten, but his caustic personality did not earn him friends. However, after his death and in the 1930s and early 1940s, Sullivan was rehabilitated by critics and historians such as Lewis Mumford, Henry-Russell Hitchcock, Nikolaus Pevsner, Hugh Morrison, and Sigfried Giedion as one of the formers of modern architecture.[46] The tendency to romanticize Sullivan as a forgotten prophet proved irresistible: As the AIA citation said: "He fought almost alone in his generation, lived unhappily, and died in poverty." In 1943, he was awarded the Gold Medal for 1944, though because of wartime conditions it was not presented until 1946. George Elmslie, a former member of Sullivan's firm and his literary executor, was selected to receive the award, but because of ill-health he could not attend. Paul Gerhardt, Jr., of Chicago accepted the medal and read an address by Elmslie and excerpts from Sullivan's writings. Elmslie claimed that Sullivan "never faltered in his efforts to liberate architecture from the scholastic thralldom evolved in traditional architectural forms and in our relics of feudalism, with their many inhibitions relative to what he believed to be the normally creative spirit of many. All this was done in the face of savage and witless criticism abroad [in] the land, which continued during the remaining years of his life."[47]

The Sullivan medal reflected the AIA trying to make amends and introduce into the roll call of the Gold Medalists an individual who was now recognized as one of the genuine American greats. The "taste" of the AIA had, in a sense, caught up with what Sullivan was doing and saying in the 1890s and 1900s. However, there is another side to the award: Americans love the underdog, the lonely and tragic fighter.

Sullivan's Gold Medal again provoked disagreement over posthumous awards, and in 1946 Ralph Walker proposed to the board they be eliminated.[48] They were not, but no further posthumous medals were given until Eero Saarinen's 1962 award.

Far more controversial was Frank Lloyd Wright's Gold Medal and his recognition by the institute. Wright had never been a member of the AIA and had publically condemned it and most American architects, living and dead. Still, many architects viewed Wright as one of the true American greats. He had received the Royal Gold Medal of the RIBA in 1941. Consequently his omission from the AIA Gold Medal list became embarrassing, no matter what some professionals thought of him. In May 1943, Wright's name was proposed by Ralph Walker for consideration for a Gold Medal in 1944. Also nominated were Sullivan and Bernard Maybeck. Submitted with Wright's name were letters of endorsement by various chapters and members, and, as the minutes circumspectly recorded, "letters opposing this award were also submitted." Both Wright's and Maybeck's nominations were subsequently ruled incomplete, since they lacked portions of a biographical statement and a "history of attainments."[49] In 1946, Wright was again proposed, along with Eliel Saarinen and Charles D. Maginnis, by a special Gold Medal committee on which Ralph Walker served. Sarrinen won the medal for 1947, and Maginnis for the next year. At the annual meeting, June 1948, in Salt Lake City, where Maginnis's presentation took place, a petition was presented to the Committee on Resolutions asking the board of directors to give the Gold Medal to Wright. Salient points of the long resolution read:

> Frank Lloyd Wright had done more than any living architect to fire the imagination of youth and to inspire the profession; BECAUSE, his great contribution to world-wide architecture has gained for him professional recognition throughout the world; BECAUSE, of his creations of great artistic beauty; BECAUSE, of his pioneering in the use of building materials and space design; AND FINALLY, BECAUSE, of his stature among the architects of our time; BE IT THEREFORE RESOLVED, it is the sense of this meeting that the 1949 Gold Medal of the American Institute of Architects be awarded to FRANK LLOYD WRIGHT.

Attached to the petition were 140 signatures by members, friends, and students, including Hugh Stubbins, Douglas Haskell, Morgan Yost, James

M. Fitch, Jr., Pietro Belluschi, Harold Bush-Brown, Turpin Bannister, Albert Martin, and John Rex.[50]

While most of the board of directors could sense the feelings of the membership, not all of the directors were convinced, and William Adams Delano was also nominated for the Gold Medal in 1949. Another special committee was set up to consider the Gold Medal and the materials submitted. At the December 1948 board of directors meeting, Joseph D. Leland, chairman of the committee, "summarized the extensive correspondence received with regard to Mr. Wright. . . . Most of the letters were in favor of Mr. Wright's and few opposed."[51] The president of the institute, Douglas William Orr, of New Haven, spoke strongly in favor of Wright's nomination, noting a concern with the institute's image in denying the award to one of the very few architects who had received public acclaim and recognition. A few board members opposed and "discussed Mr. Wright's morals (personal) and his unethical conduct, such as stealing jobs, bidding for work, and undercutting other architects in his quest for desirable commissions." The Delano nomination was dispensed with, and finally the vote came down to a single holdout, Branson V. Gamber of Detroit. Gamber, the personal architect of Henry Ford, was strongly opposed, but sensing the mood of the board, "he announced that he would absent himself from the room, and in his absence The Board could take a vote!" The board voted unanimously to give the Gold Medal to Wright. The question then arose whether he would accept it and a hurried telephone call was made, so the award could be rescinded in case he refused. "The Institute did not want that much egg on its face!"[52] Wright accepted.

Wright's Gold Medal speech showed him in top form: "It's been a long time coming from home. But here it is at last, and very handsome indeed." He lambasted American architecture as being "in the gutter," questioned the "democratic aspects" of most architecture, and trotted out and whipped once again the Cape Cod Cottage. Yet he also admitted: "I feel humble and grateful. I don't think humility is a very becoming estate for me, but I really feel touched by this token of esteem from the home boys."[53]

The Frank Lloyd Wright Gold Medal controversy led indirectly to one other result. At the Salt Lake City convention of June 22–25, 1948, where the Wright petition was presented, a convention resolution was passed asking for the establishment of an "Annual National Awards" program.[54] *Progressive Architecture* magazine had just instituted a program, which was published in the June 1948 issue. Douglas Orr, the institute president, was head of the magazine's jury. At the December 1948 board meeting Albert F. Heino of Chicago made a proposal for "Honor Awards for Current Work," which was accepted.[55] *Progressive Architecture* agreed that after their 1949 awards (the program already announced) they would discontinue the effort. The AIA Honor Awards, which got underway in 1949, were dominated by "modern" work from California, which had also dominated the *Progressive Architecture* awards.[56] The Wright medal controversy and the awards program were obviously attempts by some members to push what they perceived as a conservative establishment into a recognition of contemporary realities of modern work.

The 1949 Gold Medal did not signal the end of the Wright controversy within the AIA, for in 1956 the board of directors announced that in 1957, the hundredth anniversary of the institute, they would give, in addition to the Gold Medal, a "Centennial Medal of Honor." The intent of the Centennial award was similar to the Gold Medal, except grander, and it was "to be given only once."[57] It was to honor "the architect of the century," an individual notable for architectural design and service to the institute. Sentiment came from some members that Frank Lloyd Wright should be recognized; as Edmund R. Purves, the executive director, summed up, "It would be the worst kind of public relations for us to ignore the existence of the greatest architect the world has ever seen at the Centennial Celebration." Purves's own opinion on Wright was not positive: "I think that his influence is largely synthetic and will not be lasting."[58] After considerable discussion the board voted to give the Gold Medal for 1957 to Louis

Centennial Medal for Ralph Walker, reverse, Julian H. Harris, sculptor.

Skidmore and the superaward, the Centennial Medal, to Ralph Walker. Walker, a member of a large corporate New York firm, had designed several widely publicized buildings and had served the institute in a number of positions, including director and president. The citation to him read in part: "In this year when the Institute feels entitled, through reaching an established maturity, to express unashamedly its affection for a favorite and gifted son, this token of its pride needs no further warrant."[59]

The problem of Wright's being honored was never resolved. He still was not a member of the AIA and did not attend the convention. Several people suggested to Walker that Wright should be mentioned in his acceptance speech, but while Walker spoke of Emerson, Thoreau, Melville, Voltaire, Verne, and other writers and philosophers, the only architect mentioned by name was Bulfinch, and in reference to moldings![60]

The Wright-Walker centennial controversy had a certain irony. As noted, Walker played a prominent role in obtaining the Gold Medal for Wright, and then in 1955 he attended a testimonial dinner in Madison, Wisconsin, where Wright received a contribution of over $10,000 to help pay his taxes. At the dinner Walker was the major speaker and hailed Wright: "Call it courage, even obstinancy, if you will; it is that quality which, to all of us, will make him stand out for our emulation, and make him great for all time."[61]

For Ralph Walker personally, the Centennial Medal proved to be bittersweet. In 1959, Walker and his partners were charged with violations of the AIA's code of ethical standards, soliciting work from the state of New York for a campus plan when another firm, Moore & Hutchins of New York City, were already under contract. Walker himself was not personally involved in the violation, but he took it as a personal insult and attack upon his integrity by members of the board of directors of the AIA, who were, he felt, enemies. On November 9, 1959, the board suspended for two years the corporate memberships of Walker and his partners, Stephan Francis Voorhees, Perry Cole Smith, Benjamin Lane Smith, and Charles S. Haines II. This was rescinded by the board in 1960 after Walker and partners won a suit in the superior court of New York; and then in January 1961 a new trial was held by the board which resulted again in the suspension of Walker and his partners. Walker, whose ego knew no bounds, published two pamphlets attacking the AIA and defending his partners and himself, and after repeated attempts to resign — which were denied, since he was under charge — he finally succeeded on January 15, 1961, after the retrial. The "architect of the century," a former director and president of the AIA was no longer a member.[62] Reportedly he even melted down his medal.

A campaign began to induce Walker back into the institute and end the embarrassing situation. Finally on his eightieth birthday in 1969, Walker rejoined, though never admitting any guilt and still charging the board with "playing politics."[63]

Subsequent Gold Medals have not proved to be so disputatious as the Wright and Walker awards, though controversy has arisen. Between 1958 and 1982, eighteen Gold Medals were given, one every year except 1965, 1973 to 1976, and 1980. The procedures for the award were slightly modified by the board of directors so that a positive vote by three-quarters of the members, rather than the original unanimous decision, was required for successful nomination. Still, decisions could not be reached every year. The rules also stated: "Anyone, living or dead (not necessarily an American or an architect), who the Board believes qualified, is eligible to receive the Gold Medal."[64] One result was the award to the only nonarchitects, the medals to Nervi and Fuller in 1964 and 1970. Certainly, both had always been considered architects by the public, and both had made substantial contributions. Especially in the case of Fuller, who had never been taken too seriously by the professional architect — though he had long been a favorite of schools and students — the Gold Medal made him into a figure of substantial stature instead of a "dome-house bug."[65]

The AIA's concern with public image has been apparent in a number of cases. In 1956 at the board meeting that decided upon awarding the Gold Medal to Clarence Stein, the minutes circumspectly note that the Royal Institute of British Architects had decided to give their Gold Medal to Walter Gropius.[66] Gropius would receive the AIA medal in 1959. Richard Neutra's Gold Medal, coming in 1977, seven years after his death, did raise some questions as to whether American architecture was so bereft of direction that it had to turn to the dead. I. M. Pei would certainly have received the Gold Medal before 1979 but for the disaster of the John Hancock Tower in Boston where the glass fell out and the building was uninhabitable for several years. His triumph with the National Gallery east-wing extension that opened in 1979 brought him back to center stage and made him a logical choice (Plate 2). Philip Johnson's 1978 medal caused some argument, since Johnson appeared to be taking up the line of the so-called postmodernists. Shortly before Johnson actually received the medal, the design of the AT&T Building in New York that he had done with partner John Burgee was announced (Plate 3). The design was interpreted by many as an affirmation of the recent historicizing trend evident in the work of many younger architects, and it became a cause célèbre, making the front page of *The New York Times*.[67] In his Gold Medal speech Johnson claimed: "John Burgee and I have never done anything that caused the stir that the A. T. & T. design has. It's become sort of a symbol of our times which surprises us very much." In

Gold Medal presentation ceremony to Marcel Breuer, Portland Hilton Hotel, June 26, 1968. On right, Robert L. Durham, AIA president.

AIA Archives

the same speech, Johnson claimed the "shift in sensibility" noted in Chapter 1 and, as part of the program at the annual convention, invited eight "kids" (architects under 50 years old) to discuss their work and the "diversity" and "pluralism" present in so much of recent American design.[68]

The award of the Gold Medal has not been without controversy nor flaws, yet overall it has recognized most of the major figures in architecture for the past 100 years. It illuminates the taste of American architects and illustrates what they perceive as important, which has not been consistent in any stylistic or architectural sense, and equally has not been the same as some critics, editors, and historians would have us believe. The Gold Medal, as I. M. Pei has said, is "the greatest architectural honor in America." It represents quality in architecture, and also the changing architectural tastes of the past 100 years.[69]

Notes

1   AIA Press Release, May 16, 1923, AIA Archives.

2   Harry F. Cunningham, "The Convention as One Architect Saw It," *Journal of the AIA*, vol. XI, June 1923, p. 239.

3   AIA Press Release, May 16, 1923, AIA Archives.

4   Board of Directors, *Minutes*, AIA, June 20, 1904, AIA Archives.

5   Le Corbusier, "Remarks," *AIA Journal*, vol. 35, June 1961, p. 97.

6   Willem Marinus Dudok, "Acceptance Address," *Journal of the AIA*, vol. 24, August 1955, p. 55.

7   Richard Guy Wilson, Dianne Pilgrim, and Richard Murray, *The American Renaissance, 1876–1917*, Brooklyn Museum/Pantheon, New York, 1979.

8   Quoted in Robert Kerr, "Supplement," in James Fergusson, *History of the Modern Styles of Architecture*, 3d ed., Dodd, Mead, New York, 1891, p. 373.

9   Louis Sullivan, *Kindergarten Chats and Other Writings*, Wittenborn Art Books, New York, 1947, p. 136, 139.

10 Charles F. McKim, "Address of the President," *Proceedings of the 36th Annual Convention of the AIA*, 1902, McKim Collection, New York Public Library, New York.

11 Kerr, "Supplement," in Fergusson, *History of the Modern Styles*, pp. 351, 327–342.

12 "Sessional Notes," *Journal of the Proceedings of the RIBA*, vol. IV, new ser. 8, February 9, 1888, pp. 141–142.

13 J. Macvicar Anderson, "Presentation of the Royal Gold Medal," *Journal of the Royal Institute of British Architects*, ser. 3, vol. 1, June 22, 1893, pp. 425–428.

14 Andre Bouilhet, "L'Exposition de Chicago," *Revue des Arts Décoratifs*, vol. 14, 1893–1894, p. 68, quoted in Hugh Morrison, *Louis*

Sullivan, Prophet of Modern Architecture, Norton/Museum of Modern Art, New York, 1935, p. 189.

15   Banister Fletcher, "The Godwin Bursary Report, 1893," *Journal of The Royal Institute of British Architects,* ser. 3, vol. 1, 1894, p. 557.

16   Leonard K. Eaton, *American Architecture Comes of Age,* MIT Press, Cambridge, 1972; Dudley A. Lewis, "Evaluations of American Architecture by European Critics, 1895–1900," Ph.D. thesis, University of Wisconsin, 1962; Robert Koch, "American Influence Abroad," *Journal of the Society of Architectural Historians,* vol. 18, 1959, pp. 66–69; H.-R. Hitchcock, "American Influence Abroad," in Edgar Kaufman, Jr. (ed), *The Rise of an American Architecture,* Praeger/Metropolitan Museum of Art, New York, 1970; Dimiti Tselos, "Richardson's Influence on European Architecture," *Journal of the Society of Architectural Historians,* vol. 29, 1970, pp. 156–162; A. W. Reinink, "American Influences on Late Nineteenth-Century Architecture in the Netherlands," *Journal of the Society of Architectural Historians,* vol. 29, 1970, pp. 163–174; and *Nederlandse Architectuur 1880–1930 Americana,* Rijksmuseum Kroller-Muller, Otterlo, 1975.

17   Charles H. Reilly, "The Modern Renaissance in American Architecture," *Journal of the Royal Institute of British Architects,* ser. 3, vol. 17, June 25, 1910, p. 635.

18   Glen Brown, *Memories 1860–1930,* private printing, Washington, D.C., 1931, pp. 215–216. On the history of the AIA see above and Henry Saylor, "The AIA's First Hundred Years," *Journal of the AIA,* vol. 27, May 1957, pp. 1–181.

19   Board of Directors, *Minutes,* AIA, June 20, 1904. See also Charles H. Moore, *The Life and Times of Charles Follen McKim,* Houghton-Mifflin, Boston, 1929, p. 259.

20   Charles H. Moore (ed.), *The Promise of American Architecture,* AIA, Washington, D.C., 1905.

21   Board of Directors, Executive Committee, AIA Minutes, March 2, 1906; "By-Laws," *RIBA Kalandar,* 1904–1905, p. 51; "The Royal Gold Medal. Origin and Early History," *Journal of the Royal Institute of British Architects,* ser. 3, vol. 28, June 25, 1921, pp. 474–476.

22   Aston Webb, "Address, the Royal Gold Medal Presentation to Mr. Charles Follen McKim," *Journal of the Royal Institute of British Architects,* ser. 3, vol. 22, June 27, 1903, p. 441.

23   Board of Directors, *Minutes,* AIA, February 8, 1906.

24   Board of Directors, *Minutes,* AIA, October 24, 1906.

25   Board of Directors, *Minutes,* AIA, May 19, 1906.

26   McKim to William Boring, January 20, 1905, McKim Collection, Library of Congress.

27   Brown to McKim, May 22, 1906, AIA Archives; McKim to Webb, June 29, 1906, McKim Collection, Library of Congress.

28   Board of Directors, *Minutes,* AIA, October 24, 1906; Sidney P. Noe, *The Medallic Work of A. A. Weinman,* American Numismatic Society, New York, 1921, p. 30.

29   *Proceedings of the 40th Annual Convention of the AIA,* Gibson Bros., Washington, D.C., 1907, pp. 104–112.

30   Brown, *Memories,* op. cit., p. 217.

31   Board of Directors, *Minutes,* AIA, February 3, 1908, p. 378.

32   *Proceedings of the 42d Annual Convention of the AIA,* Gibson Bros., Washington, D.C., 1909, p. 15.

33   Board of Directors, *Minutes,* AIA, July 6–7, 1916, p. 94.

34   Board of Directors, *Minutes,* AIA, May 14–15, 18–19, 1923, p. 6.

35   Board of Directors, *Minutes,* AIA, March 4–6, 1924, p. 5; no RIBA reply has been located; *Minutes* November 18–20, 1924, pp. 11–12.

36   Board of Directors, *Minutes,* AIA, February 18–20, 1925, p. 2.

37   D. Everett Waid, "Address," *Proceedings of the 58th Annual Convention of the AIA,* AIA, Washington, D.C., pp. 95, 98.

38   Quoted in Christopher Hussey, *The Life of Sir Edwin Lutyens: The Lutyens Memorial Volumes,* Country Life, London, 1950, pp. 456–460.

39   Board of Directors, *Minutes,* AIA, December 9–10, 1928, p. 17.

40   "By-Laws Chapter XIV," *Annuary,* AIA, Washington, D.C., 1931–1932. p. 133.

41   *By-Laws and Rules of the Board,* AIA Washington, D.C., 1943, p. 63.

42   Unfortunately the minutes of the board of directors from the late 1940s on are inconsistent in recording the nominations for the Gold Medal. In some cases, the actual names are listed; in others, a simple notation that two or three nominations were made, with no listing of candidates.

43   Board of Directors, *Minutes,* AIA, November 11–16, 1957, p. 68.

44   Board of Directors, *Minutes,* AIA, December 3–6, 1935, p. 4.

45   Claude Bragdon, "Louis H. Sullivan," William L. Steele, "Louis Henri Sullivan," and Wallace Rice, "Louis H. Sullivan," all in *Journal of the AIA,* vol. 11, May 1924, p. 241, and June 1924, pp. 275–276, 294.

46   Henry-Russell Hitchcock, Jr., *Modern Architecture: Romanticism and Reintegration,* Payson & Clarke, London, 1929; Sigfried Giedion, *Space, Time and Architecture,* Harvard University Press, Cambridge, 1941; Hugh Morrison, *Louis Sullivan,* op cit.; Lewis Mumford, *The Brown Decades,* Harcourt, Brace, New York, 1931; and Nikolaus Pevsner, *Pioneers of the Modern Movement from William Morris to Walter Gropius,* Faber & Faber, London, 1936.

47   "To Louis Henri Sullivan: The Gold Medal of the American Institute of Architects," *Journal of the AIA,* vol. 6, July 1946, pp. 3, 4–5.

48   Board of Directors, *Minutes* AIA, May 8, 1946, p. 26; *Minutes,* August 7–8, 1946, p. 12.

49   Board of Directors, *Minutes,* AIA, May 22–24, 143; *Minutes,* AIA, December 1–3, 1943, p. 21.

50   *Proceedings of the 80th Annual Convention of the AIA,* AIA, Washington, D.C., 1948, p. 551.

51   Board of Directors, *Minutes,* AIA, December 1, 1948, p. 19.

52   J. W. Rankin, personal communication, May 27, 1981. Assistant secretary to the board in 1948, Rankin has served in other capacities since. His account is based upon personal conversations with the board members, including Branson U. Gamber.

53   Frank Lloyd Wright, "Acceptance Speech," *Journal of the AIA,* vol. 11, May 1949, pp. 199–207.

54   *Proceedings of the 80th Annual Convention of the AIA,* AIA, Washington, D.C., 1948, pp. 532–533.

55   Board of Directors, *Minutes,* AIA, December 1, 1948. An inaccurate account of the founding of the awards program is given in: Edmund R. Purves, "The AIA 'Honor Awards for Current Work' and its Juries," in Wolf von Eckardt (ed.), *Mid-Century Architecture in American,* Johns Hopkins Press, Baltimore, 1961, p. 29.

56   von Eckardt, *Mid-Century Architecture in America;* "Annual Progressive Architecture Awards," *Progressive Architecture,* vol. 29, June 1948, pp. 47ff.; "The Third [sic] Annual Progressive Architecture Awards, 1948," vol. 30, June 1949, pp. 43ff.

57   Leon Chatelain, Jr., "Introduction of Ralph Walker, FAIA, Winner of the Centennial Gold Medal of Honor," *Journal of the AIA,* vol. 28, June 1957, p. 146.

58   Purves to Kirby, December 14, 1956. AIA Archives.

59   "The Centennial Convention Awards," *Journal of the AIA,* vol. 27, March 1957, p. 109.

60   Ralph Walker, "Acceptance Speech," *Journal of the AIA,* vol. 28, June 1957, p. 146–148; information on Walker from William Jordy, personal communication, October 23, 1980.

61   "Wisconsin Makes Peace with Wright," *Architectural Record,* vol. 117, April 1955, p. 18; Ralph Walker, "Frank Lloyd Wright," testimonial speech, University of Wisconsin, February 10, 1955, in AIA Archives.

62   Ralph Walker, *Ralph Walker, The American Institute of Architects 1921–1961,* private printing, New York, 1961; J. Win. Rankin, personal communication, May 27, 1981; Ralph Walker File, AIA Archives.

63   Ralph Walker to Rex W. Allen, AIA president, October 22, 1969, Ralph Walker File, AIA Archives.

64   "Chapter XVIII," *Rules of the Board of Directors,* AIA, Washington, D.C., 1978, pp. xxiii–1.

65   John McHale, "Buckminster Fuller," *Architectural Review,* vol. 120, July 1956, p. 12.

66   Board of Directors, *Minutes,* AIA, March 1, 1956, p. 37.

67   *The New York Times,* March 31, 1978, p. 1, B4.

68   "Convention '78: Remarks by Gold Medalist Johnson," *AIA Journal,* vol. 67, July 1978, p. 16–22; see also, p. 22–90.

69   I. M. Pei, personal communication, January 7, 1981.

BY THE PEOPLE AND DEDICATED

FREE TO ALL

McKim, Mead & White: entrance to
Boston Public Library, Boston,
Massachusetts, 1887–1895.

BEAUX-ARTS CLASSICISM

The six Gold Medalists from the period 1907–1923— Sir Aston Webb, 1907, Charles Follen McKim, 1909, George Browne Post, 1911, Jean Louis Pascal, 1914, Victor Laloux, 1922 and Henry Bacon, 1923—reflect the orientation of the American architectural establishment toward classicism and the dominant influence of the École des Beaux-Arts. For most Americans, classicism remained the one official "American" or "national" style. The public image of America was classical, whether beginning back in the eighteenth century with Andrew Hamilton's Independence Hall in Philadelphia and the Virginia State Capitol in Richmond, designed by Thomas Jefferson, or progressing on ahead into the nineteenth century with various state capitols, city halls, post offices, and libraries. Other styles such as Gothic and Romanesque were advanced as substitutes but met with little long-term success. The reemergence of classicism in the 1880s as promoted by the American Renaissance generation of Charles McKim and George Post confirmed an earlier tendency.

The new grand scale of American classicism had a certain flavor that was particularly that of the École des Beaux-Arts.The French school provided a systematic approach to architecture that greatly influenced the Americans, so much so that all six of the Gold Medalists between 1907 and 1923 were recognized for their French sympathies, whether or not they had actually studied in Paris at the École.

Historically, the École traced its origins back to 1671 and the founda-

35

tion by Louis XIV's minister, Jean Colbert, of the Académie Royale d'Architecture. During the French Revolution, the Académie was suppressed, along with other royalist institutions, but it reemerged as the École Spéciale d'Architecture, and in 1819 the École des Beaux-Arts was established, formally uniting in one school the disciplines of painting, sculpture, and architecture. Architecture at the École always retained a separate identity, and during the nineteenth century it became the most prestigious institution for the instruction of architecture in the world. The location in Paris contributed to its standing, and while Rome and various other locations could provide inspiration, Paris became the center of the art world, a position it maintained until 1940, when it was supplanted by New York.

The École very self-consciously assumed the mantle of cultural and artistic leadership, claiming an alliance with the great traditions of earlier civilizations. In a letter written to "a young American architect" about 1900, Jean Louis Pascal suggested these themes and the universality of classicism:

> The time has passed when contemporary civilisations ignore even their nearest neighbours. There are no materials, no inventions, no new processes of one country that are not immediately known over all the world and employed everywhere. These two factors of the renaissance in art prevent us all, you as well as us, from creating significant forms or a so-called new style, which will not be a growth, a development, but one epoch simply in the upward and continuous evolution of architecture. More and more will architecture become universal — there will be little besides the conditions of climate and material which will make diversity — unless there becomes a religious evolution, and that is hardly to be looked for in this century of tolerance.
>
> It is necessary to glance at your side. Having at the first step reached the culminating point of all civilization, having had no childhood apart from ours, your composite country can offer no solutions which are not the consequences of our past conquests, which are yours now, as well as ours.[1]

The École was government-sponsored, and tuition was free to Frenchmen and to foreigners. The total number of students entering each year varied from 37 in the 1820s to approximately 100 in the 1890s.[2] Foreign attendance naturally differed from one year to the next, though from the 1870s onward Americans and Swiss became the predominant foreign nationalities at the École. Between 1892 and 1900, 700 students were admitted to the École: 124 were Americans, comprising about 17 percent of the population.[3] Open to any French student between the ages of 15 and 30, the École administered a series of tests in history, mathematics, drawing, and design which the prospective student had to pass before gaining admission. In addition, foreign students had to provide a letter of introduction from their consul or ambassador.

Instruction at the École took place in two ways. First, the École offered a series of formal lectures in the areas of history, architectural history, geometry, construction, and other subjects. Second, there were the *ateliers* (studios) and *concours* (competitions). In addition to applying to the École, students also applied for acceptance into one of the *ateliers*, which were teaching studios headed by prominent architects and were (with a few exceptions) completely independent of the École, the *patron* (head) being paid by the students. In them the student learned design. The atmosphere of the *ateliers* varied from patron to patron; Louis Sullivan claimed that the *atelier* of Émile Vaudremer was "the damnedest pigsty I ever got into."[4] A later American in Victor Laloux's *atelier* recalled the Louis XV paneling, the broad staircase and low risers, so low that "you sort of fell upstairs, it was so comfortable."[5]

At varying times throughout the year *concours* for different subjects (design, rendering, construction, and others) were announced by the École. Depending upon their year or status, students were expected to enter these competitions; it was through the design and criticism of their entries that instruction would take place. The most important competition was the *grand projet*, the Prix de Rome; the winner was granted, at government expense, a period of four to five years of study in Rome at the French Academy. This was open only to French nationals, not to the foreign students.

Officially, the École des Beaux-Arts did not teach a style of architecture; rather it taught a logical, rational system of architecture, based upon good judgment and certain rules. Classicism, with its heritage of books and learning beginning with Vitruvious Pollio and reinvigorated by individuals such as Alberti, Vignola, and Blondel, had an academic status that virtually guaranteed its dominance. Other historical styles were certainly acceptable if the program of the building or the location suggested them, as with churches or houses.

The preoccupation with style led to the establishment in 1874 of the Prix Duc, a yearly competition for the invention of a new style of architecture. Yet the major direction of the École was toward teaching monumental architecture, with a consequent stress on rules of composition that called for symmetry, clear division and hierarchy of spaces, and impressive exteriors. Planning for a rich sequence of spaces was certainly one of the main tenets of the École's system. The student was expected to have a wide knowledge of history and prototypical solutions to different problems. The manner in which students were taught to evolve a design, wherein they were put in isolation (*en loge*) and expected to come up with a *parti*, or solution, to the problem, made them depend upon a good memory of history. The result was an eclecticism based on past buildings, both in overall forms and plans and in details, whether of specific spaces or of window frames. Charles McKim's Boston Public Library is based upon the *parti* of Roman Renaissance palazzos and Labrouste's Bibliothéque Sainte-Genève in Paris.

The systemization that French instruction imparted to architecture made the École very important to Americans seeking grand traditions. A. D. F. Hamlin, a former École de Beaux-Arts student, an alumnus of the McKim, Mead & White office, a professor of architecture at Columbia University, and a critic and historian, wrote in 1892: "Meanwhile the French had been coming nearer to a true reform in architecture than any other people. Starting with the elements of classical design, they had developed out of them a more or less rational and consistent system of treatment, in which they avoided on the one hand the academic stiffness of the Vignolesque school and on the other the extravagances of the Rococo."[6]

Americans have traditionally respected education. It confers status and distinction and it is the path to advancement. This, combined with the increasing prestige of French culture and art in the latter half of the nineteenth century, made the École particularly attractive to American architects. The French offered formal instruction in architecture, whereas in both America and Britain, architecture was normally learned by apprenticeship. When Americans came to setting up schools of architecture, the École became the model.

The first attempt to teach architecture along the lines of the École came in 1857 in New York, when Richard Morris Hunt, the first American to attend the École, set up an *atelier*. His students included William Robert Ware, Henry Van Brunt, George B. Post, and Frank Furness. In 1865, Ware was appointed the first professor of architecture at the Massachusetts Institute of Technology in Cambridge. Three years later, as a result of Ware's travel in and observation of European educational methods, especially at the École, MIT offered the first systematic training in architecture in the United States. Other schools followed its lead: Cornell in 1871, Syracuse in 1873, Michigan in 1876, Columbia in 1880, Pennsylvania in 1890, and Harvard in 1895. Prominent on the faculties of all the American schools up to the latter 1930s would be Americans who had received their training at the École and French alumni of the École who immigrated to the United States. Eugene Letang came to MIT in 1871 and was followed by Maurice J. Prévot and Jean Hébrard at Cornell, Paul Cret at Pennsylvania, and E.S.A. Duquesne and Jacques Haffner at Harvard.

American attendance at the École began in 1847 with Richard Morris Hunt, who was followed in 1852 by Arthur A. Dexter and Francis Peabody, and then in 1859 by Henry Hobson Richardson. In 1867, Charles McKim, Robert S. Peabody, and Frank W. Chandler entered. Americans continued to cross the ocean in ever-increasing numbers through the 1870s and 1880s. From the later 1880s until 1922, American attendance was at its height. Between 1887 and 1906, 259 American students were officially admitted to the École. This did not include several hundred more who were in Paris studying at *ateliers,* though not officially admitted to the École.[7] The Americans generally came with a previous architectural background either from school or an office and consequently won many of the prizes open to them.

The American respect and indebtedness to the École was testified to not ony by attendance and imitation in schools of architecture but in several other ways as well. In 1887, a group of American alumni announced the Prix de Reconnaissance Architects Américains. Intended to be a prize open exclusively to French students at the École, it signified American "obligation" to the French. Among the subscribers to this prize were Richard Morris Hunt, Charles F. McKim, H. H. Richardson, Thomas Hastings, and Louis Sullivan.[8] In 1893 in New York, the Beaux-Arts Society of Architects was founded "to cultivate and perpetuate the associations and principles of the École des Beaux-Arts of Paris and to found an Academy of Architecture."[9] Among the founders were Charles F. McKim, Ernest Flagg, Richard Howland Hunt, and John M. Carrère. In 1904, the society held the first Paris Prize competition; the winner, an American student, would be sent abroad for two and a half years to study at the École. In 1916, as a spin-off of the society, the Beaux-Arts Institute of Design was founded with the purpose of carrying on "a school for giving instruction and for encouraging studies in Architecture, Sculpture, Mural Painting and other decorative arts and subjects by methods similar to those in use at the École des Beaux-Arts in Paris."[10] And finally, Americans responded to the French Prix de Rome with the American Academy in Rome, the brainchild and passion of Charles F. McKim. It gave American students the chance to study along with the French in Rome. For McKim, it amounted to a pilgrimage: "As Rome went to Greece, and later France, Spain and other countries had gone to Rome, for their own reactions to the splendid standards of Classic and Renaissance Art, so must we become students, and delve, bring back and adapt to conditions here, a groundwork on which to build."[11]

The American orientation towards classicism is aptly illustrated in a comparison of two polls of practicing architects held in the late nineteenth century on the most admired buildings in the United States. The first poll of 1885 listed H. H. Richardson's Romanesque Trinity Church, Boston, 1877, in first place and four more of his buildings in the top ten. Fourteen years later, in 1899 another poll was held. Trinity Church had slipped to number three; the number two spot was its neighbor, Charles McKim's Boston Public Library; and the number one was the Capitol in Washington, D.C. The Capitol had been number two in 1885. Between the two polls a substantial shift in taste had occurred. In the 1885 poll, seven of the top ten were in some medieval style, whereas in the 1899 poll, seven of the top ten were in some form classical. McKim, Mead & White had, in addition to the number two spot, number five, the Low Library at Columbia, and number seven, Madison Square Garden.[12]

Certainly not all American architects or critics accepted with equanimity the growing impact of classicism and the École in the United States. Louis Sullivan, in spite of his earlier supprt of the Prix de Reconnaissance Architects Américains, would find the École wanting in an overall system, but he appears not to have made this judgment until after 1900. Frank Lloyd Wright claimed "Uncle Dan" Burnham offered him, in 1894, an all-expenses-paid fellowship (including support for his wife and child) to study for four years at the École and then two years in Rome if he would then come back and work in the Burnham office. Wright replied: "Too late, Uncle Dan—It's too late now, I'm afraid. I am spoiled already. I've been too close to Mr. Sullivan. He has helped spoil the Beaux-Arts for me, or spoiled me for the Beaux-Arts. . . . I think he regrets the time he spent there himself." Wright goes on to charge the École des Beaux-Arts with being "uncreative," like a "jail."[13]

Others would also complain. Barr Ferree commented in 1893: "The work of Frenchifying American architecture goes merrily on . . . all the tremendous energy that our students are expending in this direction is so much vitality wasted." Ferree felt the major objects of the École were brilliant drawings of unbuildable buildings that did not respond to the conditions of America. "Paradoxical as it may seem, it is nevertheless a fact that though Paris possesses the foremost architectural school in the world, French architecture is, of all the others, the most frozen, the most academic, the most stationary."[14]

Obviously, such charges created a certain defensiveness in American proponents of the Ecole. Thomas Hastings, who would receive the RIBA Gold Medal in 1922, felt that classicism was the natural style of America, and the charge that it was imported French academicism denied the facts:

> When future generations look back on the work influenced by the Beaux-Arts in this country, they will find as great a difference of expression and of national character as that which existed in the sixteenth century between France and Italy. . . . This difference will be the natural and necessary outcome of the difference of our ways of living as well as of the difference of our national character.[15]

Joy Wheeler Dow summed up the debate in 1904 by declaring that Richard Morris Hunt's Biltmore was labeled "French Renaissance now; it will be American Renaissance later on."[16]

The controversy over "French" versus "American" would continue as a major issue, but undeniably the French educational system and the renewal of classicism was the mainstream of American architecture from the 1890s into the 1920s; and the Gold Medals awarded are among the most apt indications of this.

Certainly all of these Gold Medalists had designed work that falls outside of the beaux-arts and classical definition. All designed buildings with contextual relationships that called for reliance upon medieval and vernacular styles. Also, five of the medalists—Webb, McKim, Post, Laloux, and Pascal—began their careers in the 1870s during a period when medievalism and extreme picturesqueness were at their height. The careers of all these individuals are similar in that they were leaders in replacing the violently agitated architecture of the midcentury with the repose and calm classicism that held sway from the 1890s onward. Bacon, whose active design career did not begin until the 1890s, could also design buldings with a vernacular and/or medieval reference, as his shingled houses indicate, yet his major work, the Lincoln Memorial, is a dramatic restatement of classicism (Plate 1).

Henry Bacon: Donald MacRae House, Wilmington, North Carolina, 1901.

Victor Laloux: façade of Grand Prix project for 1878, "Un Cathédral."

Jean Louis Pascal: plan of Grand Prix project for 1866, "Un Hôtel à Paris pour riche banquier."

George B. Post & Sons: Wisconsin State Capital, Madison, Wisconsin, 1906–1917.

W. Cook, "Jean Louis Pascal—Institute Gold Medalist, 1913, *Journal of the AIA*, vol. 3, January 1915

Jean Louis Pascal: Faculté de Medicine, Bordeaux, France, 1876–1912.

Victor Laloux: Hôtel de Ville, Tours, 1898–1902.

L'Architecture, vol. 15, December 1902

The reigning classicism of the six Gold Medalists did differ along individual and nationalistical lines. The Americans—McKim, Post, and Bacon—tended toward a very solid, massive appearance. Ornament, while never absent, was clearly secondary to the monumental masses and deep voids. Spatially, their buildings exhibit an almost dogmatic axiality and a clear hierarchy of particulated spaces that becomes fully evident in elevation. The Americans thought and built on a scale that could only be imagined on paper by the Europeans.

Pascal and Laloux thought on the same scale as Americans in their student years, but reality was far different. Both had designed famous Prix de Rome projects which emphasized some of the unreal nature of the École educational system. Laloux's project was for a great cathedral with a towering dome, which might have inspired Post's Wisconsin State Capitol. Pascal's Prix de Rome design of 1866 was one of the famous École projects.[17] For the first time an irregular site was offered for the competition, and Pascal successfully united an unequal and asymmetrical plan and facade. French classicism of the later-nineteenth century tended toward a lightness of facade and lack of depth. Also, the surrounding context provided inspiration for the French designer. Pascal's designs tended toward a dry pedantry, a repetition of preexisting patterns and motifs. Laloux, on the other hand, had a more fertile imagination and tended to exploit surface effects. His Hôtel de Ville, Tours, and the Gare d'Orsay, Paris, have a rococo flurry and elaboration of ornament, consequently diminishing the substance of the mass of the building.

Sir Aston Webb's classicism is perhaps more widely eclectic in the assimilation of different styles. The Victoria and Albert Museum is a wild creation of Gothic and Renaissance details drawn from different sources. The complexity and elaborateness of the application of the styles is unique. Later, the classicism of Byzantium, the Georgian period, and France would attract him. Details tend to assume an importance in his work and, at times, to overwhelm the building.

Sir Aston Webb and Ingress Bell: Victoria and Albert Museum, London, 1891–1909.

Instrumental in this classicism was the connection of the six Gold Medalists to the École des Beaux-Arts. Charles McKim, Jean Louis Pascal, and Victor Laloux all studied at the École, and Pascal and Laloux later established important *ateliers*. Neither Post nor Bacon formally studied at the École, but their education and apprenticeship came from École-trained individuals. Post, as already indicated, was in Hunt's New York *atelier*. Bacon attended the University of Illinois for a few months but received his major education while working for McKim, Mead & White for nearly eight years, primarily as Charles McKim's assistant. The medals to Pascal and Laloux were in a sense recognition of the American debt to French architecture and specific repayment to the two patrons under which a generation studied. Laloux reportedly ran the most popular *atelier* for Americans; through it passed 132 American students. Pascal had the second most popular *atelier* with 48 American students.[18] The importance of the Beaux-Arts connection was emphasized at the ceremony for Laloux in 1922: When former American Beaux-Arts students were asked to stand, they numbered 25.[19]

Sir Aston Webb's Beaux-Arts connection was less direct, for he was neither a student at the École nor trained under a former Beaux-Arts student. English architecture from the 1870s on began to reflect an increasing concern with various forms of classicism. From the unsystematic Queen Anne style emerged a form of Georgian revival in the 1880s, followed in the 1890s by the so-called Wrenaissance and Imperial Baroque. This increasing classicism paved the way for the appearance of very Beaux-Arts and French buildings by English architects actually trained at the École, such as John J. Burnet, Arthur J. Davis, and others.[20] The quotation in Chapter 2 by Charles Reilly of the Liverpool School of Architecture is but one instance of the growing English interest in beaux-arts classicism. Sir Aston Webb's work, which initially was in a variety of French medieval modes, changed dramatically around 1900, becoming a full-fledged classicism with an evident

Sir Aston Webb: Queen Victoria Memorial, The Mall, 1901–1911, winning competition entry, 1901. Perspective by T. Raffles Davison.

French bias. His most dramatic work was for the crown—the Admiralty Arch, the Mall, the Queen Victoria Memorial, and the new eastern façade to Buckingham Palace. His other works indicate a beaux-arts influence in plan, emphasis on circulation, and style. He openly acknowledged these leanings, as in his AIA Gold Medal acceptance speech, where in discussing the proper placement and grand approach to buildings, he lamented the English failing and praised the Mall and the McMillan Commission's work in Washington, D.C. He went on to say that "the French, of course, are the masters of the work of arranging public buildings, and we all know how the Opera House in Paris gains by the splendid Rue de l'Opéra, and how the Rue de l'Opéra is improved by the Opera House at the end of it."[21]

Webb's selection, as noted above, was related to McKim's Royal Gold Medal award of 1903, but more importantly, he confirmed a direction toward formal, grand classicism that was very sympathetic to the Americans. That he was picked because of this is obvious; Frank Miles Day, the president of the AIA in 1907, cited in the presentation speech a number of living English architects: Ernest George, Phené Spiers, John Blecher, Norman Shaw, and George Bodley.[22] Bodley had recently been selected as the architect of the Episcopal National Cathedral in Washington, D.C. Spiers had actually attended the École, but his practice was not distinguished; he was more an educator. George and Shaw certainly had distinguished practices, yet in 1906 Aston Webb appeared to be the leading figure in classical English architecture. Webb had a connection to power through his royal works and, at the same time, confirmed the status of the new classicism: His work looked French.

Certainly the award to Bacon in 1923 does not indicate the end of the American infatuation with the École des Beaux-Arts, nor with classicism, but it can be said to be the high point; from then on there is a gradual decline in interest and influence. Many future Gold Medalists attended the École, including Paul Cret (1938), Louis Sullivan (1946), Bernard Maybeck (1951), Auguste Perret (1952), William Adams Delano (1953), Clarence S. Stein (1956), John Wellborn Root, II (1958), and Wallace K. Harrison (1967). Further, one might note that many other Gold Medalists experienced the École system secondhand, either through schooling or working in the offices of École alumni. The École and classicism will recur with respect to American architecture and the Gold Medal.

Notes

1 Quoted in "Jean-Louis Pascal: An Appreciation," *The Architect's Journal*, vol. 51, June 2, 1920, p. 710.

2 Richard Chafee, "The Teaching of Architecture at the École des Beaux-Arts," in Arthur Drexler (ed.), *The Architecture of the École des Beaux-Arts*, Museum of Modern Art, New York, 1977, p. 82.

3 Jean Paul Carlhian, personal communication, April 13, 1981.

4 Willard Connely, *Louis Sullivan as He Lived*, Horizon Press, New York, 1960, p. 62.

5 Chafee, "The Teaching of Architecture," in Drexler, op. cit., p. 90.

6 A. D. F. Hamlin, "The Battle of the Styles," *Architectural Record*, vol. 1, January–March 1892, p. 270.

7 Jean Paul Carlhian, personal communication, April 13, 1981.

8 *American Architect*, vol. 22, September 3, 1887, pp. 113–114.

9 *Articles of Incorporation*, Year Book of the Society of Beaux-Arts Architects and of the Beaux-Arts Institute of Design, New York, 1929.

10 *Constitution*, ibid.

11 Charles Moore, *The Life and Times of Charles Follen McKim*, Houghton Mifflin, New York, 1929, p. 260.

12 "The Ten Best Buildings in the United States," *American Architect and Building News*, vol. 17, June 13, 1885, p. 282–283; "The Ten Most Beautiful Buildings in the United States," *The Brochure Series*, vol. 1, January 1900, pp. 204.

13 Frank Lloyd Wright, *An Autobiography*, Faber & Faber, London, 1945, pp. 114–115.

14 Barr Ferree, "Architecture," *Engineering Magazine*, vol. 5, May 1893, p. 252.

15 Thomas Hastings, "The Influence of the École des Beaux-Arts upon American Architecture," *Architectural Record*, "The Beaux-Arts Number," January 1901, p. 83.

16 Joy Wheeler Dow, *American Renaissance: A Review of Domestic Architecture*, Comstock, New York, 1904, p. 167.

17 "Jean-Louis Pascal: An Appreciation," *The Architect's Journal*, op. cit., p. 709.

18 James Paul Noffsinger, *The Influence of the École des Beaux-Arts on the Architects of the United States*, Catholic University Press Washington, D.C., 1955, pp. 89–90.

19 *Proceedings of the 55th Convention of the AIA*, Gibson Bros., Washington, D.C., 1922, p. 76.

20 Francis S. Swales, "The Influence of the École des Beaux-Arts upon Recent Architecture in England," *Architectural Record*, vol. 26, December 1909, pp. 417–427.

21 Address of Sir Aston Webb, *Proceedings of the 40th Convention of the AIA*, Gibson Bros., Washington, D.C., 1907, p. 110.

22 Address of Frank Miles Day, ibid. p. 105–106.

Sir Edwin Landseer Lutyens: front
view of Little Thakeham, Thakeham
Sussex, 1902.

ROMANTIC IMAGERY

The Gold Medal award during the years 1925–1933 illustrates a fundamental break with the period of beaux arts classicism and indicates the reorientation of professional American architects toward a new eclecticism containing a romantic intensity. The romantic imagery of Sir Edwin L. Lutyens, Bertram C. Goodhue, Howard Van Doren Shaw, Milton B. Medary, and Ragnar Östberg has been diversely interpreted as a significant break with the past or a conservative orientation still following tradition as the only source of architectural imagery. While labels such as "period," "eclectic," "romantic nationalist," or "revivalist" have been applied to these architects at one time or another, none seems to fit them very well. What binds these Gold Medalists together as a group of kindred spirits is not a specific stylistic manner but their wide-ranging eclecticism, the ability to use a number of styles successfully. They all began in an arts-and-crafts mode and widened their vocabulary to design some very successful, classically derived buildings. All shunned the dogma of the single-track eclecticism that came to dominate beaux-arts classicists. The romantic imagists were willing to explore a variety of approaches and solutions, not in a rigid, stylistic manner but in an attempt to create images that would read as the appropriate solution to the enterprise. An intellectual justification for the stylistic choice common to the earlier group is not as apparent for these romantic imagists. They appealed to emotions through the use of transformed historical motifs.

style naturally varies. They all began as arts-and-crafts designers and then adjusted in different ways throughout their lives. Sir Edwin Lutyens has the closest relationship, since he was English, knew many of the arts-and-crafts crowd well, and was a member of the Art Worker's Guild. His youthful work, such as Little Thakeham, Sussex, 1902, was in this mode, with its reliance upon an indigenous architectural idiom—in this case, an Elizabethan manor house and its exquisite details. The interior is dominated by a large hall with mannerist classical details, a surprising shift from the

National Monuments Record

National Monuments Record

L. Weaver, *Houses and Gardens by Sir Edwin Lutyens*, Country Life, London, 1913

Little Thakeham, rear.

Little Thakeham, plan.

Little Thakeham, hall.

medieval exterior. These details indicate Lutyens's later concerns for more formalist design solutions, and by 1903 he believed Palladio was the game. Yet he always retained a certain freedom from precedent, and his plans and elevations are inventive, as with the British Embassy in Washington, D.C. or the Viceroy's House in New Delhi.

Lutyens's career cannot be taken as the exact cipher of the other romantic eclectics, for all are individual; yet it does indicate the tension between the youthful arts-and-crafts idealism of informality and the medieval and later, more formal, classical works. Milton B. Medary came from an arts-and-crafts background in the Philadelphia office of Frank Miles

Day, and his early works, such as Houston Hall at the University of Pennsylvania, 1895, are in the native Germantown schist of the area. Stylistically, its rather free treatment of Jacobean and colonial sources became an important predecessor of a regional Philadelphia idiom. Certainly similar in details and form is his Fischer House, Chestnut Hill, 1910, which has been described as a Philadelphia version of a German version of an English arts-and-crafts house.[3] More straitlaced and doctrinaire revivalist is the Valley Forge Chapel. Later, Medary could do grand-manner, high-

American Country Houses of Today, New York, 1912

Milton B. Medary: Adelbert K. Fischer House, Chestnut Hill, Pennsylvania, 1910.

classical designs, as in the Department of Justice building. Significantly, Medary completed his career with the Bok Singing Tower in Florida, a 205-foot-tall carillon in the Gothic idiom, whose ornament bears the unmistakable imprint of the Arts Décoratifs exposition in Paris (Plate 4). Edward Bok, the patron of the tower, was one of the most significant promoters of the arts-and-crafts in the United States, through his editorship of *The Ladies' Home Journal*.[4]

Bertram Goodhue came out of a similar background, not so much in the office of Renwick as in Boston in the years 1891–1903 when, with Ralph Adams Cram, he joined the *Knight Errant* group. There he did bookplates and drawings full of the vigor and aesthetic of English arts and crafts and designed parish churches in an English idiom loaded with a wealth of crafts contributions, from stained glass to reredos and stone carvings. These churches are prime examples of the Morris philosophy. Boston, along with Chicago, was one of the major centers for the introduction of the Morris philosophy into the United States: The first arts-and-crafts exposition was held there in April 1897, and two months later, the Boston Society of Arts and Crafts was founded. Goodhue was a founding member and exhibited frequently with the society.

Bertram Grosvenor Goodhue, *A Book of Architectural and Decorative Drawings,* Architectural Books, New York, 1914

Bertram Grosvenor Goodhue: cover design for *The Knight Errant,* 1891.

While for Cram the Gothic became increasingly academic—revealing the less progressive nature of the arts-and-crafts movement—Goodhue always retained a freedom of approach, a willingness to reinterpret the Gothic and medieval styles; hence, his later churches, such as the West Point Chapel (1903) or Christ Church, Cranbrook, Michigan (1923), were freer adaptions of the Gothic idiom. The Cranbrook church indicates the intimacy of Gothic revival and the arts-and-crafts style for its patron, George Booth, the Detroit newspaper publisher who also commissioned Eliel Saarinen to do the Cranbrook Institute. Goodhue had a facility in other styles, of course—Spanish colonial for houses and buildings in California and a classical vein for buildings such as the Nebraska State Capitol and the National Academy of Sciences. Yet even here Goodhue integrated the decorative arts; for example, the Nebraska State Capitol includes sculptures by Lee Lawrie, mosaics by Hildreth Meiere, and murals by Augustus Vincent Tack, among others. Goodhue summed up this approach in a letter to Paul Cret: "I should like to be merely one of three people to produce a building, i.e., architect, painter, sculptor. . . . I should like to do the plan and the massing of the building; then I should like to turn the ornament . . . over to a perfectly qualified sculptor, and the colour and surface decoration . . . to an equally qualified painter."[5]

Howard Van Doren Shaw also fits well into this pattern, for he was a founder of the Chicago Arts and Crafts Society and a member of an informal group that included Frank Lloyd Wright, Robert Spencer, and Walter Burley Griffin. His own house, Ragdale, has been described as a "twin gable, white stucco building that would have delighted C. F. A. Voysey, especially as the interiors were in the best tradition of William Morris."[6] Shaw was in many

Howard Van Doren Shaw: Ragdale, Lake Forest, Illinois, 1897–1898.

ways the midwestern counterpart to Lutyens; his biographer claimed that "perhaps the architect to whom he owed most is Sir Edwin Lutyens."[7] Similar to Lutyens's, Shaw's later work grew more formal and he designed within the various revival idioms of Georgian, Italian, and Gothic. His plans were not so inventive and idiosyncratic as Lutyens's, but comparably, Shaw never treated history in a dogmatic manner.

Ragnar Östberg's work, while frequently classified as strongly nationalistic, follows the same development as the others. His early work can best be classified as regional arts and crafts. He investigated the "folk" housing of Sweden and designed villas that betray this lineage in materials, forms, and image, but they also show the influence of outside sources and easily fit into the international arts-and-crafts movement. His best-known work, the Stockholm City Hall, is aggressively picturesque and semimedieval in outline, though none of the details are archaeologically correct (Plate 5). The building as a whole indicates his profound appreciation for details and artisanship. The impact of this building and its Scandinavian progeny on the outside world has never been properly assessed, yet a perusal of American architectural magazines from the 1920s and testimony from British architects on their admiration for Scandinavian architecture show its importance.[8] However, Östberg could also do buildings with a classical air, as in the Naval Museum in Stockholm or the crematorium at Hälsingborg. Their extreme purity and simplification of form and the almost puritanical denial of ornament recalls the romantic classicism of Ledoux or Boulee.

The usage of classicism by all of these architects certainly separates them from the medievalism of the arts-and-crafts movement. The adoption

Ragnar Östberg: Villa Ekarne, Stockholm, 1905.

Ragnar Östberg: Naval Museum, Stockholm, 1933.

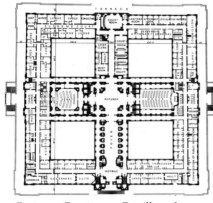

Bertram Grosvenor Goodhue &
Associates: plan of the Nebraska
State Capitol, Lincoln, Nebraska,
1920–1932.

"The Nebraska State Capital,"
American Architect, vol. 145, October 1934

Howard Van Doren Shaw: Market
Square, Lake Forest, Illinois,
1912–1917.

of classicism can, in most cases, be seen as a response to both urban and national heritages. For Lutyens, the lure of the great formal English house plans of the Wren and Georgian periods proved irresistible, but of equal importance was the need to design urban buildings. It is not without significance that the offices of *Country Life* magazine in London, his first major city building, were in a "Wrenaissance" manner. Classicism was the official public language of architecture for England, and all of Lutyens's urban and public buildings utilized it, though with an inventive spirit. Goodhue and Medary, when faced with important public commissions (other than ecclesiastical) also normally turned to a classic basis. Medary's argument for the design of the Federal Triangle and his own Department of Justice Building therein was couched in terms of the historical development of Washington under the L'Enfant plan, the McMillan commission, and the classical basis of the architecture of the early republic.[9] Goodhue's major public buildings utilize classicism as the recognized language of monumental public architecture. The Nebraska State Capitol, in spite of the tower, is basically classical in plan and composition (Plate 6). For the National Academy of Sciences in Washington, Goodhue followed the national classical tradition, though avoiding archaeological details. Howard Van Doren Shaw is the one medalist who really never built any major public buildings. His urban houses do vary in stylistic reference between arts and crafts and Georgian. The Market Square at Lake Forest, his one major commercial commission, is really beyond classification; perhaps it is best described as "suburban picturesque." The contemporary critic Peter B. Wight claimed: "The architecture of the Market Square is in Mr. Shaw's original manner. Inquisitive critics may find in it some relation or suggestion of by-gone

P. B. Wight, "The New Market Square at Lake Forest, Illinois, *Western Architect*, vol. 25, October 1917

architectural styles. But that is something he never attempts to do. . . . There is some resemblance to the old towns of Flanders and north Germany of the fifteenth and sixteenth centuries. But there is no copying."[10] While there is no direct copying, Shaw's sources are evident. The origins go back to the Queen Anne of Richard Norman Shaw in Bedford Park, and the English garden-city idiom developed by Barry Parker and Raymond Unwin. In other words, it is distinctly arts and crafts in image and typically appropriate for a garden-suburb shopping center.

Ragnar Östberg at first glance appears to be completely medieval with his Stockholm City Hall. While certainly medieval in picturesqueness and color, many of the details are classical in origin. Östberg was trying to create a building that would sum up and incorporate all of the glories of Swedish heritage, from the Huns and introduction of Christianity in the Middle Ages to the eighteenth century. He stated his position very firmly in an essay of 1908:

> In our country, as in many other lands, the excessive amount of foreign material has prevented the development of a uniform national type of architecture. It has been recognized during the last decade that this universal spirit in an art like architecture, which is influenced by climatic and local conditions, presents a distinct danger for the building art. For this reason, the problem of the day with Swedish architecture is to develop a national architecture based upon the study of national edifices.[11]

The nationalism so present in Östberg's polemic puts him directly into the lineage of the other Gold Medalists of the period. That later he would change to a more direct classical language is indicative of the importance of classicism as a language of public architecture.

A final issue involves the "modernism" of the five romantic-eclectic Gold Medalists. Their active practices all began in the 1890s and lasted into the 1920s or even the 1930s; they encompass the period when the usage of historical precedent and imagery came under severe attack as being unfunctional, untruthful, and out of phase with the "spirit of the time," or as the Germans phrased it, the *Zeitgeist*. In comparison to the next group of Gold Medalists, those from 1938 to 1958, the conservative modernists, the romantic imagists saw the spirit of the time as residing in historical styles and forms as the language of architecture. At times they disobeyed certain rules or made new combinations of forms and ornament, yet their work was understandable to the public. This issue is best pointed up in the assessment of Louis Sullivan, made in 1926 by John Harbeson: "The one-man original styles—such as the Sullivan style—have not made headway because they cannot find an audience, the forms being strange to the average beholder."[12]

The recognizability of traditional architecture was one of the major claims Sir Edwin Lutyens made:

> The modern impersonal architecture of the so-called functionalism does not seem to me to be replacing the inherited lore of centuries with anything of comparable excellence or to show yet a genuine sense of style—as style rooted in feeling for the right use of materials. One cannot make friends, through it, with the men who built it. It is all "factory and crane." I can see no wit or humor in

the "features," while the architectural relations seem to me haphazard as often as not.[13]

In his Gold Medal acceptance speech, Lutyens spelled out his approach:

> English architecture in the main follows a track of progressive retrospection. She continually refreshes her inspiration from the waters of the past, incessantly endeavoring to recover for the present the atmosphere of her history, adapting and reinvigorating its beauties in a generation that is mainly Philistinic in outlook.[14]

He went on to talk about the significance of the "association of memory" and the importance of architecture and the other arts in "service to the higher elements of national life." Lutyens was not a modernist in any way, yet he was certainly not a straitlaced revivalist; he used the language of the past in a new way. The plans in his Georgian or baroque country houses are full of surprises. The source of this is not modern architecture, but his arts-and-crafts background and personal sensibility. In form as well, Lutyens would take liberties; the simplification of elements, as in the Viceroy's House at New Delhi, 1912–1931, and the Cenotaph in Whitehall, 1919, or the extreme reductionism of the great memorial arch at Thiepval in France, 1923–1930. Lutyens's tendency towards large, massive, uncomplicated forms—especially typical of his later work—illustrates a common feeling for monumental sublimeness, typical of the 1920s and common to all the architects who received the Gold Medal between 1925 and 1933.

Milton B. Medary had a fitful association with modernism that can best be described as one of ornament and detail. The Fischer House, 1910, has as features the fenestration, extended eaves, walls of stucco or roughcast, and interior woodwork and leaded glass windows that strongly recall *Jugenstil,* or Germanic arts and crafts. These elements may be the result of the influence of the patron, Adelbert Fischer and his wife, for they had recently emigrated from Germany.[15] In the 1920s, decorative elements which today would be identified as moderne or art deco appear in the work of Medary's firm. Collaborating with the sculptor, Lee Laurie (also used extensively by Goodhue), Medary's ornament became more abstract, geometrical, and flat, recalling both neoclassicism and cubism. Flat, stylized figures and lush foliage appear at key areas in his buildings. While the resemblance to ornamental motifs appearing at the 1925 Parisian Arts Décoratifs exposition is obvious, other sources certainly contributed, including Assyrian, Aztec, and Egyptian archeological discoveries and the work of the English sculptor, Eric Gill. The Philadelphia Divinity School, while very self-consciously Gothic, contains elements of simplification that recall the work of Sir Giles Gilbert Scott in England. Basically, Medary remained strongly tied to traditional forms and styles, and while some of his ornament and forms do betray a new sensibility, it is extremely tentative and indicates the skeptical approach of most American architects to a wholesale architectural reform in the 1920s.

Medary's suspicion of the call for modernism is amply revealed in his 1927 AIA President's Address where he noted the "myriad confusions and complication of twentieth century life" and the quest for a new art: "In literature, in religion, in sculpture and painting, in music and the drama, as well as in architecture, the world is in revolt." Searching for a name for the spirit of "complete repudiation," Medary called it "jazz." "The architect hears it everywhere: Let us have a new architecture, an American architecture; let us have done with the dealers in classic and medieval forms; let us try something truly American! . . . This is plain sophistry." Medary asked his fellow American architects to look both to the past and also to international developments, including the "so-called modern movement in Central Europe and the Scandinavian countries" and he cited in this regard Östberg's new Stockholm City Hall. The problem of modernism would be solved, Medary believed, by looking beneath the surface of fast-changing fads for "roots . . . which are universal and have abiding character." Medary continued: "On these let us build in our own way, with the freest fancy, expressing our own spirits. We need not copy last year's blossomings, but we may and should take what made the blossomings beautiful as our inspiration. Our work will then surely be ours and cannot be confused with carefully reproduced expressions of great souls long since dead."[16]

Howard Van Doren Shaw's work is an example of the conservative approach that was most admired in the 1920s—by most standards he would never be considered modern. Yet Shaw was aligned with the Chicago arts-and-crafts community, and his own house, Ragdale, is an excellent example of Voysey's English-cottage style brought to America. At least partially, Shaw comes from the same milieu that produced Frank Lloyd Wright and the Prairie school phenomenon, with the difference that Shaw remained tied to the English sources, whereas Wright and followers took the conceptual basis of the English arts-and-crafts and created a unique, modern, American image. The irony should not be lost that Shaw's early work could be put into a lineage of modern design as spelled out by Sir Nikolaus Pevsner and others.[17] Shaw consistently used advanced building materials and technology in his work: The Wilson house is framed in concrete. Yet, typically, Shaw made no attempt to express the material.

Ragnar Östberg, as noted above, was concerned with breaking free of certain elements in the past and creating a unique Swedish image for his architecture—but modern in the functionalist, machine sense it was not. An English critic, writing in 1924, described Östberg's approach as a "freedom from historical pedantry and from the equally pedantic fear of employing traditional motifs." The critic notes sources in the architecture of Sweden, North Germany, Italy, England, and the Orient, though they "are so fused by the designer's imagination as to have become an organic whole."[18] Essentially, Ragnar Östberg recombined the past to create different images, but he never broke free of tradition completely or accepted the tenets of modernism.

Bertram Goodhue, during the last few years of his life and immediately after his death, was frequently thought of as modern. His modernism rests upon his final works, such as the Nebraska State Capitol, and statements such as:

> As for the theories—and professionally—I hold that while architecture should represent a decent reverence for the historic past of the art, that we should only ignore our rightful heritage for the most compelling reasons, and that one of these compelling

reasons is the modern invention of steel frame, or reinforced concrete, construction: that this form of construction does abrogate practically all known forms—at least definite constructive forms such as columns or arches: that it is not enough that a building should be beautiful, it must also be logical. Fortunately most of my buildings are honestly built. My buttresses, although I give them a little more projection than necessary, do "butt" and my columns do "col." However, I am using less and less of the latter and have devised a form, neither column, buttress nor pilaster, that is getting to be, I hope, a proper outer envelope for an inner steel vertical. It seems to me that steel, or reinforced concrete floor construction can be perfectly legitimate; that is, these don't imitate wood beams or wood floors, even though the floors themselves can be covered with wood. Contrary to what I suppose is the generally accepted view, I hold no brief for Gothic as opposed to any other style. Gothic seems to be the generally accepted spirit in which churches should be built; also, I find its forms attractive, therefore a good deal of Gothic work must be laid to my door; but I assure you I dream of something very much bigger and finer and more modern and more suited to our present-day civilization than any Gothic church could possibly be.[19]

How far Goodhue followed this direction is debatable. His buildings make use of traditional imagery, albeit in an unorthodox manner. The Nebraska State Capitol has been traced to a number of sources, including the contemporary Scandinavian architecture of Eliel Saarinen and Lars Sonck and the designs of Sir Giles Gilbert Scott and American pueblos.[20] A contemporary critic claimed Goodhue "has been bold and original but has not adopted a feature that smacks of the fantastic or the experimental. What he has done is to take the American skyscraper and with unexampled boldness and courage has fitted it into a public building.[21] Yet this should not hide the very beaux-arts Greek-cross plan, the standard binuclear arrangement of the legislative chambers, the central rotunda, a dome at the top of a 400-foot-tall tower, and the wealth of sculptural detail illustrating the usual public pieties. He uses pier buttress figures for the tower, though any informed reading of the building reveals them to be pure decoration. It was these small breaks with tradition that made Goodhue popular and seen as a modernist. As one critic wrote in an article entitled "Goodhue: The First True Modern": "The Goodhue 'style' is not one that breaks away from that fair progress called 'tradition,' but a 'style' rather that acknowledges and supplements tradition and carries it reasonably and nobly forward."[22] Fiske Kimball, writing in 1927, did not feel that Goodhue was in the artistic vanguard of his time and noted, "paradoxically, yet naturally enough, as Goodhue moved toward 'modernism,' he moved also toward classicism— the classicism of calm and ordered masses and spaces."[23] Goodhue would remain an important figure for the next decade and a half in American architecture—yet the inexorable direction of American architecture would be toward jettisoning history, and, consequently, Goodhue would be forgotten.

Obviously, it would be improper to claim that these five Gold Medalists were exclusively arts-and-crafts designers or classical revivalists or modern architects. Their work intersects these architectural approaches in a variety of ways; it does not remain within any single current. Certainly the relative freedom from the academic dogma of the École des Beaux-Arts in their early years gave them a breadth of approach that produced such designs as Goodhue's Nebraska State Capitol, Lutyens's Roman Catholic Cathedral for Liverpool, Medary's Bok Singing Tower, Shaw's Market Square at Lake Forest, and Östberg's Stockholm City Hall. Yet these designs were not modern. How to characterize architects with these wide-ranging sensibilities has been a problem; Talbot Hamlin in 1926 claimed they showed "stylistic freedom," and John Burchard and Albert Bush-Brown in 1961 typified the work as representing a "freedom from formulas."[24] In a sense they were caught between the traditions of the beaux-arts, the arts and crafts, and the modern, and their architecture is, as Fiske Kimball summed up with Goodhue, "a tardy compromise."[25] Thomas Tallmadge, writing in 1926, described Shaw as "the most rebellious of the conservatives, and the most conservative of the rebels."[26] This characterization of a rebellious conservatism is perhaps most apt and indicates the difference between these romantic imagists and the next group of traditional modernists. The romantic imagists remained tied to traditional imagery, whereas other architects of the same period who were also influenced by the arts-and-crafts movement, such as Bernard Maybeck, Frank Lloyd Wright, and Eliel Saarinen, were able to break free. And it was this breaking away that would be recognized in the next group of architects. But for the period 1925–1933, traditional imagery was the accepted and admired norm in American architecture, at least as revealed by the AIA Gold Medal.

Notes

1   A. Lawrence Kocher, "The American Country House," *Architectural Record,* vol. 58, November 1925, pp. 402–443.

2   Thomas T. Tallmadge, "Howard Van Doren Shaw," *Architectural Record,* vol. 60, July 1926, p. 73.

3   I owe this observation to Robert Judson Clark of Princeton University.

4   Edward W. Bok, *America's Taj Majal, The Singing Tower of Florida,* Georgia Marble, Tate, Georgia, 1929.

5   Quoted in Charles Harris Whitaker (ed.), *Bertram Grosvenor Goodhue—Architect and Master of Many Arts,* Architectural Book Publishing, New York, 1925, p. 27.

6   H. Alan Brooks, *The Prairie School,* University of Toronto Press, Toronto, 1972, p. 64; see also pp. 31–37.

7   Tallmadge, "Howard Van Doren Shaw," op. cit., p. 73.

8   "A Portfolio of Current Architecture in Denmark and Sweden," *Architectural Record,* vol. 60, August 1926, p. 126; Alan Devereux, "On the Philosophy of Modern Art," *Architectural Forum,* vol. 48, April 1928, pp. 482–483; Betty K. Bird, "Images of European Modernism: the Treatment of European Architecture in American Architectural Periodicals between 1920 and 1930," masters thesis, University of Virginia, 1978; John Brandon-Jones, "Britain in the Thirties," in Gavin Stamp (ed.), "AD Profiles 24," *Architectural Design,* vol. 50, 1980, p. 97.

9   Milton B. Medary, "Making a Capital City," *American Architect,* vol. 135, May 20, 1929, p. 638.

10   Peter B. Wight, "The New Market Square at Lake Forest, Illinois," *Western Architect,* vol. 24, October 1917, p. 29–30.

11   Ragnar Östberg, "Contemporary Swedish Architecture," *Architectural Record,* vol. 25, March 1909, p. 173.

12   John Harbeson, *The Study of Architectural Design,* Pencil Points, New York, 1926, p. 27.

13   Sir Edwin Lutyens, "What I think of Modern Architecture," *Country Life,* vol. 29, June 20, 1931, p. 775.

14   Sir Edwin Lutyens, "Address in Response," *Proceedings of the 58th Convention of the AIA,* AIA, Washington, D.C., 1925, pp. 97–98.

15   Information supplied to me by Charles Boney, Jr.

16   Milton B. Medary, "The President's Address," *Proceedings of the 60th Annual Convention of the AIA,* AIA, Washington, D.C., 1927, p. 6.

17   Sir Nikolaus Pevsner, *Pioneers of the Modern Movement from William Morris to Walter Gropius,* Faber & Faber, London, 1936. James D. Kornwolf, *M. H. Baille-Scott and the Arts & Crafts Movement,* Johns Hopkins University Press, Baltimore, 1972.

18   J. Murray, "The Stadshus at Stockholm," *Architectural Review,* vol. 55, January 1924, pp. 1–2.

19   Quoted in Whitaker, *Goodhue,* op. cit., p. 27.

20   Henry-Russell Hitchcock and William Seale, *Temples of Democracy,* Harcourt Brace Jovanovich, New York, 1976, p. 274.

21   "The Nebraska State Capitol," *American Architect,* vol. 121, March 10, 1922, p. 378.

22   Harry F. Cunningham, "Goodhue, the First True Modern," *Journal of the AIA,* vol. 15, July 1928, p. 247.

23   Fiske Kimball, "Goodhue's Architecture: A Critical Estimate," *Architectural Record,* vol. 62, December 1927, p. 538.

24   Talbot Hamlin, *The Pageant of America,* vol. 13: *The American Spirit in Architecture,* R. Gabriel (ed.), Yale University Press, New Haven, p. 325; John Burchard and Albert Bush-Brown, *The Architecture of America,* Little, Brown, Boston, 1961, p. 299.

25   Kimball, "Goodhue's Architecture," op. cit., p. 539.

26   Tallmadge, "Howard Van Doren Shaw," op. cit., p. 73.

FOR WISEDOMES SAKE

Paul Cret: Folger Shakespeare
Foundation, Washington, D.C.,
1929–1931.

CONSERVATIVE MODERNISM

Change in architecture — especially radical change — never occurs with lightning speed. The 1920s and 1930s have been characterized as a period of momentous architectural revolution: The old order of historicism — whether of the beaux-arts or the romantic variety — was replaced by a new architecture based upon function, modern technology, engineering, and abstract design. The opinion of the professional American architect with regard to this revolution is summed up in 1944 by William Adams Delano: "A superficial survey of the history of architecture might lead one to think that at certain periods complete revolutions took place. This was never so. Each new expression was a slow development from a previous one, and so it must be today if we would progress normally."[1] Earlier, Eliel Saarinen asked "Why revolution? Why not evolution? . . . I don't see the revolution. I see only evolution," although he added, "I think often that the evolution is too slow."[2]

These statements by two of the Gold Medalists from 1938 to 1958 illustrate the complexity of the American architectural scene in these years; in spite of the proclamation by historians and critics that the period witnessed the triumph of the revolutionary new International Style and the rejection of history, the AIA Gold Medal award to thirteen architects indicates a profoundly different orientation. Modernism in a variety of guises comes to be recognized, but there is still a lingering admiration for stylistic eclecticism — whether it be romantic or beaux-arts classical. The

61

recognition of the modern was essentially conservative, a grudging acknowledgment by the profession that, yes, Frank Lloyd Wright, Louis Sullivan, and others had altered the architectural landscape, but this did not mean a wholehearted acceptance of function, new materials, and the machine as the only determinants of design. In an inclusivist sense, these Gold Medalists might be claimed to represent modern viewpoints, but it was the "modern" of a rejuvenated and stripped classicism of Paul Cret and Auguste Perret, of a romantic combination of history and unconventional materials of Bernard Maybeck, of an essentially decorative approach through new ornament and forms of Ralph Walker, John Wellborn Root II, Eliel Saarinen, and Willem Marinus Dudok, of an updating of essentially conservative imagery of William Adams Delano and Charles Donagh Maginnis, and finally, of the revised views of the city and planning as represented by Clarence Stein and Sir Patrick Abercrombie. In a sense, all of these men, even Frank Lloyd Wright and Louis Sullivan, asserted conservative values in architecture — they rejected the implications of "radical" European modernism that called for the machine and architecture to be elements of social change. The result was that the more conservative modernism would rule for a time, but lacking both the attraction of the more radical European machine style and effective polemicists, it was replaced in the later 1950s.

Just how conservative American architects were in these years is amply testified to by an AIA poll published in the *Journal of the AIA* in 1948.[3] The buildings ranked in the top ten by 500 AIA members were: (1) Folger Shakespeare Library, (2) Lincoln Memorial, (3) Rockefeller Center, (4) Nebraska State Capitol, (5) the Federal Reserve Board Building in Washington, D.C., (6) the Parthenon, (7) Philadelphia Savings Fund Society, (8) National Gallery of Art, (9) Cranbrook Institute, and (10) Chartres. Also of interest: Paul Cret's Pan American Union captured fourteenth place, Frank Lloyd Wright's Falling Water ranked seventeenth, and Östberg's Stockholm City Hall was twenty-fifth. The Philadelphia Savings Fund Society Building is the only one that might be classified "radical modern," that is, one of the first examples of the International Style in the United States. Paul Cret emerges as the most-admired American architect with buildings in first, fifth, and fourteenth place. Polls such as this can be dismissed as an unfair sample, yet when it is compared with one conducted in 1932 by the *Federal Architect,* there is a strong similarity.[4] The *Federal Architect* asked many of the leading architectural offices in the country to list the best buildings, with the following results: (1) Lincoln Memorial, (2) Empire State Building, (3) Nebraska State Capitol, (4) Morgan Library, (5) St. Thomas's Church, New York, (6) Chicago Daily News Building, (7) Temple of the Scottish Rite in Washington, D.C., (8) Columbia University, (9) Harkness Memorial Building, Yale University, (10) Folger Shakespeare Library. Ragnar Östberg's Stockholm City Hall ranked thirteenth. Professional American architects were conservative in these years, as revealed by what they admired in both polls and the Gold Medal.

It would be inaccurate to claim that the thirteen architects who received the Gold Medal between 1938 and 1958, excluding Louis Skidmore who falls within the next group, represent a totally consistent viewpoint.

Frank Lloyd Wright: "Falling Water," Edgar Kaufman House, Bear Run, Pennsylvania, 1936-1937.

What they do reflect is American perceptions of what architecture should be in the years 1938–1958. To label them would be wrong, yet their conservatism is striking, especially with regard to the next group of Gold Medalists, the radical modernists of 1957 to 1968, who completely changed the image of architecture. The conservative modernists of 1938 to 1958 reveal the feelings of American architects that while new styles and materials must be accepted, recognizable images, scale, proportions, and ornament should not be completely abandoned. A Frank Lloyd Wright house could appear very different from a Georgian revival house, and a Ralph Walker skyscraper could articulate the skyline in a different way from a George B. Post high-rise; still the Wright and Walker buildings were understandable images.

The profile of the Gold Medalists from the years 1938–1958 that emerges from their birth dates and educational backgrounds indicates the diverse and yet similar sources of their conservatism. Their formative background of childhood and training occurred either in the late nineteenth or the early twentieth century, leaving them with a residue of cultural and architectural concepts. Louis Sullivan, who received the Gold Medal twenty years after his death, was the oldest of this group, born in 1856. The remainder were all born in the years between 1862 — Maybeck — and 1889 — Walker. Educationally, a predominant number attended the École des Beaux-Arts in Paris: Paul Cret, Bernard Maybeck, William Adams Delano, Auguste Perret, Clarence Stein, Louis Sullivan, and John W. Root II. In addition, several of the Americans, such as Delano, Sullivan, and Walker, attended American schools strongly influenced by the École. Eliel Saarinen was educated at the Polytekniska Institutet in Helsinki in a beaux-arts manner. Willem Dudok trained as an engineer. Apprenticeship or office training was still a viable method, and Frank Lloyd Wright, Sir Patrick Abercrombie, and Charles Maginnis learned architecture through the office.

The question of modern architecture and what it should be like is the central issue of the Gold Medal award in the years 1938–1958. While certainly some of the issues regarding "modern" had been enunciated as far back as the midnineteenth century, and more recently in the 1900s, much of the debate had centered upon a few individuals and was never clearly stated. Even a person such as Frank Lloyd Wright, whose early work from 1894 to 1909 would be considered a major stepping-stone of modern architecture, couched his arguments in a conservative tone. His essay "In the Cause of Architecture," accompanying a major review of his work in the *Architectural Record* for 1908, began: "Radical though it be, the work here illustrated is dedicated to a cause conservative in the best sense of the word. At no point does it involve denial of the elemental law and order inherent in all great architecture; rather, it is a declaration of love for the spirit of that law and order, and reverential recognition of the elements that made its ancient letter in its time vital and beautiful."[5] Wright carefully shades his position, claiming he is following principles — significantly he does not call for revolution.

In the early 1920s American architects begin to become aware of new currents in European modernism — both the decorative and the machine-styled. Periodicals were especially important in introducing into the United States the ideas of radicals such as Le Corbusier and Mies, as well as the more conservative and decorative, or modernistic, French, Dutch, Scandinavian, and German styles. However, for most American architects, "modern" meant the work of Bertram Goodhue, as in the Nebraska State Capitol (Plate 6), or Ralph Walker's Barclay-Vesey Building. By the later 1920s the polemical positions become more apparent, and buildings actually constructed in the United States began to challenge the mainstream. At first, they were designed by foreign émigré architects and appear in out-of-the-way places such as California, as with Rudolph Schindler's Lovell Beach House, 1922–1926, and Richard Neutra's Lovell Town House, 1928–1929.[6] Shown side by side with the stripped, "modern" classicism of a Paul Cret, confusion reigned. What exactly was "modern"? What did it stand for? The answer to this question was never fully agreed upon, except that "modern" suggested some sort of rejection of history and the traditional styles. In extreme cases it meant the actual abandonment of style.[7] Freedom from past styles was one of the messages of Le Corbusier's *Towards a New*

Sigurd Fischer, photographer; Haines, Lundberg & Waehler

Ralph Walker, for McKenzie, Voorhees & Gmelin: New York Telephone Company, Barclay-Vesey Building, New York City, 1920–1926.

Architecture, according to one reviewer of the 1927 English language edition. "He sees the greatness of our future in a scientific expression of the possibilities of steel beams, mass production units, bare concrete walls and a complete avoidance of all unnecessary detail. In a word, we must consider the function of a building, and that only, if we are to arrive at a truly new and beautiful architecture."[8]

A disclaimer for such unadorned functionalism is Ralph Walker's "A New Architecture," published in 1928, just after the completion of the Barclay-Vesey Building and his rise to prominence among American modernists. "The new architecture will not be a thing of slab-sided cubes or spheres, built-up of plane and solid geometry in which there is no element of time (something absolutely lacking in either primary forms or colors), but will have an infinite variety of complex forms and an intricate meaning that will be comprehensive to minds that are able to project thought beyond infinity." Citing Le Corbusier, Walker claimed that "the fundamental, spiritual and intellectual needs of man can never be satisfied with the thin,

65

austere design of the engineer-architect, which, while perfectly honest, fails, to take into consideration the thoughts or emotions of anyone other than a 'Robot.'"[9]

"Modern architecture," either as a concept or as an actual building, was diffuse and depended upon the personal interpretations of the polemicists and the practitioners. The problem of a definition is so difficult that a recent critic could say: "We think we know what modern architecture is—although it is notoriously difficult to define."[10] The result would be either cogently stated and rational arguments or simply personal whims and feelings. One outcome was an incestuous warfare of asserting single-line approaches and reading people in and out of various movements, bitter polemics directed as much against alternative views of "modern" as against the enemy of history and styles.

Illustrative of the warfare is an exchange that took place between Frank Lloyd Wright and George Howe in the *T-Square Journal* (later *Shelter*) in 1932. Wright decried the "internationalist" formula that he claimed was European "ready-made culture," which he saw cropping up in Japan, Brazil, and now the United States:

> I am writing this with an enemy in each eye. Two extremes. The predatory "internationalist" in the left eye. The one elects forms "ready-made" from an architecture dead. The other elects a formula derived from an architecture living, or just beginning to live, and kills the architecture. I am not at the moment cross-eyed because both the old and improved eclectic come from the same stock and amount to the same thing. I can see straight through both eyes, because the "internationalist" is only the modern improvement on the old eclectic. He is the up-to-date eclectic.[11]

George Howe replied:

> Mr. Frank Lloyd Wright, abandoning the part of Moses, is suddenly turned Pharaoh in the architectural theatre. . . . Why should he who has led us out of bondage turn and destroy his children?

Howe's defense turned on the sincerity of the "internationalist" who was "suffering jibes and stonings and starvation," in pursuit of his goals. He was, according to Howe, seeking a way out of the same "chaotic conditions that made his work not only possible but necessary," and he branded Wright as a bigot, for his criticism of the foreign internationalist.[12]

The same issue of the *T-Square Journal* carried articles by Le Corbusier, Schindler, Buckminster Fuller, and Bowman Brothers as well as pieces on Neutra and proposed "modern" housing for New York. These pieces and the Wright-Howe exchange prompted William Adams Delano to join the debate:

> I took up the Journal and read how much happier in the new era now dawning man would be—living in the skyscraping standardized apartment houses, each apartment reduced to the minimum, and spaced equally between standardized gardens, or how much more contented living in sanitary machine homes which, when shabby, he could scrap, together with his Ford car, along the

roadsides of Long Island. After centuries of struggle to evolve a culture worthy of his position in the animal kingdom, is this to be man's end? No better, no worse than the insects, ants and caterpillars he thought he had outdistanced in the race?[13]

The consequence of such vituperative polemics was the creation of artificial mainstreams and the attempt to place the opposition in eddies or stagnant pools. In spite of the polemics of Wright and Delano, by the 1930s the momentum for "modern," at least in the magazines, had been captured by critics, historians (acting as critics), and architects, who advocated the machine and the engineering-technological approach as the *Zeitgeist,* or spirit of the age. The fictive styles of the past would be replaced by an imagery directly resulting from the processes that put the building together. The International-Style exhibition, which opened at New York's Museum of Modern Art in February 1932 and traveled throughout the United States, put the stamp of approval upon the European, machine-modern style. The power of the exhibit is amply revealed in the review from *Art News:*

> Now that we have made up our minds to be honest with the steel and concrete and glass that have come to be the principal materials of our modern building, it is high time that we take accurate stock of what has been done to date in the directions that have so suddenly opened up for us toward a new architecture. No matter how monotonous or repetitious or otherwise uninspiring the new style may appear to be in its lesser manifestations — there can be no doubt about its magnificent simplicities and structural logic for a large scale work — it is probably the most powerful lever in getting us away from our jumbled aesthetic inheritances that could have been devised. After continued contemplation of the new modes, even the work of such moderns as Frank Lloyd Wright begins to look overloaded and fussy, and we begin to eye our surroundings with a fresh severity.[14]

The qualities deemed appropriate were amply summed up by Nikolaus Pevsner, writing in 1936 about Walter Gropius: "The artist who is representative of the century of ours must needs be cold, as he stands for a century as cold as steel and glass, a century the precision of which leaves less space for self-expression than did any period before."[15] The result of this mainstream categorization was well summed up by Reyner Banham in 1975:

> Willem Marinus Dudok . . . represents a strain of Dutch architecture slightly more traditionalist . . . hence his spring from thatched romanticism to square brick modern was the more spectacular. Hilversum Town Hall . . . will stand re-examination, the rest has been lost in the dust as the rest of the Modern Movement went galloping past and left him so far behind that when he died in 1974 many supposed he had been dead for years.[16]

The race to write history and the proclamation of artificial mainstreams blurs the immediate past. To anybody familiar with the architectural situation in the 1920s through the 1950s it is obvious that "modern" was not a single style or approach. Paul Cret claimed in 1923: "Modern architecture is indeed difficult to follow, because it has been borne along on

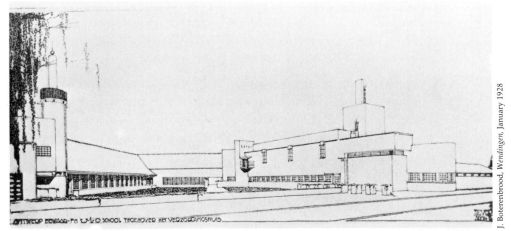

J. Boterenbrood, *Wendingen*, January 1928

Willem M. Dudok: Juliana School complex, Hilversum, 1926–1927, drawing by Dudok office.

Willem M. Dudok: Town Hall, Hilversum, 1924, 1928–1931.

Royal Dutch Embassy

many currents. It lacks that fair unity which many are pleased to find in the art of former times."[17] In 1938, *Architectural Forum* began publication of "Plus," a section to deal with "orientations of Contemporary architecture," and announced: "In all the controversy that has revolved around the subject of modern architecture, one small fact has often gone unobserved: Modern as with all architecture today, has its extremists, its moderates, and its conservatives."[18] Another article in *Forum* from the same year entitled: "Where is Modern Now?" also noted the different trends, and while nodding to Wright and Sullivan as major formers, claimed that "there is a definite trend towards modern" and that the solution would be the "International Style" and the machine image.[19] William Gray Purcell, a former Sullivan office man and partner of George Grant Elmslie, responded with a polemical letter stating that American modern architecture had never meant the machine, and that the story was far more complicated and included many figures other than Wright and Sullivan, such as Irving Gill, William Drummond, and Bernard Maybeck.[20] The issue that Purcell joined, while stated somewhat nationalistically, was, in essence, that modern architecture—if one could call it that—had numerous roots and expressions, many of which were diametrically opposed.

Somewhat earlier, Henry-Russell Hitchcock, who wrote the 1932 book *The International Style* with Philip Johnson, authored two articles and a book in which he divided the current "modern" architectural scene into two groups, the New Traditionalists and the New Pioneers.[21] The New Traditionalists, for Hitchcock, were those architects who still would borrow from the past, though not in an archaeological manner. They were romantic and humanistic, but "the practical is not to be forgotten." There were several masters of the New Tradition, including Frank Lloyd Wright, Louis Sullivan, H. P. Berlage, Auguste Perret, Willem Dudok, and Eliel Saarinen. He also included, but more peripherally, Goodhue and Östberg. The New Pioneers were the radicals, those who broke completely from the past, adopted "pure engineering," and constructed "posteclectic" buildings. Ornament was out of keeping with what Hitchcock claimed was the "contemporary spirit." This was the architecture that, in 1929, he dubbed "the international style," the proponents of which were striving "Towards a New Architecture" (the English title of Le Corbusier's *Vers une Architecture* and the title of Chapter 13 of Hitchcock's book). Included under the New-Pioneers rubric were Le Corbusier, Oud, Gropius, Lurcat, Rietveld, and Mies van der Rohe.

One of the issues that separated the conservative modernists from the more radical European International Stylists was the question of function and whether it should be raised to the position of the ultimate determinant of architectural form and beauty. "Functionalism" became the rallying cry and ideological weapon of machine-oriented architecture throughout the 1930s, 1940s, and 1950s. Louis Sullivan, with his credo "form follows function," was usually cited as a father of the new architecture, even though the romantic-nationalistic connotations of Sullivan's thought and the integral importance of ornament was misunderstood and generally cast aside as an inappropriate vestige of Victorianism. In actuality, none of the Europeans—Gropius, Le Corbusier, Mies van der Rohe, and others—ever followed the functionalist dogma to the logical end: Their artistic sensibility always intervened. Yet polemical statements such as Le Corbusier's *Machine à habiter* ("a house is a machine for living in") seemed so definitive as to preclude aesthetics.[22] Walter Gropius claimed: "The home and its furnishings are mass consumer goods, and their design is more a matter of reason than a matter of passion."[23] The conservative modernists were appalled: Eliel Saarinen questioned:

> Is the present "Machine Age" going to dominate future form-development to such an extent as to produce a form which is too much influenced by the cold and impersonal spirit of mechanization? . . . The champions of "functionalism" do not seem to be aware that when a function is raised to an "ism" its form-treatment is likely to become sophisticated and frequently used to express functions that do not exist.[24]

For Saarinen, form meant far more than expressing mere function: "Form must give forth the spirit: form is the manner in which the spirit is expressed."[25] This fear of an unbridled functionalism upset most conservative modernists; William Adams Delano, speaking at a debate on tradition versus modern in New York in 1940, worried that "our scientific knowledge —what we have learned about chemistry and physics and machinery— has outstripped our intellectual capacity to make full use of these instruments." To Delano, "architecture is an Art," and he felt "the tendency today to let the engineering element dominate is unfortunate for I do *not* believe, as many modern designers profess to believe, that to express a function frankly of necessity creates a pleasant emotion."[26]

For the conservative modernists and the traditionalists, the term *function* became a code word for an entire body of thinking that muddled together revolutionary politics and the social responsibility of architects. One critic claimed: "Fundamentally, the new architecture proclaims a radical cultural change, an alteration in the whole structure of society."[27] Housing, especially, in the 1930s became the passion of those oriented toward European machine-modern; the improvement of mankind's living standards through decent, low-cost housing appeared to be the central message of Le Corbusier's *Towards a New Architecture*, with his conclusion: "Architecture or Revolution. Revolution can be avoided."[28] With the world placed on the brink of chaos, Lewis Mumford could claim the architect had been ill-trained, he knew only "grand projects, baths, theaters, monumental railway stations; but the house itself, the most common and most functional unit of building, is left out of the architect's preparation." After lambasting the "fake" style and the impractical aspects of most American houses, Mumford advised that for the housing of the near future, "you must plan them as though you were working for a communist government."[29] Catherine F. Bauer, writing in 1931 on the International-Style exhibition at the Salon des Refusés felt architecture "is the one art that must be a social expression, impersonal anonymous, achieving its effects by adhering to time, place and function."[30]

The history of American architecture as interpreted through the architectural press in the 1920s and 1930s would seem to indicate that by 1940 the radical European architecture had triumphed. The magazines themselves tended to promote the new and unusual. During the early and mid-1920s the *Journal of the AIA,* under Charles Harris Whitaker, provided the first views of advanced European modernism.[31] In 1928, *Architectural Record,* now under the headship of A. Lawrence Kocher, took over the leadership of advanced ideas.[32] The other architectural journals gradually followed suit.

Yet in the architectural profession, and in the schools, change came more slowly. Harold Bush-Brown, for years director of the Department of Architecture at the Georgia Institute of Technology, remembered: " 'Revolution' may not be the right word to characterize what was going on in the 1930s. There was no doubt that a change was taking place in the period before World War II, but it was a gradual change without the accompaniment of violent emotions. The real revolution, as I experienced it in Atlanta, was to come later, after the war." He noted that the programs issued by the Beaux-Arts Institute of Design in New York continued to be used right into the mid-1940s. The shift, as Bush-Brown indicates, was slow and almost imperceptible, a gradual adoption of flat roofs and glass walls, removal of molding and trim, and the introduction of ideas of the Bauhaus and other European radical-modernist philosophies brought to this country by the émigrés of the late 1930s. As late as 1951 in Atlanta the adoption of these ideas caused consternation. Bush-Brown recounts an interview:

> "Don't you teach fundamentals any more?" That meant the classical orders: the Doric, the Ionic, the Corinthian. . . .
> My answer was: "Yes, of course; it comes in the history of architecture and everyone is required to take the courses in history."
> "But in design?"
> "No, we do not insist or even encourage students to use obsolete forms."
> "Obsolete forms." That really caused the furor![33]

The conservatism of American architects is amply revealed in the Gold Medal from the years 1938 through 1958. None of the individuals are easily classifiable; they generally span a spectrum. The work of Paul Cret includes his very beaux-arts classical Indianapolis Public Library, 1914 (Plate 7), his stripped-classical Folger Shakespeare Library, 1929, and the simplified, flat-roofed, thin-walled, horizontal Chemistry Building, 1940, at the University of Pennsylvania in Philadelphia. This apparent progression in the work of Cret can also be observed in that of the other Gold Medalists, though perhaps not with such a harmonious development.

Richard Guy Wilson, photographer

Paul Cret: Chemistry Building, University of Pennsylvania, Philadelphia, Pennsylvania, 1940.

The usage of traditional imagery is a common feature of all the Gold Medalists; even those who have been identified as modern, such as Wright and Saarinen, began with very traditional buildings. Wright's experiments with the Georgian revival early in his career, or later with the pre-Columbian, are well-known. Eliel Saarinen likewise began with very traditional imagery, as in the National Museum in Helsinki, a romantic composition of images drawn from the Finnish past (Plate 8). In a sense, all the Gold Medalists used traditional imagery to some degree early in their careers, and some, such as William Adams Delano and Charles Donagh Maginnis, used it extensively throughout. Delano was the consummate country-house architect of his generation; the firm of Delano & Aldrich was the logical successor to the large country-house practice of McKim, Mead & White and Charles Adams Platt. Right into the later 1930s, Delano was designing large country houses, which in imagery recalled Georgian and Palladian sources. His reliance upon this imagery was certainly because of clients' wishes but also from conviction—how else could a country house look? That he could, when called upon, also design moderne structures such as La Guardia (Plate 9) and the Marine Air Terminal (both for the 1939 World of Tomorrow World's Fair in New York) indicates his acknowledgment of different priorities, depending upon the nature of the enterprise.

Charles Donagh Maginnis's rationale for the use of traditional imagery in ecclesiastical structures, especially the scores of Catholic churches he designed, rested upon the same convictions: "The Church by its very nature is tenacious of the traditional principle and solicitous of the symbols that testify to its historical continuity," he wrote in 1944.[35] Maginnis did recognize the ecclesiastical work of Auguste Perret in France and Barry Byrne in the United States, but without major enthusiasm. None of Maginnis's Catholic churches are exact duplicates of the originals; he tended to choose widely and expand upon the original vocabulary in a manner reminiscent of the romantic imagists. A former partner of Maginnis explained, "He studied the books but then put them away when it came to the design—in contrast to Ralph Adams Cram."[35] Traditional imagery persisted in his National Shrine of the Immaculate Conception in Washington, D.C., begun in 1921 and not completed until 1959, and in the Byzantine style, though it was not a copy of any specific building. The influence of the modern movement, though, is apparent in his later works—the Law School for Boston College is a simplified, basically unornamented building in decided contrast to his earlier gothic-inspired work on the same campus.

The search for an American alternative to modernism in these years becomes obvious in considering the Gold Medal awards to Louis Sullivan, Frank Lloyd Wright, and Bernard Maybeck. Sullivan had been dead for twenty years, and his stock had risen from the nadir of his reputation in the 1920s. The change can be observed in Thomas Tallmadge's references to him in the two editions of his book *The Story of Architecture in America*. The 1927 edition had a chapter titled "Louis Sullivan and the Lost Cause"; by 1936 it had become, "Louis Sullivan Parent and Prophet."[36] Helping with the rehabilitation of Sullivan in the 1930s were the writings of Lewis Mumford, Henry-Russell Hitchcock, and finally the full-scale 1936 critical biography by Hugh Morrison, *Louis Sullivan: Prophet of Modern Architecture*. As noted earlier, what exactly was admired in Sullivan's architecture and philosophy is debatable. Most of the critics and historians who rehabilitated Sullivan admired him as the creator of the skyscraper, the master of structural expression and functionalism. That he did not "invent" the skyscraper, that his structural expression frequently was bogus, and that functionalism meant a romantic empathy with the building was ignored. His great concern with ornament, which preoccupied him all throughout his life and especially in his last works—the small-town banks—was deplored and given

Maginnis & Walsh: National Shrine of the Immaculate Conception, Washington, D.C., 1922–1955.

Maginnis & Walsh: Law School, Boston College, Newton, Massachusetts, 1949–1954.

short shrift by the cognoscenti. In actuality, it was Sullivan's ornament that made his buildings stand out from many otherwise competent structures of their day. This was only half-heartedly recognized in the 1940s and 1950s, however.

The story of the 1949 award of the Gold Medal to Frank Lloyd Wright has already been recounted, yet it is wise to remember that Wright was, by this time, 82 years old, and had an active career of over fifty years behind him in creating epoch-making designs, such as the Winslow House, 1894, the Robie House, 1906–1909, Falling Water, 1935–1936, and others. He would continue contributing to American architecture for another ten years. The Gold Medal indicates professional taste was finally catching up with him—he was safe. Also with Wright there was the special American character of his work, the relationship to nature and the organic, that he made uniquely his own and thereby American. Wright, by the early 1930s, had separated himself from European radical modernism, he claimed: "Modern architecture—let us now say organic architecture—is a natural architecture—the architecture of nature, for Nature."[37] Wright, as indicated, was highly revered as a father of modern architecture, yet his separation was complete. In 1901 he had asked for "The Art and Craft of the Machine," a title that was taken literally by many without reading the text.[39] He was appalled by what he had wrought, and as he would say for the 1932 Museum of Modern Art exhibit: "Mass-machine-production needs a conscience but needs no aesthetic formula as a short cut to any style."[39]

The shrewdness by which Wright could grab publicity and also play the underdog role has been amply noted by scholars, along with his amazing comeback in the profession, from doing practically no work in the later 1920s and early 1930s to reemerging with two of the seminal structures of the twentieth century in 1936, Falling Water and the Johnson Wax Company building in Racine, Wisconsin.

The height of Wright's fame and influence came in the 1940s and 1950s. He lived to the age of 91, and his impact upon architecture in these years was tremendous—he became a living legend.

The 1951 Gold Medal to Bernard Maybeck illustrates some of the same issues as Sullivan's and Wright's, though his architecture is more difficult to evaluate. Maybeck's active career had ceased in the 1920s, and his major buildings, the First Church of Christ Scientist, Berkeley, and the Palace of Fine Arts for the Panama-Pacific International Exposition, San Francisco, date from before World War I (Plate 10). Also, the majority of his woodsy hillside houses date from this period. Maybeck combined an arts-and-crafts sensibility with beaux-arts training, and both trends are fully evident in his work; his architecture fits most closely with the romantic eclectics of 1925–1933. However, he was not awarded the medal until 1951, and he was then viewed as a pioneer of modern regional architecture. Maybeck had been largely forgotten by most eastern critics and historians from the 1920s onward. In 1931, Lewis Mumford inserted his name rather abruptly and confusingly into a chapter entitled "Towards a Modern Architecture," in *The Brown Decades*.[40] Then a hiatus occurred, until 1947 when Mumford again returned to Maybeck with more extensive praise, claiming his work was a significant predecessor of "that native and humane form of

Bernard R. Maybeck: Hillside House, drawing, ca 1920.

modernism . . . a free yet unobtrusive expression of the terrain, the climate, and the way of life on the coast . . . [which] took root about fifty years ago in Berkeley, California, in the early work of . . . Maybeck . . . and by now is simply taken for granted."[41] This was followed by a 1949 Bay Area domestic architecture exposition showing the work of men such as William Wurster and Maybeck, with a catalog by Mumford.[42] Consequently, Maybeck became a "modern," which required ignoring the traditional sources of much of his work, whether in Rome, France, or vernacular miner's cabins, and concentrating instead upon his use of concrete and wood and the "organic" feel of many of his buildings. Maybeck's work did look different, and his use of history, as in the Gothic details of the Berkeley church, was unorthodox. Along with Sullivan and Wright, Maybeck's recognition indicates a search for roots by the contemporary American architect in the 1940s and 1950s, roots that were a relief from the rigidity, formalism, and technological determinism of the International Style.

A similar concern can be noted with the 1952 Special Citation the AIA gave to Charles Sumner Greene and Henry Mather Greene. The Greene brothers had a very active pre-World War I practice in Pasadena, California, where they designed elegant arts-and-crafts bungalows, such as the Gamble House of 1908. After World War I their practice died out, and they had been inactive for many years when they were pulled out of retirement and pushed onto center stage. Honored as predecessors of a modern California regional style, they were hardly modern in the machine image and, along with Wright, Sullivan, and Maybeck, they indicated an American alternative.

The Gold Medal to Eliel Saarinen likewise indicates the conservative nature of American modern. Saarinen's design approach has been characterized as "stylizations or simplifications of historical precedent."[43] From his earliest work in Finland to Christ Lutheran Church in Columbus, Indiana, the sources of his buildings remain obvious. In the 1920s, largely because of

Eliel Saarinen: Christ Lutheran
Church, Columbus, Indiana, 1938,
drawing by Saarinen office.

Eliel Saarinen: Chicago Tribune
Competition Entry, 1922.

the "romantic" tale of how he lost the Chicago Tribune Tower competition
through a technicality and the excessive praise it received in the architectural press by individuals such as Louis Sullivan, in one of his last writings,[44]
Saarinen became a leading modernist and his name constantly was linked,
as one critic wrote, in "a kind of kyrie eleison, Saarinen, Le Corbusier,
Neutra and Frank Lloyd Wright."[45] An architect writing as late as 1976
about the Tribune design could claim: "The astonishing thing about the
quality of Saarinen's design was that there was no trace of historical
precedent, no style with which to identify it."[46] Yet even a superficial
examination reveals that the Saarinen design is loaded with Gothic revival
and *Jugenstil* motifs and fits in with the developing setback-skyscraper
school of Ralph Walker and John Wellborn Root, II. In fact, the Tribune
competition had many more progressive and radical designs by architects
such as Walter Gropius, Adolf Meyer, B. Bijuoet, and J. Duiker. Saarinen's
entry was, in other words, a "conservative" modern example. Even Saarinen's later work, such as that at the Cranbrook Institute, which became one

of the centers for the study of modern design in the 1930s, was never radical. He might include a chromium-steel chair or two in his house, but the overpowering feeling is of a warm, cozy, and nature-related design. *Architectural Forum* magazine praised the Kingswood portion of the Cranbrook School in 1932 as follows: "There has been no effort to achieve a startlingly different or individualistic scheme of architectural design—a fact which may account largely for the undoubted success of the building."[47] His later work indicates a progressive simplification of motifs and elimination of details, yet he never disowns ornament, and traditional images are always apparent. His reputation came from being slightly on the forefront of popular architectural taste, combined with a sensitivity to materials and site.

Willem Marinus Dudok was first nominated for the Gold Medal in 1936. The award in 1955 came after his best-known work had been completed, although he was very active in the reconstruction of the Netherlands in the post-World War II years. The perception of his transformation from thatched roof to brick has been commented upon, but it should be noted that in the 1930s and 1940s he was considered one of the leading modern architects, and was extensively published. Displaying an indebtedness to both the Amsterdam expressionist school and the work of Frank Lloyd Wright, Dudok's architecture has a warm, brick, hand-crafted feel, and he utilized ornament.

Exemplified in the Gold Medal in these years was a preference for a very heavy, massive image that has gone under a variety of names, from "stripped classicism" for low-rises to "American perpendicular," "skyscraper style," and "the New York style" for high-rises.[48] Essentially a continuation of the attraction for large, sublime masses noted in the last chapter, this continued as a worldwide phenomenon in the 1930s, 1940s, and 1950s in the work of such diverse individuals as Paul Cret, Auguste Perret, Albert Sphere, and A. V. Shchusev. The essence of this massive style was covering the building with large areas of masonry, brick, or concrete panels that defined the masses. The structure in most cases was a steel frame. Opposite to the volume consciousness of the International Style, this approach eschewed large areas of glass and thin flat walls. Douglas Haskell, a polemicist for the European machine style, claimed this massy approach was "dangerous" in 1930.[49] In general, a hierarchical system of massing following rules of symmetry would be apparent. Monumentalism and bulk were positive aesthetic virtues. The Palmolive Building in Chicago by John Root and the Barclay-Vesey Building by Ralph Walker had what architects called a "good mass."[50] In both cases they responded to the zoning ordinance that required a setback above a certain height from the street. Instead of treating the mass as a base and tower, both designs attempted to integrate the forms and create large, continuous, bulky masses. The setbacks of the tower of the Barclay-Vesey are continuous. In the Palmolive Building, the superstructure of the tower is grouped at one end of the site and the base falls away in gradually diminishing steps at the other. Continuity in materials, texture, and ornament helps to unite the disparate parts of both buildings. Openings in the mass, windows, and doors were treated as voids and not as surface continuations. Ornament varied depending upon the building and the period, though generally there is a diminution in the later

Chicago Historical Society

Holabird & Root: Palmolive Building, Chicago, Illinois, 1928–1929, rendering by Gilbert Hall.

1930s and 1940s. By the 1940s a structure with no ornament had been achieved. John Root's Hotel Statler (1942) in Washington, D.C., and Ralph Walker's AFL-CIO Building, also in Washington, are good examples of the final stage of evolution.

What to call this style — really a later stage in classicism — is perplexing. While the roots are not nationalistic, it was frequently interpreted as such by Americans. In 1939, Talbot Hamlin wrote an article for *Pencil Points* on the contemporary American style. In it, he defined a generic approach that

> . . . sometimes, recognizing its classical basis, adopts frankly classical mouldings, cornices or conventional proportions, but it avoids the use of orders, and is usually free from historical precedent. . . .
> Its forms are generally stripped, clean, clear. . . .
> It believes in the greatest restraint in the use of architectural ornament, but it welcomes richness of decoration in well applied sculpture, and in lavish treatment of metal grills, window and door frames.

He identified this "American style," as having roots in the American classical impulse, but, he declared:

> Archaeological architecture was dead. . . . Yet classicism in its larger sense was not dead. People still loved noble materials, noble proportions, serenity, quietness, the sense of permanence.

Hamlin identified a number of roots for this style, from earlier American Greek revivals of the 1810s to 1840s to the Parisian Arts Décoratifs Exposition and Bertram Goodhue. As contemporary examples, he listed the host of recently completed federal buildings in the United States, "many portions of Rockefeller Center," and "almost all the work of Holabird and Root."[51]

Modern and yet not thoroughly original, accepting of certain historical images but in a simplified way, and essentially classical, this stripped-classical, or skyscraper, style is the area in which most of the Gold Medalists of the period 1938–1958 meet, at least tangentially. Auguste Perret is certainly the preeminent French example, and while he keeps his buildings more open with the concrete structural system, the essence of his work is based in classicism. Likewise, Paul Cret and his Folger Shakespeare Library, Federal Reserve Board Building, and Naval Hospital are based in classicism, though each shows a progressive simplification of ornament. Ralph Walker, who bursts onto the American architectural scene in 1927 with the Barclay-Vesey, gradually subdues his ornament with later high-rises such as the Irving Trust Company Building in New York. John Wellborn Root II, of Holabird & Root, claimed that buildings such as the Board of Trade, the Palmolive, the Chicago Daily News, and the Ramsey County Court House were all examples of "what we call 'contemporary.'" In an interview, he rejected the terms *moderne* and *modernistic* as being inaccurate.[52] Certainly, not all of Holabird & Root's work falls into his stripped-classical look, yet the influences are obvious.

Even in buildings that seem to be more open, there is the treatment of the wall as mass rather than transparency. The A. O. Smith Research

Auguste Perret: Garage in rue Ponthieu, Paris, 1906.

L'Architecture vivante, Spring/Summer 1924

Holabird & Root: Statler Hotel,
Washington, D.C., 1942, rendering
by Gilbert Hall.

Ralph Walker, for Voorhees,
Walker, Foley & Smith: AFL-CIO
Headquarters Building, Washington,
D.C., 1953–1956.

Building in Milwaukee, 1929, by Root, has large areas of glass and a remarkably open plan with 50-foot spans. However, the emphatic and decorated cornices and the strong corner piers tend to close the composition and give a feeling of weight. Root noted the change in sensibility that the International-Style dogma would have created, if followed, in a letter of 1955: "The influences of the time seem to have dictated stone pylons at the corners. The design as we look at it now would have been better if the glass and aluminum grill had enclosed the whole building from corner to corner."[53]

The conservative, modern cast of the Gold Medal in the years 1938–1958 is also revealed in the award to the two principle city planners, Sir Patrick Abercrombie and Clarence Stein. Certainly other Gold Medalists were concerned with the city; Saarinen, Wright and Cret come to mind, yet their primary interests and contributions were either more distinctly architectural or theoretical in comparison to Abercrombie and Stein. Both stood for the decentralization of cities, for low-density towns and settlements in the countryside with nature interwoven, and for thoughtful long-range, wide-scale planning. Trained as architects, both attempted to merge the sociological concerns of planning as it was developed in the 1920s with the physicality of design. Both had practices as architects: in the case of Abercrombie, only a few of his buildings were constructed, but Stein had substantially more built. Stein worked in the Goodhue office on the 1915 San Diego exposition, the Marine Corps and Naval Air Station there, and the "new" town of Tyrone, New Mexico. Consequently, Stein's early architectural work betrays the Goodhue influence. In the area of planning, both Stein and Abercrombie were greatly influenced by the garden-city concepts of Sir Ebenezer Howard, the designs of Sir Raymond Unwin and Barry Parker, and the biosociological concerns of Patrick Geddes.

Abercrombie took Geddes's "Place, Work, 'Folk' which may be classicized, Geography, Economics and Anthropology, or given active modern life as Environment, Function and Organism," and translated them into more immediate concerns of "Proper Sanitary conditions, Amenity and Convenience."[54] The import of Abercrombie's work was toward urban dispersal, and the ultimate impact was the British New Towns Act of 1946. His basic position was to preserve the character of the English landscape, or, as he said with reference to building in the countryside: "It is poor economics to bring prosperity and improvement in one direction and at the same time induce deterioration."[55] Abercrombie advocated surveys—national, regional, and rural or village—the intent of which would be a thorough revision of development practices and an end to ribbon and scattered suburbs. The recognition of place, both in planning and in architecture—the historical nature of humanity—was at the core. He was conservative in his recognition of traditional values, and the long-range impact would be widely dispersed, low-density, new towns.

The character of Clarence Stein's work was substantially the same, though in his case Lewis Mumford was a decided influence in transmitting the ideas of Geddes, Howard, and others and also creating the myth of the organic American village surrounding the common. In the 1920s, Stein and Mumford, along with Benton McKay, Catherine Bauer, and Henry Wright,

Haines, Lundberg & Waehler

Ralph Walker, for Voorhees, Gmelin & Walker: Irving Trust Company Building, New York City, 1929–1932, preliminary study of lower floors. Drawing attributed to Ralph Walker or Henry Coke Smith.

Holabird & Root: A. O. Smith Company, Research and Engineering Building, Milwaukee, Wisconsin, 1929–1931.

A. O. Smith Company

Sir Patrick Abercrombie: view of Dublin Bay from above the Howth Peninsula.

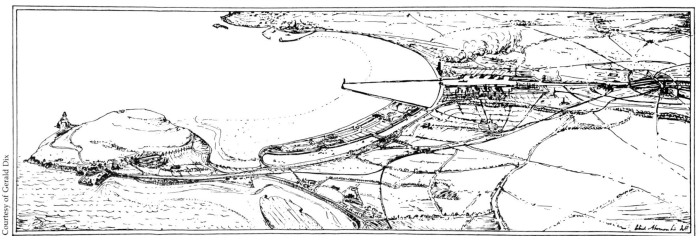

Courtesy of Gerald Dix

81

Wright & Stein: planners and
architects, Radburn, New Jersey,
plan, 1929.

founded the Regional Plan Association of America, which, according to
Mumford, "already recognized in the 1920s that a substantial dispersion of
population and industry to suburban areas would be accelerated by electric
power and the gasoline engine. It viewed the issue as one of controlled,
regional decentralization . . . or formless dispersion."[56] For Stein, the dis-
organization of the typical American city or town was anathema, and he
became a major proponent of the neighborhood unit and shopping centers.
Main Street had, according to him, "excessive congestion."[57] With the
landscape architect and planner Henry Wright, Stein designed a number of
neighborhoods or villages, such as Sunnyside Gardens in Queens, New
York (1924–1928), and Radburn, New Jersey (1928–1933). Radburn was
described by Stein as "realistically planned for the motor age."[58] Conceived
around the idea of a superblock and the separation of pedestrian and
vehicular traffic, Radburn was modern in the sense of recognizing the
impact and possibilities of the automobile, but essentially the values per-
sonified and the architecture constructed was conservative (Plate 11). Stein
frequently acted as a consultant and planner, rather than as an architect, in
later projects such as Chatham Village in Pittsburgh (1930–1935) or Baldwin Hills Village (1938–1942) in Los Angeles. The impact of Stein's "Radburn idea," as he termed it, would be immense, influencing several generations of architects, planners, and speculative builders on both sides of the
Atlantic.[59]

Abercrombie and Stein's interest in dispersion and the integration of
nature was certainly not the only planning approach in these years, yet the
idea of people going back into the landscape and of their buildings occupying only a minimal amount of ground area is a constant preoccupation of
architects from Le Corbusier to Frank Lloyd Wright. Stein and Abercrombie
rejected both the mechanistic and increased density of Le Corbusier's model
cities, Ville contemporaine and Radiant City and the rural character of Frank
Lloyd Wright's "Broadacre City" for a path between.

The Gold Medalists of the period 1938–1958, who have been
grouped together as conservative modernists were not united by a specific
style or approach to design. Their work varied wildly—Wright's Guggenheim Museum (Plate 12), Walker's Barclay-Vesey Building, Maginnis's
Boston College Law School, and Stein's Radburn, New Jersey, are radically
different—and yet there is perhaps some internal consistency. They are
united not simply by their opposition to the European machine-modern but
by a basic humanistic attitude that emphasized nature, variety, history, and
ornament. Importantly, they scaled their buildings for humans. The lack of a
clear-cut dogma, even in the case of Frank Lloyd Wright, precluded their
continued victory vis-à-vis the more aggressive and polemical radical modernists, yet for a considerable period they were heartily admired by professional American architects.

Notes

1   William Adams Delano, "A Marriage of Convenience," *Journal of
the AIA*, vol. 1, May 1944, p. 214.

2   Eliel Saarinen, "The Principles of Modern Architecture," *Journal
of the Royal Institute of British Architects*, ser. 3, vol. 39, January
1932, pp. 235–239.

3   E. B. Morris, "What Buildings Give you a Thrill?" *Journal of the
AIA*, vol. 10, December 1948, pp. 272–277.

4   "What Are the Outstanding Buildings?" *Federal Architect*, vol. 2,
April 1932, pp. 7–10.

5   Frank Lloyd Wright, "In the Cause of Architecture," *Architectural
Record*, vol. 23, March 1908, p. 155.

6   Esther McCoy, *Vienna to Los Angeles: Two Journeys,* Art & Architecture Press, Los Angeles, 1979.

7   "The modernists contend that any application of style to modern design or any buildings which reflect tradition cannot in any sense be construed as modern architecture." Howell Lewis Shay, "Modern Architecture and Tradition," *T-Square Club Journal,* vol. 1, January 1931, p. 12.

8   "On Our Library Table," *The Architect,* vol. 9, December 1927, p. 287.

9   Ralph Walker, "A New Architecture," *Architectural Forum,* vol. 48, January 1928, p. 4, 1.

10   Arthur Drexler, *The Architecture of the École des Beaux-Arts,* Museum of Modern Art, New York, 1979, p. 6.

11   Frank Lloyd Wright, "For All May Raise the Flowers Now, For All Have Got the Seed," *T-Square Club Journal,* vol. 2, February 1932, p. 6, 8.

12   George Howe, "Moses Turns Pharaoh," *T-Square Club Journal,* vol. 2, February 1932, p. 9.

13   William Adams Delano, "Man versus Mass," *The Octagon,* vol. 4 July 1932, p. 10; originally published in *Shelter,* vol. 2, May 1932.

14   Ralph Flint, "Present Trends in Architecture in Fine Exhibition," *Art News,* vol. 30, February 13, 1932, p. 6.

15   Nikolaus Pevsner, *Pioneers of the Modern Movement,* Faber & Faber, London, 1936, p. 206.

16   Reyner Banham, *Age of the Masters,* Harper & Row, New York, 1975, p. 43.

17   Quoted in Theo White, *Paul Cret,* Art Alliance Press, Philadelphia, 1973, p. 53.

18   "Plus," *Architectural Forum,* vol. 69, December 1938, pp. 1–6.

19   "Where is Modern Now?" *Architectural Forum,* vol. 68, June 1938, pp. 465–470.

20   William Gray Purcell to Meyers, June 25, 1938, Purcell and Elmslie Collection, Northwest Architectural Archives, University of Minnesota.

21   Henry-Russell Hitchcock, "Modern Architecture, I: The Traditionalists and the New Tradition," *Architectural Record,* vol. 63, April 1928, pp. 337–349; "Modern Architecture, II: The New Pioneers," *Architectural Record,* vol. 63, May 1928, pp. 453–460; *Modern Architecture, Romanticism and Reintegration,* Payson & Clarke, London, 1929.

22   Le Corbusier, *Towards a New Architecture,* Praeger, New York, 1970, p. 10.

23   Walter Gropius, "Principles of Bauhaus Production," 1925, in Ulrich Conrad (ed.), *Programs and Manifestos on 20th-Century Architecture,* MIT Press, Cambridge, 1975, p. 96.

24   Eliel Saarinen, *Search for Form,* Reinhold, New York, 1948, p. 89, 220.

25   Quoted in Albert Christ-Janer, *Eliel Saarinen,* rev. ed., University of Chicago Press, Chicago, 1979, p. 52.

26   William Adams Delano, "Architecture Is an Art," *Architectural Forum,* vol. 72, April 1940, pp. 10–11.

27   Philip Youtz, "American Architecture Emerges from the Stone Age," *Creative Art,* vol. 10, January 1932, p. 20.

28   Le Corbusier, *Towards a New Architecture,* op. cit. p. 18.

29   Lewis Mumford, "Symposium: The International Architectural Exhibition," *Shelter,* vol. 2, April 1932, pp. 3–4.

30   Catherine Bauer, "Who Cares about Architecture," *New Republic,* vol. 66, May 6, 1931, p. 326.

31   As early as 1923, the *Journal of the AIA* began reviewing foreign publications and publishing, both with and without comment, projects by Mies, Le Corbusier, and others. See, *Journal of the AIA,* vol. 11, September 1923, pp. 365–370; vol. 11, December 1923, pp. 472–475; vol. 12, March 1924, p. 122; vol. 12, May 1924, pp. 237–239; vol. 13, May 1925, p. 158.

32   Michael A. Mikkelsen, "A Word about the New Format," *Architectural Record,* vol. 63, January 1928, pp. 1–2. One of the consequences was commissioning Frank Lloyd Wright to write his series on "In the Cause of Architecture," for $10,000. See

33   Robert A. M. Stern, *George Howe,* Yale University Press, New Haven: 1975, p. 77.

34   Harold Bush-Brown, *Beaux-Arts to Bauhaus and Beyond,* Whitney Library of Design, New York, 1976, pp. 36–41.

35   Charles Donagh Maginnis, "Architecture and Religious Tradition," *Architectural Record,* vol. 98, September 1944, p. 89.

36   Eugene Kennedy, personal communication, June 17, 1981.

37   Thomas Tallmadge, *The Story of Architecture in America,* Norton, New York, 1927, chap. 9; Tallmadge, ibid., rev. ed., Norton, New York, 1936, chap. 9.

38   Frank Lloyd Wright, *An Organic Architecture,* MIT Press, Cambridge, 1970, p. 3. Lectures were originally given in England in 1939. For a number of Americans, "organic architecture" was a preferred term; see the review of the International-Style exhibition, Lewis Mumford, "The Skyline, Organic Architecture," *The New Yorker,* February 27, 1932, pp. 49–50.

39   Frank Lloyd Wright, "The Art and Craft of the Machine," an address given at Hull House, Chicago, reprinted in Edgar Kaufmann, Jr., and Ben Raeburn (eds.), *Frank Lloyd Wright, Writings and Buildings,* Meridan, Cleveland, 1960, pp. 55–73.

40   Frank Lloyd Wright, "Of Thee I Sing," *Shelter,* vol. 2, April 1932, p. 10; this was written for the International-Style symposium mentioned in note 29.

41   Lewis Mumford, *The Brown Decades,* Harcourt & Brace, New York, 1931, p. 80.

42   Lewis Mumford, "The Skyline," *The New Yorker,* October 11, 1947, p. 110.

43   San Francisco Museum of Art, *Domestic Architecture of the San Francisco Bay Region,* Museum of Art, San Francisco, 1949.

44   Alan Gowans, *Images of American Living,* Harper, New York, 1964, p. 428.

45   Louis Sullivan, "The Chicago Tribune Competition," *Architectural Record,* vol. 53, February 1923, pp. 151–157.

46   Harvey M. Watts, Letter, *T-Square Club Journal,* vol. 1, February 1931, p. 14.

46   Bush-Brown, *Beaux-Arts to Bauhaus,* op. cit., p. 24.

47   "The Kingswood School for Girls, Cranbrook, Michigan," *Architectural Forum,* vol. 56, January 1923, p. 37.

48   Sources of the various terms are: interview with Wallace K. Harrison, May 5, 1981; Philip Johnson, "The Skyscraper School of Modern Architecture," *Arts,* vol. 17, May 1931, p. 569–575; Lewis Mumford, "Notes on Modern Architecture," *New Republic,* vol. 64, March 18, 1931, p. 121; see also Cervin Robinson and Rosemarie Bletter, *The Skyscraper Style,* Oxford University Press, New York, 1975.

49   Douglas Haskell, "Architecture, Monumental Masses," *The Nation,* vol. 131, November 19, 1930, p. 35.

50   Haskell, ibid., p. 35.

51   Talbot Hamlin, "A Contemporary American Style," *Pencil Points,* vol. 19, February 1938, pp. 99–106.

52   Russell P. Whitehead, "Holabird & Root: Masters of Design," *Pencil Points,* vol. 19, February 1938, p. 121.

53   Letter, John Wellborn Root II to National Academy of Design, New York, May 17, 1955.

54   Sir Patrick Abercrombie, *Town & Country Planning,* Thornton, Butterworth, London, 1933, pp. 103–104.

55   Sir Patrick Abercrombie, *The Preservation of Rural England,* University of Liverpool Press, Liverpool, 1926, p. 53.

56   Quoted in, Henry N. Wright, "Radburn Revisited," *Architectural Forum,* vol. 135, July 1971, p. 53.

57   Clarence Stein and Catherine Bauer, "Store Buildings and Neighborhood Shopping Centers," *Architectural Record,* vol. 75, February 1934, pp. 174–187.

58   Clarence Stein, "Towards New Towns for America," *Town Planning Review,* vol. 20, October 1949, p. 203. Later republished with some modifications and an introduction by Mumford under the same title by the MIT Press.

59   Ibid., p. 220, 329, 341, and ff.

Skidmore, Owings & Merrill: Lever
House, New York City, 1949–1952.

RADICAL MODERNISM

At the awards dinner for the 1957 AIA convention, the keynote speaker, Henry R. Luce, the founder of *Time* and *Life* magazines, spoke on the "architecture of a democracy" and claimed: "The twentieth century revolution in architecture has been accomplished. And it has been accomplished here in America, no matter how great our debt to European genius."[1] Victory in the "battle" for modern architecture had been announced many times before, but the 1957 Gold Medal is the first recognition of the radical reorientation of twentieth-century architecture toward a fundamentally new and a historic expression. Luce's observation reveals the confidence, if not the hubris, of Americans of the 1950s—a pax Americana—a new architecture controlled by Americans.

Actually, in 1957 two AIA awards were given; the Centennial Medal to Ralph Walker, and the Gold Medal to Louis Skidmore. They indicate the uneasiness of many architects with radical modernism. Walker had always been an outspoken foe of radical modernism, which he regarded as a European import. His award represents a rear-guard action by those of the American architectural establishment, still unreconciled to the imperatives of radical modernism. Skidmore's Gold Medal was an ambivalent recognition of the new currents. His citation noted his accomplishments in creating the large corporate—that is, full-service—architectural practice. However, Skidmore had another ability, not in creating design but in adapting and managing it. Under his direction, the New York office of Skidmore, Owings

85

Skidmore, Owings & Merrill:
Manufacturers Hanover Trust Company, Fifth Avenue Branch,
1953–1954.

& Merrill, with Gordon Bunshaft as the principal designer, produced three of the most important buildings of the 1950s: Lever House, 1949–1952, Manufacturers Hanover Trust, 1953–1954, in New York, and Connecticut General Life Insurance, 1953–1957, in Bloomfield, Connecticut (Plate 13). Lever House with its shiny, perpetually new skin and cubist rotation of form, Manufacturers Hanover Trust, a transparent, open pavilion, and Connecticut General Life, a crisp, elegant machine set down in a verdant landscape, were adaptions of radical modern currents of the 1920s and 1930s. Through Louis Skidmore's managerial and persuasive talents, corporations ceased to clad themselves in the safety of historical images and donned images of extreme modernism. Skidmore's success was part of a change that occurred not just across America but around the world in the post-World War II years.

The continuing conservative orientation of many American architects can be seen in the 1958 medal of John Wellborn Root, II; however, thereafter the Gold Medal went with regularity to many of the masters of the new architecture: Walter Gropius, 1959; Ludwig Mies van der Rohe, 1960; Le Corbusier, 1961; Eero Saarinen, 1962; Alvar Aalto, 1963; Pier Luigi Nervi, 1964; Kenzo Tange, 1966; Wallace K. Harrison, 1967; Marcel Breuer, 1968; R. Buckminster Fuller, 1970; Richard Neutra, 1977; and Josep Lluis Sert, 1981. These architects led the way in fundamentally changing the physical world. The change was not simply an exterior alteration of style but an internal reorganization of how people lived, worked, and existed. It

Plate 1 Henry Bacon: Lincoln Memorial, Washington, D.C., 1911–1922, rendering by Jules Guerin, ca 1911.

Plate 2 I. M. Pei & Partners: National Gallery of Art, East Building, interior court, Washington, D.C., 1968–1978.

Plate 3 Johnson/Burgee: Model of the AT&T Building, New York City, 1978.

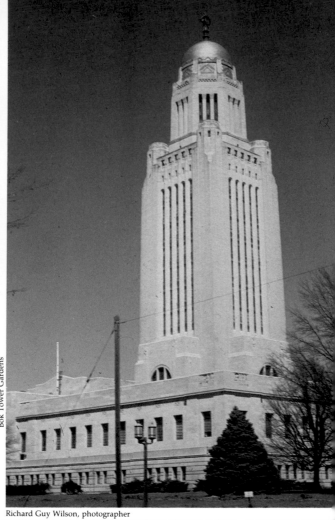

Plate 4   Milton B. Medary: Bok Singing Tower, Mountain Lake, Florida, 1922–1929.

Plate 5   Ragnar Östberg, Stockholm City Hall, Stockholm, 1907–1923.

Plate 6   Bertram G. Goodhue & Associates: Nebraska State Capitol, Lincoln, Nebraska, 1920–1932.

Richard Guy Wilson, photographer

Plate 7   Paul Cret: Indianapolis
Public Library, Indianapolis,
Indiana, 1914.

Plate 8   Gesellius, Lindgren &
Saarinen: National Museum,
Helsinki.

Plate 9   Delano & Aldrich: Marine Air Terminal, La Guardia Airport, New York City, 1939. (above).

Plate 10   Bernard Maybeck: Palace of Fine Arts, Panama-Pacific International Exposition, San Francisco, California, 1912–1915.

Plate 11   Wright & Stein: planners and architects, Radburn, New Jersey, 1929–1931, central green.

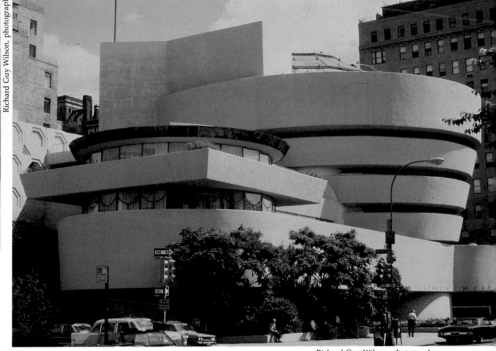

Plate 12   Frank Lloyd Wright: Solomon R. Guggenheim Museum, New York City, 1943–1946, 1956–1959.

Plate 13   Skidmore, Owings & Merrill: Connecticut General Life Insurance Company, Bloomfield, Connecticut, 1954–1957.

Kenzo Tange & Urtec

Plate 14   Kenzo Tange: Yamanashi
Press and Broadcasting Center,
Kofu City, Yamanashi, 1961–1966.

Plate 15   Harrison & Abramovitz:
First Presbyterian Church, Stamford,
Connecticut, 1953–1956, interior.

Plate 18   Willem M. Dudok:
Snellius School, Hilversum, 1932.
(opposite).

Plate 16   Alvar Aalto:
Sanatorium,
Paimio, Finland, 1928–1933,
staircase.

Plate 17   Sert, Jackson & Associates: Science Center, Harvard University, Cambridge, Massachusetts, 1970–1973, interior corridor.

Bell Laboratories

Plate 19   Eero Saarinen: Bell Telephone Laboratory, Holmdel, New Jersey, 1957–1962. (above).

Plate 20   Louis Kahn: Library, Phillips Academy, Exeter, New Hampshire, 1967–1972, interior. (below).

Plate 21   Mitchell/Giurgola: Sherman Fairchild Center for the Life Sciences, Columbia University, New York, New York, 1974–1977.

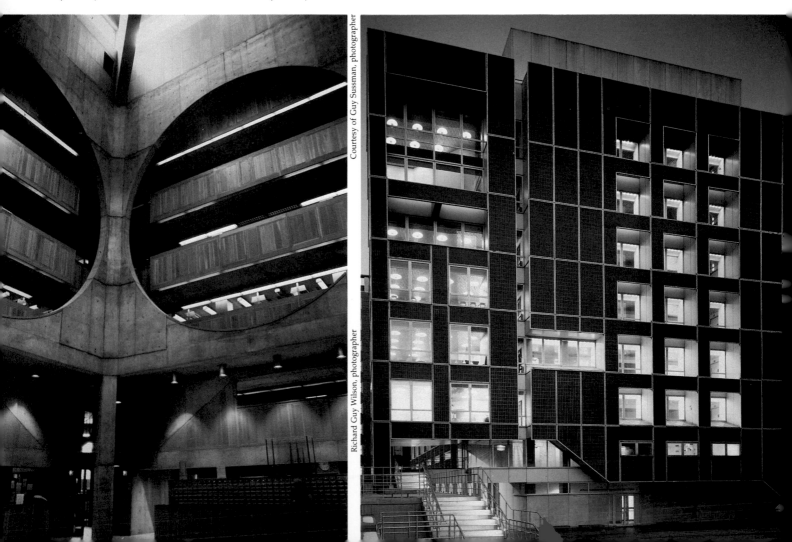

Courtesy of Guy Sussman, photographer

Richard Guy Wilson, photographer

ranged from the planning of the city to the way people sat in chairs and the type they read in books.

The strongest feature that distinguishes the thirteen radical-modern Gold Medalists is not a common style, nor a specific design approach, but the belief that a new architecture needed to be created for the twentieth century. Marcel Breuer summed up this fundamental attitude in a classic statement of 1934, and while not all the radical modernists would completely subscribe to each point, they would agree with the sentiment.

> What, then, are the basic impulses of the New Architecture? In the first place an absence of prejudice. Secondly, an ability to place oneself in immediate objective contact with a given task, problem or form. Thirdly, being unfettered by tradition and the usual stock-in-trade of the intellectual departmental store. Let those who prefer respectful transition from the principles of one school or style to those of another, adopt them if they will. What we believe is what we have perceived, experienced, thought, proved and calculated for ourselves.[2]

Behind such dogmatic statements lay a variety of approaches to the problem of architecture, as diverse as the new architecture itself. Two concerns were fundamental: the need to escape from the past, and the social responsibility of the architect. The coalescence of the ideas of newness, freedom from history, and social concern gave radical modernism not a style or approach but the quality of a controlling belief. Supposedly, questions of image, style, art, taste, and usage of history would be sublimated to a new architectural order defined by the approach to design. The approach: "function," "structure," "technology," and many others (in reality, slogans) would replace the older concerns. Architects claimed their designs were governed by specific processes: Mies, the craft of building; Aalto, abstraction; Nervi, structure; Le Corbusier, science and the machine (in the 1920s); Fuller, technology; Saarinen, the program of the building; Harrison, truthfulness; Neutra, biology and behavior; and Sert, urbanism. Such condensation of the complex process of design to single words is unfair to many of the architects, yet it does serve to illustrate the radical nature of their modernism. These architects sought a new expression based upon the reformulation of architectural principles, free from the fictions of the past. The impossibility of completely rejecting history, and the realization that all of the radical modernists were products of tradition and at times broke faith in their designs and pronouncements was, in general, ignored. As some generations do, the radical modernists saw themselves in opposition to their forebears; they defined their work as free from history. The academy was overthrown and a new academy erected in its place.

Central to the concept of radical modernism was the realization that twentieth-century culture and technology had broken so decisively with the past — perceptually, narratively, and behaviorally — and created not simply new possibilities of living but a new person and a new consciousness. The various experiments and successes in music by Schönberg, Stockhausen, and Cage, in literature by Joyce, Pound, and Sarraute, in painting by Picasso, Mondrian, and Pollock, in science by Einstein and Bohr, in social science by Weber, Mannheim, and Parsons, in psychology by Freud, Jung, and Skinner, and in philosophy by Wittgenstein, Heidegger, and Sartre all contributed to the concept of twentieth-century change. While it is fashionable and indeed correct to see radical-modern architecture as coming into focus in the 1920s, the idea of continual change and progress is fundamental. The arts or psychology did not stand still, so neither should architecture. The consequence was a continually changing or evolving architecture, never static, always dynamic.

The diverse images of the new architecture ranged from simple pavilions set in midwestern river valleys, as in the Farnsworth House by Mies van der Rohe, to urban landscapes of complex and competing forms, as in the Yamanashi Press and Broadcasting Building of Kenzo Tange (Plate 14). The designers themselves changed through their careers. Le Corbusier's early white boxes—flat, transparent, and elegant in detail, as in the Villa Stein at Garches, 1927—gave way in his later years to the density, crudeness, and sculptural massiveness of the chapel of Notre-Dame-du-Haut, Ronchamp, 1950–1955. This shift upset many, as the reaction of one critic

Le Corbusier and Pierre Jeanneret: Villa de Monzie-Stein, Garches, 1926–1927.

Le Corbusier: Notre-Dame-du-Haut, Ronchamp, 1950–1955.

indicates: "To some it may seem strange that such a robust, primitive movement of shapes and textures, with some of the pulse of Africa in them, should come from a man who was once so fascinated by the forms of modern industry and transportation."[3] Other designers were able to change even more rapidly. Eero Saarinen could, within the space of a few years, create images that ranged from the thin membrane walls of the rectilinear General Motors Technical Center, Warren, Michigan, 1948–1956 to the curving, high, sailing roof of Dulles International Airport, Chantilly, Virginia, 1958–1962. Wallace K. Harrison saw different building programs as having fundamentally different images; hence, rectangular slabs and towers for the city, as in the United Nations Headquarters, New York, designed under his guidance, 1947–1954, and the free-form, organically shaped First Presbyterian Church, Stamford, Connecticut, 1956–1959 (Plate 15). In spite of such challenging diversity, others such as Richard Neutra or Buck-

Eero Saarinen: General Motors
Technical Center, Warren, Michigan,
1948–1956.

Eero Saarinen: Dulles Airport
Terminal, Chantilly, Virginia,
1958–1962.

minster Fuller were able to retain a remarkable degree of internal consistency in their architecture. However, their approach was remarkably different and illustrates again the diversity of radical modernism.

Though some commentators and architects have tried to pen specific stylistic labels and to formalize radical modernism, the diversity was apparent right at the very beginning. For most writers the canonical image, the base reference point of the 1920s and the beginnings of radical modernism, is the International Style. The image of the International Style as ahistoric, abstract, and machine-produced is apparent in three of the buildings by leaders of the 1920s: Walter Gropius's Bauhaus, 1925; Le Corbusier's Villa Stein at Garche, 1927; and Mies van der Rohe's Barcelona Pavilion, 1929. However, these examples represented only a narrow stratum of the alternative approaches to the radical reformulation of architecture proposed in these years. Le Corbusier actually presented several possibilities, as can be seen in his Maisons Citrohan and Monol, both of 1920. The Citrohan — the name being a pun on the Citroën motor car and intended to evoke the

Le Corbusier: Maison Monol, project, ca 1920.

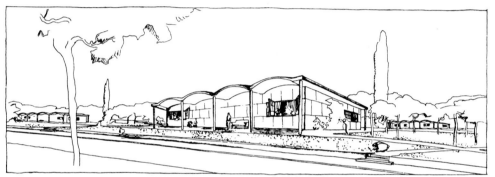

Mies van der Rohe: German Pavilion, world exposition at Barcelona, Spain, 1929.

90

possibilities of mass production—became a prototype of the machinelike, rectilinear International Style. Le Corbusier's Maison Monol was designed to use local, semiskilled labor, the only modern material being asbestos sheeting. The curving shell roof, covered in sod and grass, the wall of local stone rubble, and the overall primitive feeling came from the Algerian vernacular houses. Throughout the 1920s Le Corbusier explored the possibilities of the Citrohan type of housing; however, by 1930 he began to shed the extremes of the machine image and lost faith in the beneficent possibilities of technological civilization. The result would be a building that began to incorporate sensuous and muscular curves, local, vernacular construction, and greater density of image, all prefigured in the Maison Monol.

Mies van der Rohe's Barcelona Pavilion is frequently taken as the epitome of the new rationalism of the 1920s: regular, ordered, instantly perceivable. The Schinkelesque, neoclassical overtones were generally overlooked and ignored at the time.[4] Yet, earlier Mies had explored neoclassical elements in several of his pre-World War I houses, and it did reappear in the 1920s in several apartment houses. An expressionist tendency of extreme shapes and angles was fully apparent in his two glass skyscraper designs, an angular one of 1919, and a curved, faceted one of 1920–1921.

Gropius, and, for that matter, the entire Bauhaus, was more expressionistic than rationalistic in the years 1919–1922. The Sommerfield House in Berlin, 1921–1922, designed by Gropius and Adolph Meyer and built by Bauhaus students, is a romantic, crafty log cabin, filled with faceted, crystalline details—far different than the Bauhaus in Dessau, which is a polemical statement of the efficiency and rationality of the machine age and distinctly nonexpressionist.

Walter Gropius and Adolf Meyer: Sommerfield House, Berlin, 1921–1922.

The Architects' Collaborative

91

In addition to Le Corbusier, Mies, and Gropius, there were other designers working in the 1920s — Nervi, Aalto, and Fuller — who suggested other alternatives or approaches to the question of a new architecture. Pier Luigi Nervi explored the possibilities of reinforced-concrete designs which had no relationship either to the International Style or to most other defined styles. The Florence Stadium of 1929–1932 exploited structure as architectural expression and in its daring cantilevers went far beyond the paper dreams of Mies, or the Russian Constructivists.

Alvar Aalto initially appeared to be a rather doctrinaire International Stylist, as in the Turun Sanomat Building, Turku, 1928–1930, though the press room had huge sculptural piers. The sanatorium at Paimio, 1929–1933, also seemed to be International Style in its form, fenestration, color, and details (Plate 16). The fracturing of the building into a series of wings was prefigured by the functional split of parts, as in Gropius's Bauhaus. Yet, in Aalto's hands the wings were not aligned rectilinearly, but

Pier Luigi Nervi: Municipal Stadium, Florence, Italy, 1929–1932.

seem almost awkward and crude in their juncture, reminiscent of the plan of Hadrian's villa. He claimed the arrangement came from the determinants of sunshine and view and, accordingly, gave each wing "a special position in the landscape according to the demand of the rooms."[5] Yet there is no apparent consistent approach; the same functions—for example, stairs and patients' rooms—receive different treatments. It is a picturesque composition. His almost simultaneous library at Viipuri, 1928–1934, also reflects the same attitude. He later described how the composition at Viipuri came through a series of "childlike drawings representing an imaginary mountain." The arrangement of forms, and indeed the interior landscape of the conical roof lights for the reading room and the undulating ceiling of the conference room, were abstractions of this approach, reached not totally through logical processes but through "feeling."[6] Instead of a logical rationalization of functions, the design came through intuition.

Buckminster Fuller presents a completely different alternative, for he

Alvar Aalto: City Library, Viipuri, Finland, 1927–1935, lecture hall.

Alvar Aalto: Sanatorium, Paimio, Finland, 1928–1933.

claimed his designs were not concerned at all with visual values, intuition, or the subconscious but only with the maximization of existing technology. The Dymaxion House of 1927 was expressive of "maximum gain of advantage from minimal energy input" and was a series of decks supported from a central mast of high-pressure, inflated duraluminum that contained all the mechanics: elevator, waste disposal, energy outlets, and air conditioning.[7] This and Fuller's other designs, such as the Ten Deck Building, 1927, while only existing in model stage, served as a conscience to many of the designers of radical modernism. If the statements and proclamations on architecture coming to terms with the revolution of the machine and technology were to

Buckminster Fuller: "Dymaxion House," 1927, drawing.

Courtesy of Buckminster Fuller

94

be believed, those factors would need to be taken as determinants. Aesthetics for Fuller really did not exist or, alternatively, his attitude was typically American pragmatism: "beauty as the promise of function."[8]

These various approaches to architecture in the 1920s indicate the lack of stylistic unity apparent in radical modernism from its very formation and why, even when a new academy had been created, the architecture still could take on so many different expressions. Radical modernism had both strengths and weaknesses. It was both heroic and foolhardy in the attempt to start all over again. Agreement could be reached on the need for a new architecture, the important role that modern technology should play, and the social responsibility of the architect, but stylistic agreement was elusive. Without a common stylistic model and with the architect seeking individual expression, a not-unexpected result occurred. Agreements on polemics did not transfer into buildings; diversity in construction overwhelmed paper consistency.

One of the common agreements among most radical modernists—though a few wavered at times—was the issue of social responsibility of architecture. Radical modernism was serious architecture concerned with issues of recycling housing, saving cities, and providing a better life for all people. The word *science* had the air of systematic thoroughness and objective observation. Consequently, for most radical modernists the "scientific" approach became a key attitude for their architecture. Traditional architects, whether of the beaux-arts, arts-and-crafts, or conservative-modernist persuasion, seemed excessively preoccupied with style, the depth of moldings, proportions, and other ephemeral matters. Replacing such frivolous concerns, radical modernists looked to fundamentals; minimum housing standards, green space for the cities, hygiene, the relation between economics and buildings production, and large-scale housing projects. The writing of the radical modernists reflects this social concern, with the implication that Armageddon is just around the corner unless the remedies are followed: Walter Gropius, *Rebuilding Our Communities* (1945) and *The Scope of Total Architecture* (1955); Josep Lluis Sert, *Can Our Cities Survive?* (1941); and Richard Neutra, *Survival through Design* (1954).

Buildings and projects were represented not as unique art objects but as research and prototypical solutions to serious and real problems. Consequently, much of the early work was either projects or demonstration buildings: Le Corbusier's Voisin Plan for Paris, 1925, and the Maisons Citrohan and Monol, 1920; Buckminster Fuller's Dymaxion House, 1927; Richard Neutra's Rush City Reformed and Diatom Prefabricated House, 1923; and the Stuttgart Weissenhofsiedlung (housing exposition), 1927, with Mies van der Rohe in charge and buildings by him, Gropius, Le Corbusier, and others.

International expositions have always been showcases of advanced architectural ideas and polemics. In the 1930s the expositions became modern in appearance and adopted the themes of salvation through design. The Century of Progress Exposition in Chicago of 1933, with Louis Skidmore as chief of design, was daring in its radicalism—demonstration houses, art deco buildings, and the message that science and technology lead to the good life. While many of the designers, such as Paul Cret, Ralph

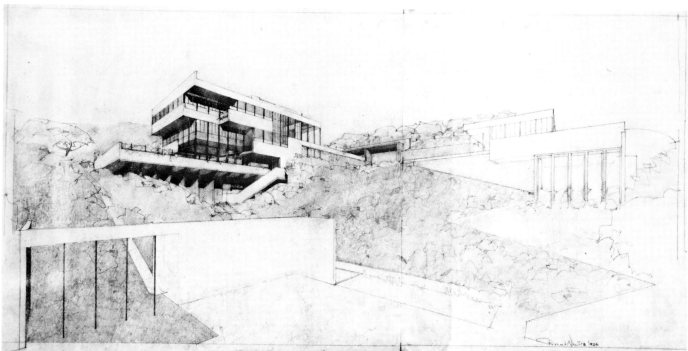

Richard Neutra: Lovell House, exterior perspective.

Richard Neutra: ''Health House,'' Dr. Philip Lovell House, Los Angeles, California, 1929, construction photograph.

Walker, and John Root, were conservative modernists, they can be seen responding to the new imperatives of radical modernism. The 1939 New York exposition was titled "The World of Tomorrow" and was filled with projects for radical transformations of the landscape, from gigantic high-rises to superhighways. Expo 67 at Montreal had Buckminster Fuller's dome as the U.S. pavilion. Expo 70 in Tokyo was dominated by a large space-frame that Kenzo Tange used as the central ordering device.

Important to this prototypical identification design would be labeling, taking the house or the building out of the realm of the individual client. Richard Neutra called his house for Doctor Philip Lovell in Los Angeles, 1929, the "Health House," indicating its more far-reaching consequences. Physiological and psychological benefits could actually accrue to the occupants of a well-designed home. While some of the ideas of health, physical fitness, and hygiene are common to radical modernism (In 1930, Le Corbusier produced a movie, *Esprit Nouveau,* that showed calisthenics on the roof of one of his houses!), Neutra made them a major theme of his architecture with the title "Biological Realism."[9] It might be noted that Dr. Lovell was a health faddist and wrote a newspaper column on care of the body. The Lovell house, an elegant steel-framed pavilion, infilled with either glazing or steel panels covered with hose-poured concrete — gunite — was also a demonstration house as far as techniques of prefabrication and new technology. Bethlehem Steel gave a discount on its product if the house could be used in advertisements. Neutra would continue with the idea of designs as statements of research problems, perhaps most apparent in his own house of 1932 in Los Angeles, labeled the V. D. L. Research House in honor of its sponsor.

Acting as a guide to the social consciousness of radical modernism was CIAM (Congrès Internationaux d'Architecture Moderne), founded in 1928 under the guidance of Le Corbusier and Sigfried Giedion and continuing until 1956. Nearly all of the radical modernists attended at least one of the ten CIAM meetings held between 1928 and 1956. CIAM can be seen in one sense as part of the academization of radical modernism, and while there was never an overt attempt to throw a blanket of style over the members, the interaction at various meetings and the definitions of the important problems and solutions tended to create a conformity of viewpoints. The social responsibility of CIAM is evident from several points of the 1928 La Sarraz Declaration:

> The idea of modern architecture includes the link between the
> phenomenon of architecture and that of the general economic sys-
> tem. . . . The most efficient method of production is that which
> arises from rationalization and standardization. . . . Urbanization
> cannot be conditioned by the claims of a pre-existent aestheticism;
> its essence is of a functional order. . . . The chaotic division of
> land, resulting from sales, speculation, inheritances, must be
> abolished by a collective and methodical land policy.[10]

Later CIAM congresses abandoned some of the 1920s socialist polemics, but never the essential social responsibility of architecture. The question of architecture's concern with the city noted in 1928 became paramount in 1933 at the "Functional City" meeting. The Charter of Athens, composed by Le Corbusier, Sert, Giedion, and others as they cruised the Mediterranean on the *S.S. Paris,* codified Le Corbusier's view of town planning, later reformulated as *La Ville radieuse* (*The Radiant City*). The general apocalyptic air was one of "chaos." Cities today did not "satisfy the primordial biological and psychological needs of their inhabitants." "The new mechanical speeds have disrupted the urban environment, creating permanent danger, causing traffic jams and paralysing communications, and interfering with hygiene." The solution was of course planning, zoning, restructuring the city into "a functional unit." For architecture this meant tall towers, thus freeing the ground for green space. "Private interest will be subordinated to the collective interest."[11]

Still later CIAM congresses, especially those under the leadership of Sert, moved away from the doctrinaire and sterile aspect of the functional city and, as at the 1947 Bridgewater Congress, toward "the creation of a physical environment that will satisfy man's emotional and material needs and stimulate his spiritual growth."[12]

The results of CIAM, or the CIAM method of thinking, are not hard to find, and while it is inaccurate to assign all the redevelopment and rebuilding of cities from the 1930s onward to its pronouncements, certainly its principles have guided many. Rockefeller Center, not a CIAM project became an icon of radical modernism and another demonstration of the possibilities of large-scale inner-city redevelopment. With Rockefeller

Reinhard & Hofmeister; Corbett, Harrison & MacMurray; Hood, Godley & Fouilhoux; and Harrison & Abramovitz, associated architects: Rockefeller Center, New York, 1929–1939, 1953–1974.

Center and CIAM as a guide, many cities in Europe and America rebuilt themselves. In Europe the destruction of the war made it both possible and feasible; in the United States a brand of liberalism led to urban renewal. Walter Gropius's Boston Back Bay project, Wallace K. Harrison's Empire State Mall in Albany, and Mies van der Rohe's Lafayette Park in Detroit are examples of CIAM attitudes toward the city. Today, most such massive projects are viewed with critical disdain as failures to preserve the life of the city, and certainly there are real questions about such approaches. Some of the blame lies with the architects, but politicians and planners were also at fault. And perhaps as time passes and these seemingly alien objects gain the slight patina of age and familiarity, as Rockefeller Center has, they may gain a certain approbation and following.

One consequence of this increasingly urban interpretation of the social responsibility of the architect has been the tendency to move away from the rather stark, alien, and puritanical aspect of many of the earlier examples of radical modernism and see the building as part of the city or as a small city or village in itself. Instead of the finite quality of much earlier work, Kenzo Tange's Yamanashi Press and Broadcasting Center, 1961–1966, has an almost anthropomorphic quality of change capable of growth or contraction. The service and communication shafts support flexible floor levels. Josep Lluis Sert's Science Center at Harvard University, 1970–1973, draws up on the later work of Le Corbusier, it is a picturesque

Sert, Jackson & Associates: Science Center, Harvard University, Cambridge, Massachusetts, 1970–1973.

Hillel Burger, photographer; courtesy of Josep L. Sert

are for the most part unknown. They are part of the trend of our time towards anonymity. Our engineering structures are examples. Gigantic dams, great industrial installations and huge bridges are built as a matter of course, with no designer's name attached to them. They point to the technology of the future."[21] "Technology is rooted in the past. It dominates the present and tends into the future. It is a real historical movement."[22] "Architecture is a historical process; it has little or nothing to do with the invention of interesting forms or with personal whims. I believe that architecture belongs to the epoch, not to the individual."[23] Mies's architecture sought this position. Anonymous and machinelike, its roots lay in the industrial vernacular raised up to the level of art. The essence of the architectural expression lay in the industrial materials, the I-beam mullions

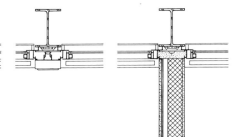

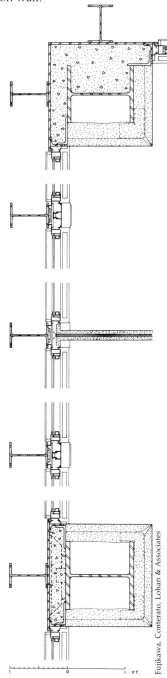

Ludwig Mies van der Rohe: 860–880 Lake Shore Drive, Chicago, Illinois, 1948–1951, horizontal section wall.

Fujikawa, Conterato, Lohan & Associates

and outrigging of 860–880 Lake Shore Drive, the columns of the Farnsworth House, the deep-plate girders of Crown Hall, fitted together in a logical sequence.

Assisting in the attempt to free architecture from the past, or at least the western postmedieval tradition of rejuvenated styles and ornament, were historians who acted as polemicists. Their writings not only influenced the future direction of architecture but became a foundation of the radical-modern academy. The importance of the work of historians such as Sigfried Giedion, Nikolaus Pevsner, and Henry-Russell Hitchcock cannot be overstressed. They gave an air of legitimacy to radical modernism, for they claimed, in a Germanic philosophical and historiographic idealistic stance, that the new architecture expressed the *Zeitgeist*, or spirit of the age. The consequence was a skewing of history, the creation of an exclusivist viewpoint—as noted in the last chapter—where only a small minority of architects, historical and contemporary, were deemed of value and worthy of study. In the rush to exclude, some extreme positions were taken, as reflected in Sigfried Giedion's writing in 1957:

> From Chicago flows the life-blood of American architecture. No architecture either in Europe or elsewhere in America developed so closely in accord with the time or had such courage to tackle new problems as in Chicago between 1883 and 1893. . . . After 1893 Chicago went into a deep sleep. Houses by Frank Lloyd Wright grew as if by magic in the environs of Chicago at the beginning of the century, but they stood alone. . . . Nothing of any value to the history of architecture was produced between the end of the Chicago School in 1893, and the advent of Mies van der Rohe at the Illinois Institute of Technology.[24]

That Giedion completely ignored John Root could be expected, but he was factually incorrect. Wright's houses were not alone but part of the Prairie School, and at least one of Sullivan's most important buildings came after 1893, the Carson, Pirie, Scott and Company Store, 1899–1904.

Giedion was instrumental in forming the taste of several generations of architects, Americans as well as Europeans. He was a participant in the creation of the new architecture in that he was a personal friend of Le Corbusier, Mies van der Rohe, Gropius, Neutra, Breuer, Sert, and Aalto, and he helped to found one of its academies, the CIAM, in 1928. He commissioned the Doldertal Apartments in Zurich, 1933–1936, designed by Marcel Breuer in collaboration with Alfred and Emil Roth. A prolific writer throughout the later 1920s and 1930s in the promotion of the European modernists, Giedion was invited to deliver the Charles Eliot Norton Lectures in 1938 at the instigation of Walter Gropius, the head of the Department of Architecture at Harvard University since 1937, With some alteration, they served as the basis of *Space, Time & Architecture* (1941), certainly the most influential work on architectural history in the United States throughout the 1940s, 1950s, and 1960s. *Space, Time & Architecture* provided a whole host of mechanical sources for radical modernism, from the balloon frame to robots. It promoted large-scale reconstruction of cities, attempted to link Einstein's theories of the universe with the new architecture, and stretched the history of radical modernism back to baroque architecture. This last was certainly in response to the more sculptural work of Le Corbusier and others, and in its own right became a powerful influence in releasing radical modernism from the straitjacket of the International-Style aesthetic.

Nikolaus Pevsner's *Pioneers of the Modern Movement: From William Morris to Walter Gropius* (1936) was, as its title suggests, more restricted chronologically and added a range of later nineteenth-century sources. The linkage of the arts-and-crafts movement, and especially architects like C. F. A. Voysey, to radical modernism became widely accepted, though it was largely incorrect.[25] Pevsner was explicitly moral, arguing for a puritanical simplification of architecture, a dying away of excess, individuality, and frivolity. His essentially cold, machine preferences, needless to say, did not accord well with the rise in post-World War II of the robust baroquelike individualism of later works by Le Corbusier, Saarinen, or Tange.

As important as Pevsner and Giedion in legitimatizing radical modernism was the exhibition held at the Museum of Modern Art in New York in 1932. This exhibit and accompanying books, especially *The International Style* by Henry-Russell Hitchcock and Philip Johnson with a preface by Alfred Barr, provided a name and introduced many Americans to a segment of radical modernism. The Museum of Modern Art organizers claimed that the designs of Le Corbusier, Mies van der Rohe, Gropius, and J. J. P. Oud represented a complete reorientation of architecture and that a new "controlling style" had emerged in Europe. Historically, this architecture grew out of "the unconscious and halting architectural developments of the nineteenth century [and] the confused and contradictory experimentation of the beginning of the twentieth." Now there was "a directed evolution . . . a single body of discipline."[26] The principles of the new architecture—the International Style—were three: "architecture as volume rather than as mass"; "regularity rather than axial symmetry serves as the chief means of ordering design"; and the absence of "arbitrary applied orna-ment."[27] These three principles, it will be noted, have little to do with some of the expressed ideas of the radical modernists, nothing about structure, technology, function, or social responsibility. Hitchcock and Johnson's argument for their primarily aesthetic approach was complex, for while they recognized the importance of the ideas of function and the incorporation of the expressive possibilities of (supposedly) twentieth-century materials and structure, these were not the determinants, for a style—or an aesthetic—had developed that provided a method of arranging facades, fenestration, plans, and details. The International Style became in Hitchcock and Johnson's hands, an aesthetic approach that did not depend upon the ideas of function and materials, which of course was proven by buildings that looked like thin-walled volumetric containers but were stucco-covered brick. This was perfectly acceptable to Hitchcock and Johnson: "From an aesthetic point of view, brick is undoubtedly less satisfactory than any other materials, including stucco."[28] Gropius's Dessau-Torten Siedlung and Le Corbusier's Pessac housing, both 1926–1928, are examples of such "fictive" rendering of brick and concrete block. Interestingly, the concept of a new interpenetrating space was recognized by Hitchcock and Johnson; however, it was not elevated to the height of a principle, but rather sublimated under architecture as volume.

Essentially *The International Style* was a recipe book filled with do's and don'ts on how to design up-to-date buildings: "Flat roofs are so much more useful that slanting or rounded roofs are only exceptionally justified."[29] Treating the parts of a building as objects was stressed: The fireplace became separate from the wall as in Le Corbusier's interiors; stairs were architectural objects in themselves. A new architectural order, a new classicism, as Hitchcock wrote, was being sought.[30]

The book with its rules and photographs made a significant impression, and the International Style was interpreted by critics as "an expression of the fast-growing band of scientific-minded who believe in the universal efficacy of machine efficiency."[31] Another critic wrote: "No matter how monotonous or repetitive or otherwise uninspiring the new style may appear to be in its lesser manifestations—there can be no doubt about its magnificent simplicities and structural logic for large scale work—it is probably the most powerful lever in getting us away from our jumbled aesthetic inheritances that could have been devised."[32] In spite of Hitchcock and Johnson's attempt to disown function and technology as determinants, the International Style became the functionalist expression; its seeming ahistorical image was the expression of necessity and not art. Severity, flat, spartan surfaces, revealed structure, and mechanics became the identifying features. The manufactured object in the landscape and the white interior were its trademarks. It was the machine style, no matter that the forms were rarely dictated or made by the machine.

The identification of the International Style and the writings of Pevsner and Giedion tended to circumscribe the alternatives of radical modernism, and contributed to the academization of radical modernism. Left out were the alternatives, whether Nervi, Fuller, the conservative modernists, or the more expressionist works of Mies, Gropius, Le Corbusier, and other variations: Mendelsohn, Schroon, and the Russian constructivists. While many architects flocked to the banner of the International Style, the more creative talents recognized that a fundamental premise of radical modernism was not a style but the continuous reformulation of architecture.

Revealing the open-ended nature of radical modernism are the alternative proposals by Wallace K. Harrison for the central theme pavilion at the World of Tomorrow Exposition, New York, 1939. Harrison was a convert to the new radicalism. He began his career in the offices of McKim, Mead and White, studied for a brief time at the École des Beaux-Arts, and then worked for Bertram Goodhue. In the late 1920s and early 1930s Harrison worked on Rockefeller Center under Raymond Hood. He had first become aware of Le Corbusier while in Paris in 1921, and in 1935 he and Philip Goodwin were instrumental in bringing Le Corbusier to the United States. With the death of Hood in 1934, Harrison gradually assumed leadership on the later design stages of Rockefeller Center. The Eastern Airlines Building, 1938, is more simplified in shape with less ornament and sculptural setbacks than earlier Center buildings; it is a sheer slab rising from a simple base. For the central theme of the 1939 New York fair, Harrison, his partner Max Abramovitz, and their staff brought forth a variety of proposals which explored the expressive possibilities of modernism. In their complete disregard of history and conventional laws of structure, the projects recall the wilder dreams of Melnikov and Tatlin's Russian-constructivist proposals, Boulée, Ledoux,

Harrison & Fouilhoux: The Trylon and Perisphere, New York world's fair, 1937–1939.

Werner Drews of Harrison & Fouilhoux: drawings for Central Theme Pavilion, New York world's fair, 1937.

and Piranesi's visionary schemes, Buckminster Fuller's suspended buildings, Nervi's cantilevers and science-fiction illustrations. The result: The Trylon and Perisphere rejected some of the technological rhetoric in favor of basic geometrical forms. The Perisphere actually contained a large exhibit, a model city of the future. The inherent dynamism of the forms was enhanced by their juxtaposition and the interpenetrating curved ramp used for egress. Their scale, especially when lit at night, gave the entire enterprise a feeling of high drama, of confidence in the future.

By the late 1930s two trends emerged within radical modernism: the increasing academization and, alternatively, the increasing search for new expressions. The academy can be briefly summarized as consisting of the various historians and critics—Hitchcock, Giedion, and Pevsner—CIAM, and the institutionalization of radical modernism in the architectural schools. Following liberal ideology, radical modernism had always tried to change the world through education, the Bauhaus being the prime example. However, the Bauhaus had always been unstable, riven with cliques and dissenters, and, certainly at least in its later years, at odds with the state. In 1933, the Bauhaus was closed for the last time by the Nazis. In 1937, Walter Gropius was offered the chairmanship of the Department of Architecture at Harvard University, and he brought with him Marcel Breuer. Harvard University, the most prestigious university in America, put its name behind radical architecture. In 1938, Mies van der Rohe, at the suggestion of John A. Holabird (John Wellborn Root II's partner), became the director of architecture at the Armour Institute in Chicago, which would shortly be renamed Illinois Institute of Technology. He brought with him Ludwig Hilbersheimer and Walter Peterhans. A year earlier, Laszlo Moholy-Nagy, a former Bauhaus "master" founded the New Bauhaus in Chicago, the Institute of Design. In 1940, Alvar Aalto accepted a teaching post at MIT, where he remained intermittently until 1950. In succeeding years other schools also accepted Europeans: Erich Mendelsohn at the University of California at Berkeley and Konrad Wachsmann at the University of Southern California. The impact was tremendous, and while the change did not come all at once, by 1950 most American schools were under the sway of radical modernism. Abroad, the same process took place: Nervi taught from 1946 onward at the University of Rome and Tange, beginning in 1946, developed a powerful studio in conjunction with his practice at the University of Tokyo. Le Corbusier never did formally accept a teaching post but lectured constantly and ran an atelier through his office in Paris. This academization would continue in the 1950s and 1960s. Most of the radical modernists spent some time lecturing and teaching at various schools of architecture around the world. Perhaps the ultimate indication of radical modernism as an academy would be the establishment by several architects of foundations to preserve their papers and works and perpetuate their ideas: Le Corbusier, Aalto, Neutra, and Gropius.

While some architects did follow the dictates laid down by the academicians, and some leaders did successfully institute a consistent approach, such as Mies at IIT, the other side of radical modernism and indeed its fundamental premise was continual change, the search for new expressions and forms aided by modern structure and technology. Gropius and Breuer came to the United States as somewhat doctrinaire International Stylists, yet even in their earliest buildings, such as the houses they jointly designed for themselves at Lincoln, Massachusetts, the designs are more relaxed. Native wood, stone, and brick appear, and the smooth, geometrical box of the 1920s becomes more sculptural. This rejection of the 1920s and an increasing sculptural appearance would lead to a new posture, the muscular drama of exposed structure and a renewed search for an abstract monumentalism, as in Breuer's dense, almost solid Whitney Museum, New York, 1963–1966, and Gropius's peripteral American Embassy in Athens, 1956–1961. Eero Saarinen searched more widely and rapidly than the others in the 1950s; hence, he was the most open to criticism. The General Motors Technical Center, Warren, Michigan, 1948–1956, was essentially a

Walter Gropius and Marcel Breuer: Gropius House, Lincoln, Massachusetts, 1937–1938.

Marcel Breuer and Hamilton P. Smith: Whitney Museum of American Art, New York, 1963–1966.

The Architects' Collaborative: United States Embassy Building, Athens, Greece, 1956–1959.

prewar International-Style solution, based to some degree on Mies van der Rohe's Illinois Institute of Technology. In contrast to Mies's solutions, Saarinen suppressed the structure and added color and highly reflective materials. The design he claimed "is based on steel—the metal of the automobile. Like the automobile itself, the buildings are essentially put together, as on an assembly line, out of mass produced units. . . . The Center was, of course designed at automobile scale and the changing vistas were conceived to be seen as one drove around the project."[33] Saarinen moved from this in succeeding projects through a wide variety of forms and images: a thin steel-concrete dome for the MIT Auditorium, 1950–1955, the hung roof of Ingalls Rink at Yale University, 1953–1959, the interlocking concrete vaults of the Trans World Airlines Terminal at John F. Kennedy International Airport, 1956–1962, and finally, the soaring forms of Dulles International Airport, Chantilly, Virginia, 1958–1962. Saarinen described Dulles as "monumental," "the national and international gateway to the nation's capital." Instead of the "static" quality of most federal architecture, he believed "a jet-age airport should be essentially non-static, expressing the movement and excitement of travel."[34]

Against Saarinen's highwire act there stood the more consistent work of Mies van der Rohe, who succeeded in establishing his own academic idiom. Mies's power was summed up by one critic in 1960: "He has influenced present day American architecture more than any other architect. His is an architectural order which can be *learned*. . . . Less able architects have been released from the imperatives of originality and architecture is the better for it. They have found in the reasonable, detached clarity of Mies a system of architecture within which they are able to do a decent job."[35]

Mies's own feelings were stated thus: "Education must lead us from irresponsible opinion to true responsible judgement. It must lead us from chance and arbitrariness to rational clarity and intellectual order."[36] This rebuke to the search of designers such as Saarinen is exemplified in Mies's own work that comes straight from the logic of building. To a collaborator he once said: "I had the idea that buildings ought to look the way they went together."[37] The consequence was that in his later American career Mies confined himself to the parameters of structure and essentially the trabeated system of posts and lintels. While it is true he did depart with the girder-hung roof of Crown Hall or the various space-frame projects, they all developed around the logic of revealed supports. With structure as a basis, the designer was left free to investigate the realm of space, proportions, and the integration of art into the building. The result was a body of work, from the Illinois Institute of Technology to the Seagram Building, that while containing individual differences, had a unity and consistency unmatched by any other radical modernist.

The success of radical modernism in its various guises during the post-World War II years was on an international scale. The world-shrinking advances in communication technology allowed architects in the most obscure and improbable locations to digest the latest expression, style, or slogan, no matter how recondite. The increasing speed and efficiency of air travel allowed for the true international practice. Earlier, Lutyens could build in India, or Wright in Japan, but only through laborious time-consum-

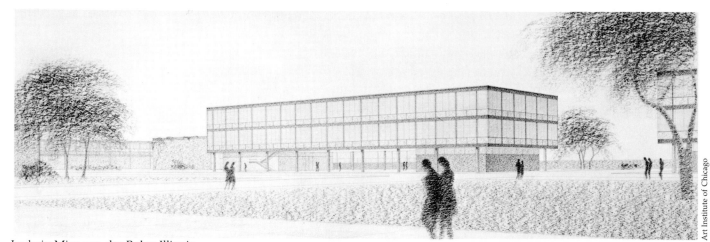

Ludwig Mies van der Rohe: Illinois
Institute of Technology, studies for
buildings, ca 1940.

Mies van der Rohe and Philip
Johnson, associate architect:
Seagram Building, New York City,
1954–1958.

ing weeks of voyages at sea; now, Le Corbusier could be in India overnight and Tange in the Mideast or the United States in a day.

Accompanying and contributing to this international success would be the increasing identification of radical modernism as American. Henry R. Luce was perceptive when he noted that no matter the European origins, the revolution in modern architecture had been accomplished in America. The United States, emerging from World War II as the most powerful country militarily, economically, and politically, accepted radical modernism in its various expressions and then in turn reexported it to the world. The transference of the impetus of modern architecture paralleled a corresponding shift in the other visual arts such as painting; the Paris School lost its dominance to the New York School.

The career patterns of the Gold Medalists tend to support this increasing Americanization of radical modernism. Of the thirteen Gold Medalists, only three — Skidmore, Harrison, and Fuller — were native to the United States. Of the remaining ten, six immigrated to the United States. Of these, only Eero Saarinen came as a child at the age of 12. Neutra arrived in 1923 at the age of 31, his education completed and with a knowledge of advanced European radical modernism, though he had built little. The remaining four all came in the 1930s, fleeing repression at home and with American job offers. After the war they could have returned, but that Mies, Gropius, Breuer, and Sert chose to stay in the United States testifies both to the reception they experienced and their perception that the United States would lead the world in building.

Radical modernism as an increasing American expression inevitably took on certain political attributes and came to be viewed as an expression and ultimately as a symbol of capitalist freedom and democracy. Ironically, though largely forgotten, some of the architects — Mies, Le Corbusier, Gropius, and Nervi — had built, or attempted to build, for fascist regimes. They appear not to have been motivated by political commitment, but rather the force of circumstances and political naiveté. These imprecations were largely unknown, and to their credit Mies, Gropius, and Breuer did leave Nazi Germany. Hitler and many of his subordinates did depreciate modernism, whether in painting or architecture. The question was more complicated in Italy, since Mussolini wavered between a renewed classicism and the International Style. Finally, it should be noted that the Soviet Union had experimented with forms of radical modernism in the 1920s, but by 1932 Stalin had imposed a tight straitjacket of social relevance — that is, traditionalism — on Soviet architecture and art. This brief Russian interlude, actually well-known to many of the architects, historians, and critics of radical modernism — Le Corbusier's Centrosoyus Building was erected in Moscow, 1929–1933 — became submerged in the attempt to sell radical modernism in the United States. Interest in and historical knowledge of the Russian involvement with radical modernism only began to emerge in the later 1960s.

The association of radical modernism with political freedom and democracy came from the negative Nazi attitude toward it and from projects such as Le Corbusier's 1937 Monument to Vaillant-Couturier, a predecessor of the Open Hand in Chandigarh and Josep Lluis Sert's Spanish Pavilion at

111

Josep Lluis Sert and Luis Lacasa:
Spanish Pavilion, Paris world's fair,
1937, interior court.

the 1937 Paris world's fair. The Spanish Pavilion, an open, prefabricated, steel-framed structure, housed Picasso's *Guernica,* and was commissioned by the Spanish Republican government, then in a losing fight with the fascist General Franco.

The United Nations Building in New York, 1947–1952, confirmed the liberal-democratic associations of radical modernism. The choice of Wallace K. Harrison as the director of planning, in reality the head architect, made the choice of radical modernism inevitable. Harrison's selection certainly came partially from his relationship with the Rockefeller family, and he had helped purchase the site they presented to the United Nations, but also because of his reputation as one of the foremost American modern architects. He was largely responsible for selecting the international advisory board composed of representatives from various countries, including Sven Markelius from Sweden, Oscar Niemeyer from Brazil, Matthew Nowicki from Poland, and Le Corbusier from France. In spite of Le Corbusier's reputation as a notoriously difficult collaborator, Harrison insisted on his presence on the committee; Harrison believed that Le Corbusier had been treated unfairly in the League of Nations competition of 1927, when the Parisian's winning proposal had been disqualified on a technicality. Le Corbusier's reputation did prove true. He would later claim major credit for the United Nations design; however, in 1948, when the official announce-

Wallace K. Harrison, chairman of the board of design and director of planning: first sketch for United Nations.

United Nations.

ment of the approved design came, he approved and issued a statement declaring the project was a true team effort.[38] Le Corbusier certainly influenced the form of the buildings and also the concentration into small plots, leaving a vast amount of the 17 acres free for gardens. Harrison, though, is the man who actually designed the complex, chose the details, rejected *brises-soleil* for plate glass, and chose the works of art donated by different countries. The 39-story, slab-shaped Secretariat contrasts with the two low-rising buildings, the curved and domed Assembly Building and the rectangular, cantilevered Conference Building. The complex is uncompromising in its acceptance of the tenets of modernism. It is ahistorical, and its monumentalism comes not from any applied ornament, but simply from size and scale. At its completion it was inevitably hailed as symbolizing peace, freedom, and the modern spirit of the twentieth century.

The United States was perhaps foremost in utilizing radical modernism as a political expression. New American embassies were embarked upon in many countries: England and Norway by Eero Saarinen, Greece by Walter Gropius and The Architects' Collaborative, Brazil and Cuba by Wallace K. Harrison and Max Abramovitz, and the Netherlands by Marcel

Eero Saarinen: United States Embassy, London, 1955–1960.

Breuer. Bucky Fuller's domes were adopted by the armed forces for a variety of uses, including the DEW Line. Military bases around the world were designed by Skidmore, Owings & Merrill. These buildings became implicit symbols of the pax Americana, the cold-war warrior confronting communist aggression around the world. Accompanying this acceptance of radical modernism by the United States government was its acceptance by most western-aligned nations, and by business. The role of Skidmore, Owings & Merrill in repackaging American corporations has been already stressed. However, others — Mies, Aalto, Saarinen, Tange, Gropius, and Harrison — also designed seminal buildings that became corporate icons and identity symbols.

The question of whether these buildings of radical-modern architecture itself had any inherent symbolism was never fully addressed. An example is Vincent Scully, Jr.'s book, *Modern Architecture: The Architecture of Democracy* (1961), a highly idiosyncratic examination of modern architecture, not as a symbol of democracy but as existentialism. A revised version in 1974 keeps the same subtitle, but now the mood is one of despair and anger. Modern architecture has become representative of power and bureaucracy.

Buckminster Fuller: geodesic dome for U.S. Marine Corps, 1954.

Obviously, modern architecture was open-ended symbolically, avoiding any reference outside of itself; it could adopt any meaning, as it could adopt any program. What people did within or controlled from a building became its meaning. A housing project could represent well-meaning social intentions, yet if it failed, it came to be viewed as a symbol of the failure of an entire architectural approach. Seldom examined were contributing factors: economics, changing lifestyles, and a priori decisions. The architects of radical modernism claimed too much for their architecture; it could solve too many problems. The result was a failure of expectations.

Such judgments on the death of modern architecture completely belie the stunning successes of an architecture that has succeeded in conquering the world. Radical modern architecture provided a new approach to architectural problems, a new way of thinking and of designing. Architecture, though, is always more than theory, doctrine, or pronouncements; it is real buildings that can stand the test of time. From Ronchamp to the Lovell Town House, from Lever House to the Hiroshima Peace Center, radical modernism has provided a set of monuments that inspire not only architects but people, and that is the test of a real architecture.

Kenzo Tange: Hiroshima Peace Center, Hiroshima, Japan, 1949–1950.

116

Notes

1 Henry R. Luce, "The Architecture of a Democracy," *Journal of the AIA*, vol. 28, June 1957, p. 149.

2 Marcel Breuer, "Where Do We Stand?" Lecture given in Zurich, 1934, subsequently reprinted many times, *Marcel Breuer Buildings and Projects, 1921–1961*, Praeger, New York, 1962, p. 259.

3 "Corbu Builds a Church," *Architectural Forum*, vol. 103, September 1955, p. 120.

4 Philip Johnson, *Mies van der Rohe*, Museum of Modern Art, New York, 1947, p. 58, noted the Schinkle elements.

5 Alvar Aalto, *Paimio*, Alvar Aalto Museo, Jyväskylä, 1976, originally written 1933.

6 Alvar Aalto, "The Egg of the Fish and the Salmon," *Architectural Design*, vol. 49, December 1979, p. 16, originally written 1944.

7 Quoted in John McHale, *R. Buckminster Fuller*, Braziller, New York, 1962, p. 17.

8 John McHale, "Buckminster Fuller," *Architectural Review*, vol. 120, July 1956, p. 14.

9 Richard Neutra, *Survival through Design*, Oxford University Press, New York, 1954, p. 171.

10 Quote in Ulrich Conrads (ed.), *Programs and Manifestoes on 20th-Century Architecture*, MIT Press, Cambridge, 1970, pp. 109–111.

11 Ibid., pp. 137–145.

12 Sigfried Giedion, (ed.), *A Decade of New Architecture*, Girsberger, Zurich, 1951, p. 7.

13 Le Corbusier, *Towards a New Architecture*, Praeger, New York, 1960, p. 210.

14 Le Corbusier, "Twentieth Century Living," (1930), reprinted in Dennis Sharp (ed.), *The Rationalists*, Architectural Press, London, 1978, pp. 73–74.

15 Colin Rowe, *The Mathematics of the Ideal Villa and Other Essays*, MIT Press, Cambridge, 1977; the major essay was originally published in 1947.

16 Breuer, "Where Do We Stand?" op. cit., p. 259.

17 Walter Gropius and Kenzo Tange, *Katsura: Tradition and Creation in Japanese Architecture*, Yale University Press, New Haven, 1960, p. 11.

18 Josep Lluis Sert, "Gold Medal Speech," *Proceedings of the 113th Annual Convention of the AIA*, AIA, Washington, D.C., 1981.

19 Walter Gropius, "Blueprint of an Architect's Education," 1939, in his *Scope of Total Architecture*, Collier, New York, 1962, p. 57.

20 Kenzo Tange, "Creation in Present-Day Architecture and the Japanese Tradition," 1956, reprinted in Robin Boyd, *Kenzo Tange*, Braziller, New York, 1962.

21 Mies van der Rohe, "Architecture and the Times," 1924, reprinted in Philip Johnson, *Mies van der Rohe*, Museum of Modern Art, New York, 1947, p. 187.

22 Mies van der Rohe, 1950 address at IIT, reprinted in Philip Johnson, *Mies*, 3d ed., Museum of Modern Art, New York, 1978, pp. 203–204.

23 Peter Carter, "Mies van der Rohe," in Dennis Sharp (ed.), *The Rationalists*, Architectural Press, London, pp. 70–71.

24 Quoted in Henry-Russell Hitchcock, "Introduction," in *Architecture of Skidmore, Owings & Merrill, 1950–1962*, Praeger, New York, 1963.

25 See my review of Hermann Muthesius, *The English House*, in *Progressive Architecture*, vol. 62, November 1981, pp. 168–172.

26 Henry-Russell Hitchcock, Jr., and Philip Johnson, *The International Style*, Norton, New York, 1932, p. 20.

27 Ibid.

28 Ibid., p. 52.

29 Ibid., p. 44.

30 Henry-Russell Hitchcock, Jr., "Frank Lloyd Wright," in *Modern Architecture: International Exhibition*, Museum of Modern Art, New York, 1932, p. 37.

31 Kenneth K. Stowell, *Architectural Forum*, vol. 56, March 1932, p. 253.

32 Ralph Flint, "Present Trends in Architecture in Fine Exhibit," *Art News*, vol. 30, February 13, 1932, pp. 5–6.

33 Aline B. Saarinen (ed.), *Eero Saarinen on his Work*, Yale University Press, New Haven, 1968, pp. 30–32.

34 Ibid., pp. 102–104.

35 "Mies van der Rohe," *Architectural Record*, vol. 121, April 1960.

36 Mies van der Rohe, IIT inaugural address, quoted in Werner Blaser, *After Mies*, Van Nostrand Reinhold, New York, 1977.

37 Alfred Caldwell, personal communication, January 1977.

38 Herbert Warren Wind, "Profiles Architect," *The New Yorker*, December 4, 1954, p. 36.

Kenzo Tange & Urtec

Wurster, Bernardi & Emmons: Pope
Ranch House, Madera, California,
1958.

NEW IMAGES

Shifts in taste and how and when the critical juncture occurs becomes increasingly problematical the closer one comes to the present. "Modern architecture," as indicated, never was a monolithic movement with a clear direction, but rather a series of conflicting ideals and approaches encompassing both conservative and radical modernism. The antipathy and unease many American architects found with many aspects of radical modernism in spite of its seeming success was evident throughout the 1950s and 1960s. Beginning in 1969 with the Gold Medal award to William Wurster, a subtle shift becomes obvious, and the succeeding awards to Louis I. Kahn in 1971, Pietro Belluschi in 1972, Philip Johnson in 1978, I. M. Pei in 1979, and the most recent award to Romaldo Giurgola in 1982 indicate a significant redirection in the award. No common label, style, or approach can be placed upon this group. However, their recognition by professional American architects raises the possibility a new synthesis may be in the making and a critical juncture has occurred.

The sense of change and of new possibilities is evident everywhere, perhaps most openly in the acceptance speeches of two of the medalists. Philip Johnson declared in 1978: "We stand at an enormous watershed."[1] The next year, I. M. Pei claimed: "Liberated after 50 years of dogmatic rigidity, architects are exploring alternatives to accepted modes of design."[2]

This sense of a reorientation has been obvious for at least the past decade—never as a violent break, but rather as a slow change. The earlier

Wurster, Bernardi & Emmons

observation in 1931 by Eliel Saarinen of evolution, not revolution, was echoed in 1981 by I. M. Pei: "We are in an evolutionary process, not a revolutionary process at all. Continuity is much more important than change."[3]

Certainly there are major differences between the six Gold Medalists, both in their work, their periods of practice, and their perceptions of themselves and each other. Negative definitions such as *dissent* or *alternative* do not create a homogeneous group. Present in their work, whether consciously or unconsciously, is the affirmation of architecture as concerned with creating image, rather than being exclusively concerned with structure or function. All have placed value on the recognition of the surrounding environment and history. They cannot be labeled by current terms such as *postmodernists* or *inclusivists,* yet some of them—Johnson, Giurgola, and Kahn—have sometimes been so grouped. The six Gold Medalists represent various strains in their work: regionalism, eclecticism, beaux-arts composition, at times, classicism and minimalism, and, finally, a new urban sense of fitting within the context. And there is an undeniable modernist strain.

Pietro Belluschi: Equitable Building, Portland, Oregon, 1943–1948.

All six of the Gold Medalists were heavily influenced by radical modernism and all have produced buildings that might be considered within this group. Pietro Belluschi's Equitable Building in Portland, Oregon, 1944–1947, was one of the first International-Style high-rises in the United States, an elegant statement of the principles Mies van der Rohe would shortly make evident. Louis Kahn's extension to the Yale Art Gallery, 1953, has anonymous and abstract exterior walls of brick and glass, typical of radical modernism and heavily indebted to Mies. On the interior, the tetrahedron-shaped ceiling is derived directly from Buckminster Fuller, and space is typically undefined in the best International-Style manner. William Wurster's urban work of the 1950s and 1960s frequently reveals the reductivist radical-modernist extremes, as in the Coleman House, San Francisco, 1961–1962, with its glazed walls. Philip Johnson was one of the more ardent followers of Mies van der Rohe, collaborating with him on the Seagram Building in New York, 1954–1958, and producing on his own the glass house in New Canaan, Connecticut, 1949, an extreme statement of the marvels of technological civilization in freeing the inhabitant from almost all sheltering enclosure. Much of I. M. Pei's work can be seen as "still on the track laid down in the 1920s."[4] His Kips Bay Apartments and the Society Hill Towers are basically Miesian in inspiration with their revealed frames. Romaldo Giurgola's University of Pennsylvania parking garage, 1963, with its long span of reinforced-concrete beams framed into the diagonal exterior truss, has a clear derivation from the rhetorical structural overstatement of Pier Luigi Nervi. Yet despite these radical-modernist connections, it is also evident that these buildings can be otherwise interpreted in some cases, and that these buildings represent only a few examples from careers which have encompassed many other concerns.

Both Pietro Belluschi and William Wurster had significant pre- and post-World War II careers as designers of houses that were far-removed from the orthodoxy of radical modernism. They made an aesthetic out of native materials and vernacular forms. They created a "woodsy" modern architectural vernacular — the ranch house — that proved to be extremely popular on the Pacific coast. Wurster in fact was part of the "Bay Region Style" that Louis Mumford enunciated back in 1948.[5] More recently, Wurster and Belluschi collaborated on the Bank of America building in San Francisco, which with its setbacks and undulating granite and glass-sheeted surface, was an important and early departure from the strict Miesian orthodoxies of the post-war high-rise. The faceted surface recalls the great period of Chicago skyscraper architecture of the 1880s and 1890s, and also the San Francisco bay-window tradition.

Louis Kahn's work after the Yale Art Gallery extension moved increasingly toward a strong geometrical order reminiscent of Rome. The Salk Institute in La Jolla, California, 1959–1965, has a plan that has been likened to Hadrian's Villa. The composition makes references to mythical elements, with the stream of water representing the flow of life that bisects the central court.

Romaldo Giurgola's work is frequently urban in nature and recognizes the context of the surroundings. The Philadelphia United Fund Building, 1971, has three different facades, each oriented to its particular direc-

Pietro Belluschi: Bank of America World Headquarters, San Francisco. An early Belluschi sketch, May 6, 1964.

Pietro Belluschi: Bank of America, San Francisco, 1964–1970.

122

Salk Institute, view of central court.

Jim Cox, photographer; Salk Institute

Louis Kahn: Salk Institute, La Jolla,
California, 1959–1965, plan.

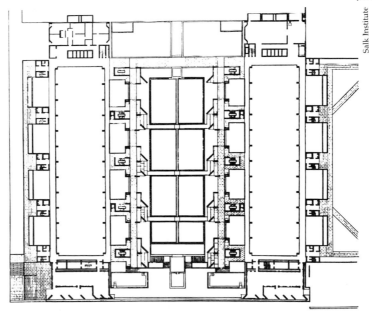

Salk Institute

Mitchell/Giurgola: United Fund,
south and west façades.

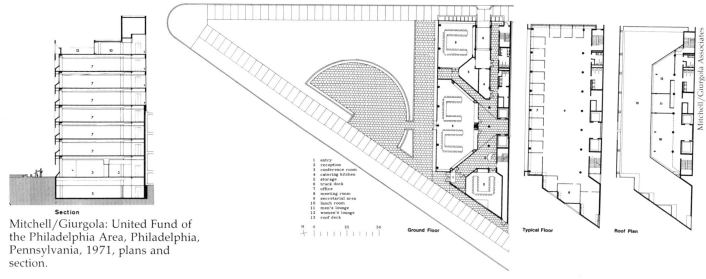

Section

1 entry
2 reception
3 conference room
4 catering kitchen
5 storage
6 truck dock
7 office
8 meeting room
9 secretarial area
10 lunch room
11 men's lounge
12 women's lounge
13 roof deck

N 0   25   50

Ground Floor   **Typical Floor**   **Roof Plan**

Mitchell/Giurgola: United Fund of
the Philadelphia Area, Philadelphia,
Pennsylvania, 1971, plans and
section.

I. M. Pei & Partners: National
Center for Atmospheric Reseach,
Boulder, Colorado, 1961–1967.

Philip Johnson: Glass House, New Canaan, Connecticut, 1948–1949.

Johnson/Burgee: AT&T Building, New York City, 1978, drawing of entrance.

tion: to the north, a glass wall; to the west, a *brise-soleil* with large horizontal punctures to be read by the fast-moving traffic on the Benjamin Franklin Parkway; and to the south, a heavy concrete frame with deep vertical openings, indicating both its structural character and function as entrance.

I. M. Pei's architecture is generally the closest to radical modernism, with its abstraction and removal from the surrounding context. The National Center for Atmospheric Research (NCAR), Boulder, Colorado, 1961–1967, is abstract without apparent human scale; rather, its scale is the Flatiron mountain range, which serves as NCAR's backdrop and context. Pei has testified that his inspiration came from the Mesa Verde ruins in southwestern Colorado where the Indians, unintimidated by the scale of their surroundings, built massive towers of stone.[6] At NCAR, tall-hooded towers, complex volumetric and plastic shapes, echo the surrounding landforms and archaic sources.

In spite of the radical-modernist appearance of Philip Johnson's glass house at New Canaan, Connecticut, the building was essentially an eclectic assemblage of parts. This he openly acknowledged in an article he wrote at the time, wherein he cited precedents ranging from Van Doesburg to Schinkel, Mies, and Choisy.[7] Subsequently, Johnson has investigated and designed in a variety of expressions: neoclassicism for the Sheldon Art Gallery, Lincoln, Nebraska; Mies's expressionist Glass Tower of the 1920s for the IDS Center in Minneapolis, and the streamlined *moderne* of the 1930s for the Post Oak Central complex in Houston, Texas. One of his latest historicizing buildings is the AT&T headquarters in New York, which combines, he claims, the two greatest periods of New York City architecture, the American Renaissance of McKim, Mead & White and the Skyscraper school of the 1920s and 1930s (Plate 3). The building has a classical Renaissance logia base and a broken pediment of a crest.[8]

Dating the beginning of this dissent from radical modernism is problematical, since to some degree it represents a resurgence of earlier attitudes that had lain fallow during the success of radical modernism. Changes in architectural journalism and the rise of architectural history and the historic preservation movement provide some clues to the changing attitudes.

Beginning in the 1930s and reaching a peak in the 1950s, most American architectural journals eschewed critical articles, lengthy exegesis, and history in favor of "practical" and "functional" articles on techniques or brief encomiums on recent buildings, pictured with a centerfold delight. Photos and drawings increasingly dominated, and significant commentary crept to a bare minimum. This news-magazine approach corresponds, to some degree, with the purifying imperatives of the radical modernists which tried to reduce architecture to pure technique. In the 1960s a number of architectural journals, especially *Architectural Forum* under the editorship of Douglas Haskell, began to reassert some intellectual and critical content. Haskell, at a time when few others would dare, began to question certain of the accepted values and works of radical modernists. He criticized the Pan American Building in New York, a collaboration between Walter Gropius, Pietro Belluschi, and Emery Roth and Sons, as a "disaster", with no feeling for the context and a poor design.[9] The January 1960 *Forum* questioned the lack of continuity in American architecture and claimed radical modernism was blighting the landscape. An essay entitled "Main Street's Vanishing Patina" pointed to the colorful juxtapositions of forms, colors, and images which could be observed in practically every town and was in the process of being lost.[10] One of the significant outcomes of Haskell's editorship was Jane Jacob's *The Death and Life of Great American Cities* (1961), a scorching criticism of many of the accepted radical-modernist notions about urban renewal and the rebuilding of American cities. Considered heretical when published, by the early 1970s most of Jacob's criticisms, such as the value of the older, messy context and the failure of most urban-renewal programs, had been accepted by the more thoughtful in the architectural community.

Robert Venturi's *Complexity and Contradiction in Architecture* (1966) picked up on some of the themes enunciated by Haskell and Jacobs and at the same time enunciated a literary theory of architecture which stressed communication as an ultimate concern. *Learning from Las Vegas* (1972), a later book by Venturi in conjunction with Denise Scott Brown and Steven Izenour, attempted to enlarge the area of architectural responsibility and also the vocabulary upon which to draw by emphasizing the "strip" environment. The essential message was the same: Architecture communicates through recognizable forms and imagery, and radical modernism had forgotten this goal, with its extreme abstraction and concentration upon function and structure.

Accompanying the journalistic resurgence was the growth of interest in architectural history, which revived fitfully in the 1960s and mushroomed into a growth industry in the 1970s. The appearance of *The Prairie School Review* in 1964, a periodical devoted to chronicling the forgotten architecture of the midwestern contemporaries Frank Lloyd Wright and Louis Sullivan, signified an important enlargement of historical concerns. Later there would be *Classical America* (1971) which attempted to rehabilitate the despised beaux-arts. *Oppositions,* which first appeared in 1973, took the European modern movement as a field for historical debate. In various ways these publications enlarged the field of debate and added some degree of intellectual discourse. In 1971 a large traveling exhibit on art deco signified its coming of age. Similarly the exhibit on the École des Beaux-Arts by the Museum of Modern Art in 1975 and the growing interest in the American equivalent, as in the American Renaissance exhibit of 1979 at the Brooklyn Museum which featured the work of Richard Morris Hunt, Charles F. McKim, George B. Post, Henry Bacon, and others, indicated other rehabilitations. Romaldo Giurgola claimed the architects needed "a sense of the past, to which the modern movement in architecture belongs as well, and an awareness of history not as a fashionable and disposable commodity, but as a space for humanity which will endure and expand as long as there are people on earth."[12]

At the same time, and greatly influencing these developments, was the growth of the historic-preservation movement in the United States. Historic preservation in the 1940s, 1950s, and 1960s had been generally seen by architects — especially those with radical-modernist sympathies — as peopled by pedagogues and antiquarians exclusively concerned with the homes of famous people. It appeared to have little architectural relevance.

Actually, the foundations of historic preservation in the United States in the later quarter of the nineteenth century had been actively led by architects such as Charles F. McKim, and the AIA in the 1930s had formed a Historic Resources Committee. Yet this concern had little overall impact in the 1940s and 1950s, and radical modernism, while paying lip service to certain historic structures and the vernacular, was concerned basically with building a totally new world disconnected from the past. In the 1960s and 1970s historic preservation developed a much wider constituency, and actual programs concerned with teaching the principles of historic preservation were founded in 1964 at the University of Virginia and Columbia University in their respective schools of architecture. They were followed in succeeding years with programs at many other schools, and, perhaps most importantly, the impact began to be felt in architectural studios, were students were asked to design buildings in historic contexts.

The passage of the Historic Preservation Act of 1966 made the federal government an active participant in preservation and mandated a state-by-state survey of all buildings and objects of historical, cultural, and architectural significance. The shift in architectural orientation was already evident in the mid-1960s when William Wurster, in conjunction with his partners Theodore Bernardi and Donn Emmons and the landscape architect Lawrence Halprin, converted the old Ghirardelli Chocolate Factory in San Francisco into a market square by reusing the old turn-of-the-century buildings. The popularity and success of Ghirardelli Square could not be

Wurster, Bernardi & Emmons: Ghirardelli Square, San Francisco, California, 1967.

missed by any architect or city planner. By 1976 the AIA had recognized the implications of historic preservation for architecture and included a new category in the annual awards to designs that creatively used the original historic fabric of buildings.

Demonstration of an increasing historical consciousness came in a 1976 poll conducted by the *Journal of the AIA.* The poll asked forty-six practitioners, historians, and critics to nominate what they felt to be the greatest achievements of American architecture.[13] The results were as follows:

In first place was the University of Virginia campus, Charlottesville, 1817–1826, Thomas Jefferson. In second place was Rockefeller Center, New York, 1929–1940. Associated architects included Corbett, Harrison & MacMurry; Hood & Fouilhoux; and Reinhard & Hofmeister. Tied for third place were Dulles International Airport, Chantilly, Virginia, 1958–1962, Eero Saarinen & Associates, and Falling Water (Kaufman House), Bear Run, Pennsylvania, 1935–1936, Frank Lloyd Wright. Fifth was the Carson, Pirie, Scott and Company Store, Chicago, 1894–1904, Louis Sullivan. Sixth, a tie between the Seagram Building, New York, 1954–1958, Mies van der Rohe and Philip Johnson, and the PSFS Building, Philadelphia, 1929–1932, Howe & Lescaze. Eighth was a tie between Trinity Church, Boston, 1872–1877, H. H. Richardson, and the Boston City Hall, 1962–1969, Kallman, McKinnell & Knowles. Ninth place was a five-way tie: Lever House, New York, 1949–1952, Skidmore, Owings & Merrill; Robie House, Chicago, 1906–1908, Frank Lloyd Wright; Johnson Wax Company buildings, Racine, Wisconsin, 1936–1937, 1947–1950, Frank Lloyd Wright; Brooklyn Bridge, New York, 1867–1883, John A. and Washington A. Roebling; and the Ford Foundation Building, New York, 1963–1967, Kevin Roche, John Dinkeloo & Associates. Finally tenth place was a tie between Johnson House, 1948–1949, New Canaan, Connecticut, Philip Johnson and Grand Central Station, New York, 1903–1913, Warren & Wetmore and Reed & Stem.

Such polls must be carefully evaluated. They represent the mood of a particular group at a specific time. However, they do give some clues as to the status of the American architectural mind. The concern with large-scale design issues is obvious. The popularity of the University of Virginia campus may reflect the bicentennial fever, but it also remains as one of the few successful American attempts to create a total environment. Rockefeller Center in second place has certain admirable features in its skyscraper styling, ornament, and materials; however, one suspects it was largely admired as a successful, cohesive, architect-created, inner-city development. It is noteworthy that further down the poll, below the top ten but receiving substantial votes, were several other large-scale urban designs: the plan of Savannah, Georgia, circa 1735; Central Park, New York, Frederick Law Olmsted, 1858; the plan of Radburn, New Jersey, Clarence Stein and Henry Wright, 1929; and the Illinois Institute of Technology, Mies van der Rohe, 1940. Such listings indicate a substantial shift of opinion from twenty years before. In 1956 in honor of the AIA's hundredth anniversary, *Architectural Record* magazine took a similar poll of architects, critics, and historians, asking them to list the most significant buildings of the past 100 years.[13] The differences in time span do not make the polls exactly comparable. Jefferson's campus would not have been eligible in the 1957 poll. Even so, it is significant that while the buildings of Rockefeller Center are listed in third place in 1957 and the General Motors Technical Center in seventh place, there are no other urban, suburban, or large-scale groupings of buildings so noted.

The 1976 poll reveals a surprising historical consciousness with regard to American architecture. As evidenced by Eero Saarinen's Dulles International Airport, Mies van der Rohe's Seagram Building, and others, radical-modernist buildings rank high, as they should. Yet, it is striking that out of the sixteen buildings in the top ten places, only five date from the post-World War II years. For a profession that is frequently accused of believing "the last work is the best work" and lacking any historical perspective, the poll offers a different view.

This historical revisionism in architecture should be put into the context of the period. The vigorous spirit of political dissent evident in the later 1960s and early 1970s in the United States was certainly a contributing factor. There also emerged a new concern with ethnic identity that challenged the traditional melting-pot assumptions of American history. The study of American history moved away from an exclusive concern with consensus to look at the submerged histories of minorities, women, and other forgotten subjects. The environmental movement certainly influenced, and was in turn influenced by, historic preservation. The result was a climate wherein many of the imperatives of radical modernism came under question. The new direction, which the six Gold Medalists represent, shows this spirit of questioning and revision. To some degree their work reflects the reestablishment of ties with earlier periods that had been broken by radical modernism. Some, such as William Wurster, never really broke with their conservative-modernist heritage. Others, such as Philip Johnson, are converts, discovering the riches of history they had expelled in the 1930s. All of them, in one way or another, represent a connection with the École des Beaux-Arts. Five of the six—Wurster, Kahn, Belluschi, Pei, and Giurgola—attended schools with pronounced Beaux-Arts leanings. The importance of certain Beaux-Arts notions, such as the plan as a generator and the primacy of design, are common inheritances. Philip Johnson has significantly enlarged upon the critical Beaux-Arts notion of *marche* with his writing on procession: "Architecture is surely *not* the design of space, certainly not the massing or organizing of volumes. These are auxiliary to the main point, which is the organization of procession. Architecture exists only in time."[14] Some, such as Kahn, Belluschi, and Wurster, actually learned the styles of and then worked for Paul Cret (Kahn) and William Adams Delano (Wurster). Pei attended MIT from 1936 to 1940, before the school made a shift to modernism. Giurgola's schooling in Rome, 1945–1948, was still largely controlled by a Beaux-Arts-oriented faculty, and additionally, his father was a well-known stage-set architect who was thoroughly familiar with the styles. Only Philip Johnson never attended a Beaux-Arts-oriented school; rather, he studied architecture at the center of American radical modernism, Harvard University, from 1940 to 1944 under the guidance of Gropius and Breuer. Previously, of course, Johnson had helped to form the American synthesis of radical modernism, the International-Style exhibit and book of 1932. His earlier career as a critic-historian-curator is crucial in understanding his attitude and later embrace of certain beaux-arts principles, for Johnson is a supreme connoisseur and has tried to recognize aesthetic quality, no matter what its source.

A significant dimension to the career of the Gold Medalists has been their role as educators, theoreticians, and spokesmen for different architectural positions. Four of the Gold Medalists—Wurster, Kahn, Belluschi, and Giurgola—have made a major impact upon architectural education as teachers and administrators. Only Pei has consistently devoted himself to practice and, except for a few years in the later 1940s, has stayed out of education. Consequently, Pei has spoken less and written little about his work. Philip Johnson has never been formally connected with a school of architecture for any extended length of time, yet in another sense, he has conducted an ongoing public seminar wherever he has been located. Johnson's realization, dating from his early days at the Museum of Modern Art, of the power of the spoken and printed word in forming architectural judgments made him one of the leading spokesmen for the rejection of radical modernism.

Johnson's theoretical approach with his quick repartee often undercuts the seriousness of his pronouncements and makes him sound at times like a stand-up comedian. "The Seven Crutches of Modern Architecture," delivered in 1954, denounced the reliance upon structure, cheapness, comfort, and other functionalist considerations as the formers of architecture. He noted: "They said a building is good architecture if it works. Of course, this is poppycock. All buildings work."[15] Much more crucial for architecture was its traditional role as art: "I like the thought that what we are to do on this earth is to embellish it for its greater beauty, so that oncoming generations can look back to the shapes we leave here and get the same thrill that I get in looking back at theirs—at the Parthenon, at Chartres Cathedral."[16] He has described himself as a "functional eclectic."[17] For him this has meant both a certain radical-modernist residue of belief in trying to fulfill the program of the building under design, and also, "I am free to roam history at will." Essentially, Johnson is within the American architectural tradition of a pragmatic eclecticism. For Johnson this has come to mean a study of place or the "genius loci." "What look does the ambience call for? What do the surrounding buildings look like? What is the local scale?"[18]

I. M. Pei's theoretical position can be formulated from both his statements and the work he has directly controlled. Pei's designs have oscillated between two poles, the building as a unique object and the building in relation to context. The Society Hill Town House, 1964, Philadelphia, was an "intentional" recall of the past: "The use of brick and arches was characteristic of the townscape of old Society Hill." He explained: "In my view no building can stand alone without reference to its surroundings. I would like to make clear, however, that I recognize the importance of the individual building. Villa Savoye and the Barcelona Pavilion are two such examples that come readily to mind."[19] This seemingly contradictory attitude is reconciled in several of Pei's buildings, especially the east-wing extension to the National Gallery of Art in Washington, D.C., 1969–1978.

I. M. Pei & Partners: National
Gallery of Art, East Building, Washington, D.C., 1968–1978.

I. M. Pei & Partners: National
Gallery of Art, East Building, Washington, D.C., plan.

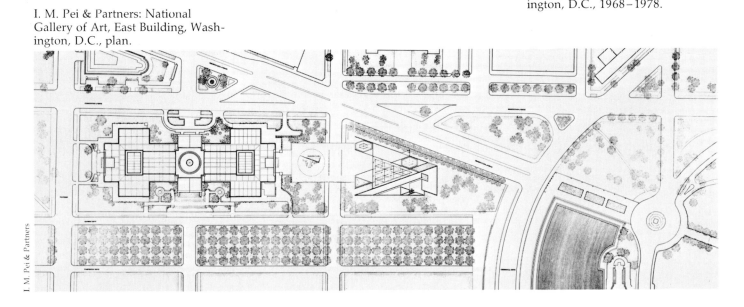

The building is reminiscent of a large piece of minimalist sculpture. Yet in context, both its profile and massing echo the surrounding beaux-arts buildings and complete the end of the Federal Triangle where it is located. The plan, while highly abstract, does have a circulation pattern that puts onto diagonals both the peripheral and central paths possible in its neighbor, the original National Gallery of Art by John Russell Pope.

The architectural positions of William Wurster and Pietro Belluschi have certain similarities, since both came from the west coast and were known for their regionalist concerns. Their acknowledgment of the special demands of the locale brought both of them during their academic careers to emphasize the larger environmental concerns of architecture. First at MIT, 1944–1950 and then at the University of California at Berkeley, 1951–1963, Wurster formulated a new architectural curriculum that while drawing upon European examples, such as the Bauhaus, for some aspects, refused a dogmatic formalism. Consequently it was more eclectic and open-ended stylistically. He succeeded in changing the College of Architecture at Berkeley in 1957 into the College of Environmental Design, which became the model for many American architectural schools in the 1960s and 1970s. Wurster defined his position as: "Environment surrounds and controls our buildings, so to produce inspired architecture, it is necessary to know and interpret, and perhaps to change the frame in which we live and work."[20] Wurster, more than any other of the Gold Medalists, accepted the radical-modernist belief that architecture should and could change human behavior.

Pietro Belluschi followed Wurster as dean at MIT in 1951, and he remained in the position until 1965. His educational stance was similar: a belief in a regional response where possible and an expanding role for architecture. His essentially eclectic position allowed him to become a spokesman for "good design" that was not based upon the formalism postulated by radical modernism. His long and distinguished career as a church designer gave Belluschi a sensitivity for the traditional symbolic role of architecture. He could never accept the contriving of symbols, yet they were the ultimate concern: "They are born out of the deep passions of people who are willing and capable of penetrating into the essence of things, who have vision to find its ultimate meaning and have the power to give it expression."[21]

More than any of the others, Louis Kahn attempted to provide a theoretical foundation for an architectural position fundamentally opposed to the radical-modernist mainstream. Kahn wanted to return to the beginning: "Actually my whole purpose has been to read volume *zero*, the unwritten volume, because I am certain it contains a very old, cut-off kind of beginning—a source of sources which when reclaimed, will also be very new."[22] An example of such beginnings is Kahn's poetic musings on the development of the column:

> Out of the wall grew the column.
> The wall did well for man.
> In its thickness and its strength
> it projected him against destruction.
> But soon, the will to look out

made man make a hole in the wall,
and the wall was very pained, and said,
'What are you doing to me?'
I protected you; I made you feel secure —
and now you put a hole through me!'
And man said, 'But I will look out!
I see wonderful things,
and I want to look out.'
And the wall still felt very sad.

. . . .

Such realizations come out of nothing in nature.
They come out of a mysterious
Kind of sense that man has
to express those wonders of the soul
which demand expression.[23]

Such complex and almost mystical ruminations are part of Kahn's search for an order in architecture that lay beyond simple geometry, structure, or function. For him it was the essence of what the building should be; hence, the questions, What does this building want to be? What is the nature of brick? The ultimate source was in the human soul, or "existence will," or the psyche, an unmeasurable quality akin to the soul. The crucial aspect was the realization of this "existence will" and then the translation into a measurable quality or design.[24]

In his later life, Kahn was recognized as a major theoretician. However, the poetic difficulty of his ideas, for a generation — or generations — not overly given to poetics, not to say complex thoughts, diluted his impact. For many Kahn was more important as a form giver or a reinterpreter of modernism, heavy, exposed structure, and the separation of servant and served spaces, as in the Richards Medical Laboratory. Yet, he provided architecture with the first creditable system of architectural thought for many years, and he will certainly stand as a major force in loosing the bonds of radical modernism and the orthodoxy of functionalism.

Romaldo Giurgola is frequently labeled a successor to Louis Kahn; while there are certainly influences, Giurgola's approach is sufficiently divergent. A reason is that Giurgola never experienced a hiatus in career in his late thirties and forties as did Kahn. At the age of 38 he became an active member of a growing firm, and his thought is more accessible and less abstract and mystical. He is uneasy about overtheorizing: "From a literary theory good novels were never made. . . . Too often a theory of a competent principle counts more in essence than in realization. Results derived from preconceived positions are identifiable in high schematization of plans; in pedantic separation of traffic routes; in definite specialization of areas . . . we should work with the idea of a city rather than a theory of it."[25] While Giurgola has been frequently thought of as concerned principally with the city, his fundamental concern has been with the idea of place: "A place embodies a desire which is a mediation on the past, but is also made up of the thoughts, the will, and the dynamics of life and the present. . . . To make a place means to resolve a human proposition in poetic terms."[26] As with Kahn, Giurgola searches for an order, but his order comes "from a realistic apprehension of the facts that make the city — facts that extend from the historical experience of human events to the functional logic of its structures,"[27] or, as he later elaborated, "if they are not urban, are the land, trees and nature."[28] Giurgola's order comes from the attempt to understand a place, not as a single unit in time but as a reflection of overlapping concerns of "partial visions." He explicitly contradicts the rational dogmatism of so much of radical modernism, as with his celebration of place: "Architecture may have started even before man erected four posts to make a roof. It started when he chose where to make it. Thus, a sense of place was generated from the context of human issues together with a natural site."[29] Even though Giurgola displays a verbal reluctance to accept any dogma of form, geometry, or style, there is a crucial classical thread that runs through his work. It is never classicism as a style, but a strong sense of geometrical order, deformed at times by the surroundings and yet insistent.

No common style, label, or manner can be cast as an umbrella over these six Gold Medalists. The length of their careers — Wurster stretching back into the 1920s, Giurgola beginning active practice as late as 1958 – and the diversity of their output make tight connections impossible. Yet, the striking feature that emerges is the concern with place or environmental context of a building. Examples of departures from this can be cited with all six Gold Medalists, and their approaches have differed from the regionalism of the Pacific coast to the new expanse of Houston where the absence of context allows the design of large, minimal sculptures as inhabitable buildings. Such divergences are hard to reconcile, yet the new interest in architectural history, historic preservation, and the recognition of cities as living entities with their own traditions may be seen in retrospect, along with the six Gold Medalists, as a significant shift in the direction of architecture in the later twentieth century and the beginning of a new consensus that reaches back to the earlier concerns of architecture.

Notes

1   Philip Johnson, "Remarks," *AIA Journal*, vol. 67, July 1978, p. 16.

2   I. M. Pei, "The Two Worlds of Architecture," *AIA Journal*, vol. 68, July 1979, p. 29.

3   Pei quoted in Rosalie Merzback, "Gold Medalists Share Insights to Architecture, Cities, Energy," *F. W. Dodge, Construction Report*, June 12, 1981, p. 13.

4   Ibid.

5   Louis Mumford, "Skyline," *The New Yorker*, October 11, 1947, p. 110.

6   Bernard P. Spring, "Evaluation: From Context to Form," *AIA Journal*, vol. 68, June 1979, p. 71.

7   Philip Johnson, "House at New Canaan, Connecticut," *Architectural Review*, vol. 108, September 1950, pp. 152–159.

8   Johnson, "Remarks," op. cit., p. 18.

9   Douglas Haskell, "The Lost New York of the Pan-American Airways Building," *Architectural Forum*, vol. 119, November 1963, pp. 106–111.

10 "Main Street's Vanishing Patina," *Architectural Forum*, vol. 112, January 1960, pp. 108–115.

11 Quoted in *AIA Journal*, vol. 68, May 1979, p. 162.

12 *AIA Journal*, vol. 65, July 1976.

13 "One Hundred Years of Significant Buildings," *Architectural Record*, vol. 119, June 1956, pp. 117–118.

14 Philip Johnson, "Whence and Whither: The Processional Element in Architecture," *Perspecta*, vol. 9/10, 1965, reprinted in *Philip Johnson Writings*, Oxford University Press, New York, 1979, p. 151.

15 "The Seven Crutches of Modern Architecture," *Perspecta*, vol. 3, 1955, reprinted in *Writings*, ibid., p. 137.

16 Ibid., p. 140.

17 *Writings*, op. cit., p. 108, 271.

18 Ibid., p. 271.

19 Quoted in, Andrea O. Dean, "Conversations: I. M. Pei," *AIA Journal*, vol. 68, June 1979, pp. 64–65, 67.

20 William W. Wurster, "Architecture Broadens Its Base," *Journal of the AIA*, vol. 10, July 1948, p. 36.

21 Pietro Belluschi, "Architecture as an Art of Our Time," in Harry S. Ranson (ed.), *The People's Architects*, University of Chicago Press, Chicago, 1964, p. 105.

22 Quote in William Marlin, "Within the Folds of Construction," *Architectural Forum*, vol. 139, October 1973, p. 27.

23 Louis I. Kahn, "Talks with Students," *Architecture at Rice*, vol. 26, 1969, pp. 4–5.

24 Jan C. Rowan, "Wanting to Be, The Philadelphia School," *Progressive Architecture*, vol. 40, April 1960, pp. 131–163; this is still the best article on Kahn's philosophy.

25 Romaldo Giurgola, "Reflections on Buildings and the City: The Realism of the Partial Vision," *Perspecta*, vol. 9/10, 1965, p. 108.

26 Romaldo Giurgola, "The Aesthetics of Place," in "Mitchell/Giurgola Architects," *Process: Architecture*, vol. 2, 1977, p. 36.

27 Giurgola, "Reflections on Buildings," op. cit., p. 108.

28 Romaldo Giurgola, "The Discreet Charm of the Bourgeoisie," in "Five on Five," *Architectural Forum*, vol. 138, May, 1973, p. 57.

29 Romaldo Giurgola with J. Mehta, *Louis I. Kahn*, Westview Press, Boulder, 1975, p. 12.

The AIA Gold Medal, A. A.
Weinman, sculptor 1906.

BIOGRAPHIES

GOLD MEDAL FOR 1907 SIR ASTON WEBB

AWARDED ON JANUARY 8, 1907
AT THE CORCORAN GALLERY
WASHINGTON, D.C.

Sir Aston Webb.

On the score of amplitude, your achievement lacks nothing, for no architect in England, save Sir Christopher himself, has been entrusted with the conduct of so many and such vast works. . . . Through your hands, also, the British nation is giving to the world an example of municipal improvement upon a vast scale and under circumstances the most fortunate. . . . But in the midst of these large affairs, you have not neglected to perform a labor of love in the restoration of ancient edifices.[1]

Aston Webb was born in 1849 in London, the son of a successful watercolorist, Edward Webb. After a public school education, he was articled, in the typical manner of the day, to Banks & Barry (Robert Richardson Banks and Charles Barry, Jr., the son of Sir Charles Barry). In 1871, Webb won the Pugin Scholarship of the RIBA and spent a year traveling on the continent. In late 1873 he set up a London practice and began a long intermittent association with E. Ingress Bell (1837–1914). During Webb's later career, he was assisted by his son Maurice. He died in 1930.

Early in his career, Webb exhibited a social and professional astuteness that placed his name in the forefront. He became a member of the Architectural Association in 1873, and president in 1884. He joined the RIBA as an associate in 1874, in 1883 he became a fellow, and in 1902–1903 he was president. Edward VII knighted Webb in 1904, and in 1905 he received the Royal Gold Medal. Webb became a strong supporter of professionalism in architecture and the registration of architects. In 1899 he was elected an associate of the Royal Academy, then full academician in 1903, and president in 1919–1924.

Webb's architecture can be characterized with the same astuteness of style. He moved with aplomb

1   "Address of Mr. Frank Miles Day, President, AIA," *Proceedings of the Fortieth Annual Convention of the American Institute of Architects,* Gibson Bros., Washington, D.C., 1907, pp. 104–107.

Sir Aston Webb: Admiralty Arch, London, 1906–1911, perspective by T. Raffles Dawson.

through a variety of expressions. The basis of his design was classicism with an emphasis on plan; in this he was the most beaux-arts English architect of the period. One critic claimed "Plan, with main focus and primary factors, was to him the basis of all architecture, and embodied the eternal unchanging principle."[2] Webb was a younger member of the group that included Nesfield, Shaw, and Bodley, the group that challenged the reigning high-Victorian idioms and introduced a new concentration upon accurate historical details, a calming of visual agitation, and a reassertion of mass. His particular contribution was a wide-ranging eclecticism and emphasis upon plan. As with most English architects of the period, Webb did a few churches and restorations (St. Bartholomew the Great, London, 1880–1897), but his major work was for the government. Beginning in 1882 and continuing for many years, Webb and Bell provided designs for the Crown Agents for the Colonies. In 1887 they won the competition for the new Law Courts in Birmingham, with a red-brick and terra-cotta design that is stylistically Franco-Flemish, or, as it was then termed, *free style.*

The new main front to the Victoria & Albert Museum in South Kensington, won in competition in 1891, continued the same eclectic combination — Gothic and early Renaissance details combined, and topped by a stepped, baroque corona. According to one critic, it was the "most outstanding example of the New Renaissance."[3] This continuing assimilation of a variety of styles for elevations can be seen in buildings such as the Metropolitan

Life Assurance Society in Moorgate, London, 1890–1893, which is nominally Gothic; the Royal United Services Institute in Whitehall, London, 1893–1895, which is late Italian baroque; the Royal Naval College, Dartmouth, 1899–1905, which is Wren-baroque; and Birmingham University, 1900–1909, which is Byzantine. Underlying all is a strongly organized plan, symmetrical and hierarchical, which is unique in English architecture for the period.

His greatest work began in 1901 with the winning of a limited competition for the Queen Victoria Memorial and approach to Buckingham Palace. Analogous to contemporary "American City Beautiful" plans Webb eventually succeeded in designing the Admiralty Arch, the Mall, the Queen Victoria Memorial (with Sir Thomas Bock as sculptor), the *rond point,* the forecourt, and the new east façade to Buckingham Palace. Webb's planning genius allowed him to mask the shift of axis from the Strand and Trafalgar Square into the Mall by using curved façades on the Admiralty Arch. The arch with offices in the wings is a great example of urban civic architecture. The new façade for Buckingham Palace had as a requirement the retention of the fenestration from the 1840 wing. Webb skillfully masked the old building with a new classic and austere façade that, while called Georgian, is more analogous to the Louvre in Paris. Webb described the new building as the "Heart of Empire" and indicated the appeal his work would have had for an American audience seeking their own empire and formal architectural traditions. The grand manner of Webb had a certain inconclusive yet systematic order of plan that put him at the forefront of English architecture in the turn-of-the-century period.

2   William Luca, "The Architecture of Sir Aston Webb, President of the Royal Academy," *The Building News,* vol. 118, January 1920, p. 63.

3   Ibid.

Sir Aston Webb: Buckingham Palace, London, 1912–1913, Queen Victoria Memorial, 1901–1911, Thomas Brock, sculptor.

National Monuments Record

GOLD MEDAL FOR 1909 CHARLES FOLLEN MCKIM

AWARDED ON DECEMBER 15, 1909
AT THE CORCORAN GALLERY
WASHINGTON, D.C.
ACCEPTED BY WILLIAM R. MEAD

Library of Congress

Charles Follen McKim.

His monuments in bronze and marble will long enrich his native land; his benefactions, not measured alone in the standards of commerce, have laid the sure foundation of even greater monuments in the hearts of his countrymen. But it is not for these alone that we offer this token of our praise and love. The award of this medal can add nothing to his honor. Tiles, nor decorations, nor medals, nor any worldly thing can add to worth. Character and merit are intrinsic. They are not conferred. Nothing we can do or say can add to their sum. Nobility is of the soul.[1]

Born in 1847 in rural Pennsylvania, the son of a radical abolitionist father and a Quaker mother, McKim was brought up in the Philadelphia vicinity in an atmosphere of high-toned morality and genteel poverty. After a year at Harvard, he arrived in Paris at the École des Beaux-Arts in 1867 and enrolled in the studio of Honoré Daumet. In 1870 he returned to the United States to the New York office of H. H. Richardson, and two years later began his own practice. A partnership was begun in 1877 with William R. Mead and William Bigelow; in 1879, Stanford White joined, replacing Bigelow. McKim had already met with some success, but with Mead as the office manager and Stanford White as the decorator, the firm of McKim, Mead & White became the leading American architectural firm. Initially they were known for their designs of resort and city houses for wealthy society and robber barons; their later success came with large-scale public and private urban commissions. With a main office in New York, their work was concentrated in the northeast; however, they designed buildings in the midwest and west. McKim's personal life was unhappy: A first marriage ended in divorce in 1879, and his second wife died shortly after their marriage in 1887. The consequence was an extremely public life, and in spite of being a poor public speaker, he became involved in the Columbian Exposition in Chicago, the American Academy in Rome, the McMillan Commission for Washington, D.C., and the AIA. Privately, he was an extremely persuasive

individual, loved the company of women, and traveled almost yearly in Europe. He died in 1909.

The consequence of McKim's early background and later interests was an architecture with a certain moralistic didacticism; he had read and absorbed many of the historians and philosophers on art and architecture—Ruskin, Viollet-le-Duc, Taine, and Burckhardt—and while he did not always agree with their stylistic choices, he believed architecture was a permanent record of a nation's greatness and aspirations. Integral to his personal philosophy was a search for the appropriate image or expression for America, which for McKim eventually became classicism, especially Italian Renaissance and Roman classicism. The consequence was that McKim's architecture, rich though it was in fine marbles, color, and luxury, had a certain monumental aloofness and drama that separated it from the more decorative approach of his partner, Stanford White.

The earliest work of McKim from the 1870s and early 1880s, the so-called shingle style, was a synthesis of English Queen Anne and American colonial of the sixteenth century and displayed the usual picturesque restlessness of the period.[2]

The Boston Public Library (1887–1895) is

1 "Address of Cass Gilbert, President, AIA," in Glenn Brown (ed.), *Charles Follen McKim Memorial Meeting of the American Institute of Architects*, Gibson Bros., Washington, D.C., 1910, p. 16.

2 Richard Guy Wilson, "The Early Work of Charles F. McKim, Country House Commissions," *Winterthur Portfolio*, vol. 14, Fall 1979, pp. 235–267; Vincent Scully, Jr., *The Shingle Style*, Yale University Press, New Haven, 1955.

McKim's first major essay in the Italian-Renaissance idiom for public buildings. Designed to be seen opposite Richardson's agitated and polychromatic Trinity Church, the library exhibits a new restraint and calmness. As with all of McKim's work, certain sources can be identified—in this case, Labrouste's Bibliothèque Sainte-Genève in Paris, Alberti's San Francesco in Rimini, and Roman palazzos. For McKim and his patrons, the building was more Italian Renaissance than French, and the form of the library has a masonry substantiality not present in the Bibliothèque. An elaborate sequence of spaces, richly decorated by the foremost artists of the day, leads to the impressive reading room, Bates Hall, across the front of the building. A large courtyard in the center provides orientation; it is based upon Italian prototypes but is American in planning and usage.

The University Club (1896–1900) is one of the eight major men's clubs McKim, Mead & White designed in New York City. McKim's initial sketch illustrates what his office man, Henry Bacon, de-scribed: "In the sketch his idea was evident, but most indefinitely drawn, and in no stage of planning and designing did he make a definite line or contour."[3] The completed building is a synthesis of Sienese, Florentine, and Roman palazzos. Behind the façade that reads as three major floors are actually six floors. An interior courtyard, or cortile, on the first floor and its vestiges on the upper floors provides orientation.

McKim's large-scale planning can be seen in projects such as Columbia University in New York (1892) or the Washington, D.C., plan of 1901–1902. His desire to provide an order for American architecture extended to the city. The approach in all of these was a classical order of direction, axis, closed vistas, and images of great monuments of the past. His success can be gauged by the wave of classical beaux-arts buildings that spread across the country in the first four decades of the twentieth century.

3   Henry Bacon, "Charles Follen McKim—A Character Sketch," *The Brickbuilder,* vol. 19, February 1910, p. 38.

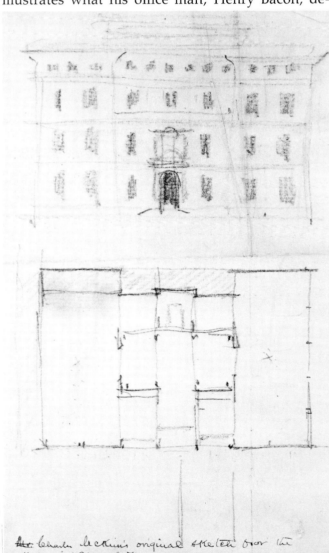

University Club, exterior.

Charles Fullen McKim: original sketch for the façade of the University Club, New York City, 1896–1900.

GOLD MEDAL FOR 1911 GEORGE BROWNE POST

AWARDED ON DECEMBER 13, 1911
AT THE NEW NATIONAL MUSEUM
WASHINGTON, D.C.

George Browne Post. Portrait by
Edwin H. Blashfield.

From first to last he has acted upon a principle which may appear simple enough when expressed, but is not of such an habitual application as to have become banal; the principle that a building is not an abstract composition raised mid-air for the delectation of fleshless spirits, but is a reality holding fast to the ground, and to a particular sort of ground, in the midst of definite surroundings, in view of certain uses, with all of which it must agree: there must be harmony. . . . Sixteenth century French architects created an admirable style which they did not invent outright, nor copy from anybody, but evolved from previous and from foreign ones, and modified as taste and necessity told them. . . . The same will take place here, owing to the efforts, energy and clear artistic insight of men like Mr. Post. An American style will develop if local circumstances are sufficiently taken into account and buildings are vested with beauty—another word for harmony.[1]

In 1911, when Post received the Gold Medal, he was the head of one of the largest and most respected architectural firms in the United States, producing large, commercial high-rises, or skyscrapers—a building type he helped to create—and classically derived public buildings such as the Wisconsin State Capitol and Manufacturers and Liberal Arts Building at the Columbian Exposition in Chicago. He served as president of the AIA from 1896 to 1899 and president of the New York chapter in 1904. He was director of the Municipal Art Society of New York from 1901 to 1909. In 1901 he received the Chevalier de la Legion d'Honneur. Other honors included honorary doctor of laws from Columbia University, 1908, and academician of the National Academy of Design, 1908.

His practice was widespread and active, with work not only in New York, but also in New Jersey, Connecticut, Pennsylvania, Ohio, Michigan, Wisconsin, Washington, D.C., Virginia, and Canada. Primarily a commercial architect, he also built fashionable residences for the Vanderbilt and Huntington families on Fifth Avenue in New York City, more than thirty houses for his neighbors in his home of Bernardsville, New Jersey, and many more on the east coast. He designed churches, hospitals, apartment complexes, restaurants, theaters, munici-

pal buildings, college campuses, and most of the original structures for City College in New York. In 1905 he was joined by his two sons, and the firm became George B. Post and Sons. He died in 1913.

Born in 1837 to an old New York family, Post was educated at Churchhill's Military School, Ossining, New York, and then in civil engineering at New York University. Being chiefly interested in architecture, he entered the studio of Richard Morris Hunt, remaining until 1860 when he formed a partnership with Charles D. Gambrill. The Civil War put an end to this arrangement; Post was commissioned as a captain, subsequently becoming an aide to General Burnside and rising to the rank of colonel.

In 1868, Post resigned his commission and opened an office in order to compete for the Equitable Life Assurance headquarters being planned for New York City. In this he was only partly successful: The prize went to Arthur Gilman and Edward Kendall, but Post was asked to change the structural system. His solution so reduced the cost that the project became possible financially. The success of this first "elevator building," as the early sky-

---

1   "Address of M. J. J. Jusserand, Ambassador of France," *Proceedings of the Forty-fifth Annual Convention of the American Institute of Architects*, Gibson Bros., Washington, D.C., 1912, pp. 180–181.

scrapers were then called, catapulted Post to fame and led him into the field of commercial architecture.

Shortly after the completion of the Equitable headquarters in 1870, Post received the commissions for the Troy Savings Bank, Troy, 1872, and the Williamsburg Savings Bank, Brooklyn, 1874, the latter of which featured a Renaissance-style dome. At the same time, he was designing the Western Union Building in New York, 1873, which at the height of 260 feet was one of the tallest buildings in the world. Like many architects, Post in this period of his professional life did not exhibit any stylistic consistency; details would be drawn from a variety of sources and plastered over pragmatic and functional cores.

In the early 1880s, Post arrived at a solution that can be termed the earliest example of the modern business building, or the "commercial style," because in plan, elevation, and decor, buildings such as the Mills, 1881–1883, aimed first and foremost at fulfilling the requirements of commerce. They broke away from the block plan so common in the 1820s through the 1860s to the U-shaped formula which made possible greater amounts of well-lighted office space and enhanced revenue. Decoration in the Mills Building is kept to a minimum, and subservient to the overall grid. In these buildings, an interior iron frame is encased in outer walls of brick and stone; terra cotta was used as a fireproofing material.

While Post would continue with major high-rise structures in a variety of styles, such as the Richardson Romanesque in the Prudential Life Insurance Company Building, Newark, 1890, his lower structures increasingly reflected the more austere classicism of the American Renaissance. One of his most famous structures was the New York Stock Exchange, 1901–1904, which enclosed the major capitalist trading institution in a Roman temple. The Wisconsin State Capitol, topped by a great colonnaded dome, was designed with four equal wings, whose pedimented fronts lined up with diagonal streets radiating outward from Capital Square. Four other curved porticoes are nested between the wings and align with perpendicular streets entering the square. The gleaming white-marble exterior contrasts with the richly colored interior decorated by prominent artists. Montgomery Schuyler claimed Post

> . . . personally fulfilled the function which Viollet-le-Duc assigns to the Roman engineer, that is to say, of the maker of the "parti," or the "layout," which he devised with a view not only to economy and convenience but also to dignity and impressiveness. The man who does that, call him what you will, is an architect, even though he should leave all his buildings in the rough or turn them over to a decorator for their ornamentation.[2]

CONTRIBUTED BY WINSTON WEISMAN

2   Montgomery Schuyler, "George Browne Post Obituary," *Architectural Record*, vol. 35, January 1914, pp. 94.

Courtesy of Winston R. Weisman

George B. Post: Mills Building, New York City, 1881–1883.

GOLD MEDAL FOR 1914 **JEAN LOUIS PASCAL**

AWARDED ON DECEMBER 3, 1914
AT THE PAN AMERICAN UNION
WASHINGTON, D.C.
ACCEPTED BY AMBASSADOR JUSSERAND

W. Cook, "Jean Louis Pascal—Institute Gold Medalist, 1913," Journal of the AIA, vol. 3, January 1915

Jean Louis Pascal.

In conferring the highest honor of the Institute upon one of the most distinguished French architects of the present time . . . we have not only honored him but we are honoring his country as well, and acknowledging with greatful feelings the vast debt we are under to her in so many ways, and most especially the architectural debt.[1]

Pascal was born in Paris in 1837, and he studied architecture at the École des Beaux-Arts from 1855 to 1866. He was in the atelier of E.-J. Gilbert, 1853–1855, and Charles Questel, 1855–1872. These men were rationalists, as opposed to classicists, and as such were more concerned with the new needs of society than with the old traditions of Greco-Roman architecture. In 1866, Pascal won the highest prize possible for a young French architect, the Grand Prix de Rome, and his project, a combination palace and office for a "rich banker" in Paris, shows in its arrangement what rationalism meant then. Beneath roofs and walls that, incidentally, call to mind the ornate additions to the Louvre in the 1850s and 1860s there is a plan that is an imaginative response to an awkward, nonrectangular site. Separating the different parts of the project are cylindrical turrents, which serve as hinges in the composition, linking and giving clarity to the different masses.

After four years at the French Academy in Rome, Pascal returned to Paris and in 1872 took charge of the atelier where he had been a student. He was its master until his death in 1920. Like many of the great *patrons*, he produced relatively few buildings. The best-known of them was for the Faculty of Medicine and Pharmacy at Bordeaux. The result of a competition in 1876, it went up slowly, in several stages, and was completed only on the eve of World War I. In appearance sober, it looks like a restrained, sixteenth-century Roman palace. Pascal's façades for the Bibliothèque Nationale, Paris, (on the rue Vivienne and the rue Colbert), which became his responsibility after the death of Henri Labrouste, are likewise unostentatious, being similar to the older parts of the building. Pascal's architecture is not assertive; it is less grandiloquent than Laloux's.

Pascal is more important for his teaching than for his buildings. Students entered his atelier because of his reputation as a *patron:* American students flocked to him: Fifty-five Americans are known to have been there between 1873, when William B. Bigelow arrived, and 1910, when Eugene H. Klaber left. In between were Joseph C. Hornblower, John Stewardson, William A. Boring, E. L. Tilton, Guy Lowell, Paul A. Davis, Harvey Wiley Corbett, Charles Collens, Robert P. Bellows, George B. Ford, Francis J. Swales, and others. Among his French students were two who became famous professors

1   Walter Cook, "Jean Louis Pascal—Institute Gold Medalist, 1913," *Journal of the AIA*, vol. III, January 1915, p. 19.

of architecture in the United States: D. Despradelle at MIT and Paul P. Cret at the University of Pennsylvania.

In his teaching Pascal encouraged his students to avoid current architectural fashions and to seek the best qualities of older architecture. He considered these qualities to be strength and refinement (or, as he put it, distinction). He saw them best expressed in the buildings of Brunelleschi and Bramante.

By his last decade, Pascal was the grand old man of the *section d'architecture* at the École des Beaux-Arts. He had been elected to one of the eight seats for architects in the Institut de France in 1890 and had been president of the whole body in 1904. He had been the president of the jury in the international competition for the design of the University of California and had traveled to Berkeley in 1899 for the judgment. His Gold Medal from the AIA in 1913 was the greatest honor his American admirers could bestow on him. He died in 1920.

CONTRIBUTED BY RICHARD CHAFEE

Jean Louis Pascal: Bibliothèque Nationale, Paris, rue de Richelieu façade, 1875–1902.

W. Cook. "Jean Louis Pascal—Institute Gold Medalist, 1913," *Journal of the AIA*, vol. 3, January 1915

VICTOR LALOUX

AWARDED ON JUNE 9, 1922
AT THE FINE ARTS BUILDING
CHICAGO, ILLINOIS
ACCEPTED BY A. BARTHELEMY

Courtesy of Jean Labatut

Victor Laloux.

The Architects of America have been rarely privileged in the opportunity afforded to them by a sister country. Many years ago the artistic sense of the people of France led them to endow and establish a school of art and architecture. With a rare generosity they opened its doors to all who would come. With but very little restriction every privilege of the school was opened to those who came from different nationalities to worship at the Shrine of French Art and to profit by her lessons and teachings, to learn the architecture of classic times, the architecture of plan and design and study as it has been there taught. With rare skill her teachers have taught methods of expression. . . . The pupils of Monsieur Laloux are numerous in this country. They felt the debt of gratitude they owe to him as well as to the school.[1]

Born at Tours in 1850, Laloux studied architecture in Paris at the École des Beaux-Arts from 1869 until 1878. His *patron* was Jules André, who had been H. H. Richardson's master. André's architecture (for example, the museum at the Jardin des Plantes in Paris) is big in scale, and so is Laloux's: Such largeness seems to have been a principle André taught. It was not a new principle but was in the tradition of grand classicism long central to the École's teaching. In 1878, Laloux won the Grand Prix de Rome with a design for a cathedral that would have been enormous in both size and scale, a grandiose neoclassical version of J. H. Mansart's church of the Invalides.

After his four years at the French Academy in Rome, Laloux returned to France and began to practice architecture. Several important commissions came to him from Tours: the reconstruction of the basilica of Saint Martin, the city hall, and the railroad station. In Paris he did another railroad station (with a hotel attached), the Gare d'Orsay, put up for the International Exposition of 1900. These four works differ from one another in style: the church is Byzantine; the city hall is French Renaissance, like the one in Paris; the Tours station is a variation of the Gare du Nord in Paris (Laloux doubles Hittorf's central motif, the arch of the

shed); and the Gare d'Orsay echoes the Louvre almost directly across the Seine in the use of high mansard domes. All four buildings have similar oversized details, such as cartouched dormers above the cornice line and heavily rusticated stonework at eye level. Big details are Laloux's signature.

Laloux's reputation owed more to his teaching than to his buildings or Grand Prix. Soon after coming home from Rome, he began informally assisting his *patron*, Jules André. In 1867, André had been put in charge of one of the three official ateliers established in 1863 within the École itself; thus, when he died in 1890, the government had the duty of naming his successor. The students expected Laloux to get the post. When another man got it, the majority of them walked out, as was their right, and invited Laloux to become their *patron* in a private atelier of his own. This he did, and from 1890 until his death in 1937 he taught. In one sense he was the school's most successful *patron* ever: Sixteen of his students won the annual Grand Prix de Rome; no other atelier took the prize as often. (Five of Pascal's

1 "Address of Henry H. Kendall, President, AIA, *Proceedings of the Fifty-fifth Annual Convention of the American Institute of Architects,* Gibson Bros., Washington, D.C., 1922, pp. 75–76.

students were winners.) Awarding the Grand Prix to his students, the Institut de France recognized Laloux as the main proponent of its values, the custodian of what the Institut hoped was the continuing French tradition. In 1909, Laloux himself was elected to one of the eight places for architects in the Institut, and for the year 1923 he was president of all of it. At his death in 1937 he was the patriarch of French academic architecture.

In his teaching Laloux emphasized composition, primarily the composition of plans. He suggested to his students that a good plan, a plan with a strong, clear idea and balanced, well-proportioned parts, would so much as generate good façades and good details. His students often postponed drawing their elevations and sections in order to give more time to problems of organization and planning. The plan was what mattered; it determined the whole composition.

Laloux is known to have had 132 American students from 1890 to 1928, from Edward P. Casey to Alfred V. Dupont. In between were many Americans who became well known: John Galen Howard, Arthur Brown Jr., William Emerson, William E. Parsons, William A. Delano, Otto Faelten, William Graves Perry, George Howe, William L. Bottomley, Lawrence Grant White, William Van Alen, Henry R. Shepley, Lloyd Morgan, and more. Also among his pupils were three Frenchmen who were to become important teachers of architecture in America: Jacques Carlu at MIT, J.-J. Haffner at Harvard, and Jean Labatut at Princeton. Laloux was the foremost of the École *patrons* in the very years when the most Americans were there.

CONTRIBUTED BY RICHARD CHAFEE

Victor Laloux: La Gare d'Orléans
and Le Quai d'Orsay, Paris,
1896–1900.

GOLD MEDAL FOR 1923 **HENRY BACON**

AWARDED ON MAY 18, 1923
AT THE REFLECTING POOL
LINCOLN MEMORIAL
WASHINGTON, D.C.

Henry Bacon.

There never was a more profoundly considered design. That building was studied, and re-studied, and re-studied again. Its smallest detail, as well as its mass, represents ceaseless meditation. And here I would emphasize once more the man behind the building. What is the style of the Lincoln Memorial? A natural reply would be: "the style of ancient Greece." But for my own part I would prefer to call it "the style of Henry Bacon." The great principles of the Lincoln Memorial, its majesty, its strong refinement, its simplicity, its beauty, its monumental serenity, you will find running through the entire long procession of Bacon's buildings. We must call him I suppose a classicist, but he has made the classic idiom absolutely his own and gives to his designs a superb individuality.[1]

Henry Bacon was born in Watseka, Illinois, in 1866. After a short period, his father, an engineer, moved the family to Wilmington, North Carolina, where Bacon grew up. He studied architecture briefly at the University of Illinois, 1884–1885, then moved to Boston to work for Chamberlin & Whidden. Shortly thereafter he departed for a place in the New York firm of McKim, Mead & White. Between 1889 and 1891, Bacon held the Rotch Traveling Scholarship and traveled and sketched abroad. He returned to McKim, Mead & White in 1891, becoming Charles McKim's personal assistant. In 1897, Bacon left the firm to form a partnership with James Brite, another McKim office man; the partnership lasted until 1903 when Bacon began independent practice. He died in 1924.

The long period spent with the McKim office naturally influenced Bacon, and his work is, in many ways, a logical continuation of that office. He worked on shingled country and resort houses, then was exposed to issues of artistic collaborations while assisting on the Boston Public Library. For the Chicago Columbian Exposition, Bacon was McKim's personal, on-site representative and consequently gained more exposure to collaboration, civic art, urban planning, and landscaping. While at the fair he designed independently the exhibition building for the Pennsylvania Railroad Company. Returning east, he was a designer under McKim on the Rhode Island State House and did many of the presentation and working drawings. His close relationship

continued even after he left the office, and he was asked to contribute to the McMillan Commission, but the press of work prevented him.

Bacon's own work shows the stylistic range and variety of McKim, Mead & White, from bases for statues to major public buildings and individual houses. For houses, he followed the semivernacular prototypes set down by McKim: semi-Georgian, as in the Daniel Chester French House and studio in Stockbridge, Massachusetts, 1900; and shingled, as the Donald MacRae House in Wilmington, North Carolina, 1901. Bacon's more urban work followed the classical idiom, as in the Union Square Savings Bank, 1907, New York, the Public Library, Paterson, New Jersey, 1906, and Wesleyan University, in Middletop, Connecticut. From 1905 until his death, Bacon would act as campus architect and planner for Wesleyan University, attempting to bring order out of a disparate group of buildings. The architecture is a reticent Georgian.

It is as a collaborator with sculptors designing settings and bases that Bacon is perhaps best-known. In this activity he inherited the mantle of Stanford White and did several bases for Augustus Saint-Gaudens, Carl Bitter, and Charles Niehaus. Far better known is his collaboration with Daniel Chester French; together they did the Melvin Me-

---

1   Address of Royal Cortissoz," *Proceedings of the Fifty-sixth Annual Convention of the American Institute of Architects* Gibson Bros., Washington, D.C., 1923, p. 86.

morial, Concord, Massachusetts; the Francis Parkman Memorial, Jamaica Plain, Massachusetts; the Lincoln Memorial, Lincoln, Nebraska; the Spenser Trask Memorial, Saratoga Springs, New York, and numerous others.

The collaboration continued with his best-known work, the Lincoln Memorial in Washington, D.C., 1911–1922, where French did the statue and Jules Guérin provided the murals (Plate 3). The Lincoln Memorial had originally been projected by the McMillan Commission in 1901–1902, and Bacon's selection as architect indicated his close connections with the now-deceased McKim, who had intended for the site a large, rectangular, colonnaded structure with a stepped attic. In 1911, Congress set up the Lincoln Memorial Commission, and while there was some small sentiment to move the site of the memorial elsewhere and to engage another architect, Bacon from the beginning appears to have been assured of the commission and the site. In this, he was assisted by the Commission of Fine Arts, set up in 1910 as a result of the McMillan report, and headed from 1910 to 1912 by Daniel Burnham, and from 1912–1915 by Daniel Chester French. While Bacon considered a number of alternatives, including an open colonnade, and a round structure, ultimately he returned to a rectangular peripteral temple of thirty-six Doric columns, containing a central atrium and flanking sanctuaries. Details were carefully studied, from the inclined columns and walls through the terraces, the circular traffic pattern, and the elimination of the side basins to the Reflecting Pool, which had been projected by the McMillan Commission. He chose French as the sculptor in 1915 and succeeded in convincing him that the seated Lincoln should be of marble rather than brass. He viewed the artist as a collaborator, however, not merely someone to embroider his designs or fill in waste spaces. The design was continually modified and refined to show not just his and their work at its best, but to insure a harmonious whole.

The concept of artistic collaboration has become a byword for the period of the American Renaissance, and many of the projects are well known, but perhaps none have had the lasting popularity or impact of the Lincoln Memorial. In design and execution it matches the best work of Bacon's contemporaries, and its placement and acclaim have played no small part in the preservation of the Mall as central to the plan of Washington, D.C. It continued to evoke the character and greatness of Abraham Lincoln for a constant stream of visitors and has served as both symbolic and actual backdrop and stage for some of the great dramas of the last fifty years. While it is unfair to judge Bacon on the basis of one building, it is perhaps fair to say that not many architectural works so completely fulfill their reason for being.

CONTRIBUTED BY TONY WRENN, LESLIE BONEY,
AND RICHARD GUY WILSON

Henry Bacon: Lincoln Memorial, Washington, D.C. 1911–1922.

Henry Bacon: Lincoln Memorial, interior.

SIR EDWIN LANDSEER LUTYENS

AWARDED ON APRIL 24, 1925
AT THE METROPOLITAN MUSEUM OF ART
NEW YORK CITY

Sir Edwin Landseer Lutyens.

Royal Institute of British Architects

His function it has been first to speak of the heart of Great Britain, that heart which lives and breathes in the quiet homes of the British people, where are born those elemental virtues of courage, and perseverance and steadfastness, and adventurous pride out of which has come the British Empire on which "the sun never sets." He has spoken again of the power and majesty of Great Britain, and today in sight of the ruins of seven empires, he builds at Delhi monumental buildings which testify not only to the far flung law which England has carried throughout the world . . . he expressed in his Cenotaph the soul of Great Britain in the moment of her greatest grief and her greatest pride.[1]

Sir Edwin Landseer Lutyens was easily the most popular and famous English architect of his day, commonly referred to as the greatest architect since Sir Christopher Wren, and in some people's minds, even greater. Honors came readily to Lutyens: the Royal Gold Medal in 1921; vice-president of the RIBA, 1924–1925; Knight Commander, Order of the Indian Empire, 1930; Legion of Honour, 1932; president of the Royal Academy, 1938, and Order of Merit, 1942, along with membership on the Royal Fine Arts Commission, and honorary degrees from Liverpool University and Oxford. While revered as a guardian of tradition and an outspoken antagonist of the modern movement, Lutyens commanded respect from architects, critics, and historians of both camps. Even Frank Lloyd Wright, notorious for expressing negative opinions about his contemporaries, could claim an "admiration of the love, loyalty and art with which this cultured Architect, in love with Architecture, shaped his buildings."[2]

Lutyens's father was a painter of horses and the hunt, and his son's name derived from his friendship with the great Victorian painter of animals, Sir Edwin Landseer. Born in 1869 and sickly as a child, Lutyens was privately educated and decided to become an architect. He attended the Kensington School of Art for two years and then spent a year in the office of Ernest George & Peto, leading practitioners of the Queen Anne, Pont Street Dutch, and Olde-English idioms. Lutyens's own practice began in 1890 with several small commissions in his native Surrey. His big break came in collaborating with

Gertrude Jekyll, a leading landscape gardener of the time, and together they became a team. In 1899 another fortuitous link was made when Lutyens met Edward Hudson, the editor and publisher of *Country Life,* and for years practically anything that Lutyens designed was featured in the magazine. He would design three buildings for Hudson. Lutyens's early manner was in the arts-and-crafts idiom of Philip Webb or Norman Shaw, though transformed by his own sense of exaggerated scale and features, historical and local imagery, geometry, and materials. Many of the best were located in Surrey, such as Tigbourne Court—a neovernacular classical composition, with the U-shaped court, reiterated gables, and local materials of Bargate stone, ironstone chippings inserted into the mortar, brick quoins, and thin horizontal bands of Roman tiles. From this earlier informal manner, Lutyens progressed toward a more classical image, as the fascination of axial planning, the geometry of interrelated spaces and forms, and the idea of known orders and proportions attracted him. In 1903 he wrote: "In architecture Palladio is the game! It is so big—few appreciate it now, and it requires training to value and release it."[3]

1   "Address of John W. Davis, Ambassador to Great Britain," *Proceedings of the Fifty-eighth Convention of the American Institute of Architects,* AIA, Washington, D.C., 1925, p. 96.

2   Frank Lloyd Wright, "Review of the Memorial Volumes," *Building,* vol. 26, July 1951, p. 260.

3   Letter of February 15, 1903, quoted in Christopher Hussey, *The Lutyens Memorial Volumes,* vol 1: *The Life of Sir Edwin Lutyens,* Country Life, London, 1950, p. 121.

Lutyens's output was phenomenal—approximately 500 realised commissions and another several hundred unexecuted projects. Best-known for his country-house work, Lutyens slowly built up a substantial urban practice, especially in the 1920s as economies foreclosed the country house as a field for new work. His best-known urban work was the offices for *Country Life*, 1904, in a "Wrenaissance" manner, and then a series of buildings for the Midlands Bank. In 1917, Lutyens was appointed to the Imperial War Graves Commission and subsequently designed the majority of the cemeteries and memorials for the 750,000 British dead and missing from the Great War. Concurrently he designed his most popular public work, the Cenotaph in Whitehall, 1919–1920, to commemorate the British missing. This, together with his Memorial to the Missing of the Somme, the Thiepval Arch, 1927–1932, illustrates his later elemental classic mode, a drastic simplification and reduction of ornament and form. Two great projects consumed much of his later life, the incomplete Liverpool Cathedral, 1929, and the planning and design of the new imperial capital at New Delhi, India, 1912–1931. The New Delhi Commission and especially the Viceroy's House, the central building of the new planned city, show Lutyens's attempt to merge the western forms of classicism with Indian ornament. A great elemental mass of red and cream Dolphur sandstone is deeply pierced by porticos and openings and banded by thin, protruding cornices, responses to both the environment of heat and harsh sunlight, and the need to make a statement about the permanence of the classical tradition. Unfortunately, it was to be the swan song of the British Empire: the English left in 1947, sixteen years after completion. Lutyens died on January 1, 1944, and while he never really passed from public or architectural memory, his reputation was eclipsed for a number of years, until the 1970s when his genius again became recognized.

Sir Edwin Lutyens: Cenotaph, Whitehall, London, 1919–1920.

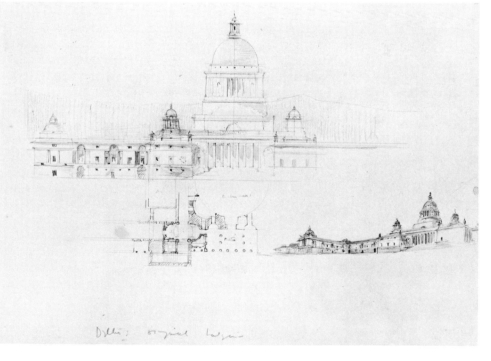

Sir Edwin Lutyens: Viceroy's House, New Delhi, 1912–1931, drawing by Lutyens, September 1913.

153

GOLD MEDAL FOR 1925 BERTRAM GROSVENOR GOODHUE

AWARDED ON APRIL 24, 1925
AT THE METROPOLITAN MUSEUM OF ART
NEW YORK CITY
ACCEPTED BY MRS. GOODHUE

National Academy of Design

Bertram Grosvenor Goodhue.
Portrait by Kenneth Frazier.

The story of Bertram Goodhue, as an artist (and I use that generic word deliberately), is the story that has been told in allegory of the hunter who set out in the face of the high mountains of Dry Facts and Actualities to snare the white bird of truth beyond, having seen its reflection one day in a lake by which he stood in his own valley, and who, after years of climbing, at times digging out the stones with the bare shuttle of his imagination, mounting one cliff after another, at last lay down in death at a great, bare height—the eternal mountains still rising with walls to the white clouds—but holding in his dying hands a silver feather that had fluttered down from the pinions of that great white bird of truth, and knowing that when enough of these feathers had been gathered by the hands of men to make a cord and that cord woven into a net, in that net, Truth would be taken, since "nothing but the truth can hold truth."[1]

Bertram Grosvenor Goodhue was a strikingly romantic and individualistic architect. Standing outside the mainstream of American classicism, which he regarded as a fait accompli, Goodhue searched for an architecture that embraced modern materials, inventions, and ideas, and also that embodied the idealism and often the forms associated with medieval life. He stressed that a building be designed with a careful regard for its physical and social context, that it be built with a judicious array of proven as well as innovative construction techniques, that it include the work of allied artisans, that it be composed of simplified, sculpted masses, and that it display ornament as a finishing touch.

Born in 1869, Goodhue was raised in the rural town of Pomfret, Connecticut, where he developed a precocious talent for drawing and a deep knowledge and appreciation of medieval life and lore. At 15, he moved to New York City to apprentice under James Renwick, architect of St. Patrick's Cathedral.

In 1891, Goodhue began a twenty-two year association with Ralph Adams Cram, first as part of Cram, Wentworth & Goodhue (1892–1897) and then as part of Cram, Goodhue & Ferguson (1898–1913). Goodhue found a sympathetic and ardent compatriot in Cram. Together they created an office worthy of attention, and they worked in extracurricular literary endeavors. Goodhue played a central role in a renaissance of fine bookmaking, designing several books and the typeface Cheltenham.

All Saints Ashmont (1891–1895) was the first major building completed by Cram and Goodhue, and it established the firm's reputation as Gothic church architects. However, the building was only part of an oeuvre that included a series of impressive libraries, houses, apartment houses, and schools in varied styles.

In 1903, Cram, Goodhue & Ferguson won the competition to design major additions to the United States Military Academy at West Point with a scheme that integrated the existing midnineteenth-century castellated Gothic buildings with several new buildings. Prominent among these was the rugged Cadet Chapel (1903–1910), set high upon a hill. Required to establish a local field office, Goodhue moved back to New York where he developed a wide acquaintance with the powerful individuals who were at the heart of American culture.

St. Thomas Church (1906–1915) in New York was the last collaborative effort between Goodhue and Cram, and it is an extremely distinguished work of architecture. The chunky exterior forms are an expression of the eccentric plan and were designed to give the church a great presence among the tall skyscrapers that were anticipated to surround the building. The interior is dominated by the unusually large and dramatic reredos, designed by Goodhue in close collaboration with the sculptor, Lee Lawrie.

1   Address of Hon. John H. Finley, *Proceedings of the Fifty-eighth Annual Convention of the American Institute of Architects*, AIA, Washington, D.C., 1925, p. 98.

Goodhue designed a series of churches with a style, structure, and use of material and craft that seemed especially his own. Of these, the First Baptist Church (1909–1912) at Pittsburgh was the most strikingly original. For the Panama-California Exposition (1911–1915) at San Diego, Goodhue designed a group of buildings in a Spanish idiom, in which voluptuous ornament was densely massed in counterpoint to broad blank walls, forming a backdrop for the green and floral landscape. The imagery of this fair gave impetus to the Spanish colonial revival in California in the 1920s.

In 1913, Goodhue visited the modern Gothic cathedral at Liverpool, designed by Giles Gilbert Scott. This daunting building forced Goodhue to reassess his attitudes about architectural form. He thus began to abandon architectural tradition in favor of new, original forms.

Soon after establishing his own office in 1914, Goodhue received three important commissions. For St. Bartholomew's Church (1914–1918) in New York, Goodhue moved away from Gothic to a Romanesque-Byzantine idiom. St. Vincent Ferrer Church (1914–1919) in New York at once summarized his Gothic designs and suggested his new direction. For the National Academy of Sciences Building (1916–1924) in Washington, D.C., Goodhue employed stripped classical forms on the exterior, balanced by a polychromed, tiled, central rotunda.

His greatest achievement was the design for the new Nebraska State Capitol in Lincoln, Nebraska, (1920–1932) (Plate 8). The audacious design, admired as a daring departure from the typical classical precedent, was a vigorous composition of freely styled stepped masses piling up to a central tower that embodied the romantic image of a skyscraper.

His last buildings were usually free in style, exotic in aura, and composed of stripped forms adorned only with integral sculpture and inscriptions: his entry in the Kansas City War Memorial competition (1921); the Los Angeles Central Library (1922–1926); and the Sterling Library (1920–1924) at Yale University. Goodhue's passion for the skyscraper was developed in a proposed eighty-story ecclesiastical office building for New York (1921), which would have been the tallest building in the world at that time, and in a distinguished entry in the Chicago Tribune competition (1922).

When Goodhue died in 1924, his position as an American modernist was not yet confirmed by completed buildings. Nevertheless, his influence on a younger generation of architects had been substantial, and with his last designs he had helped to establish both the broad stylistic characteristics and philosophical intentions of American modernism in the 1920s and 1930s.

CONTRIBUTED BY RICHARD OLIVER

Cram, Goodhue & Ferguson: Panama-California International Exposition, San Diego, California, 1911–1915. Drawing of approach by Goodhue, ca 1911.

Bertram Grosvenor Goodhue, *A Book of Architectural and Decorative Drawings*, Architectural Books, New York, 1914

GOLD MEDAL FOR 1927 HOWARD VAN DOREN SHAW

AWARDED ON MAY 13, 1927
AT THE U.S. CHAMBER OF COMMERCE
WASHINGTON, D.C.
ACCEPTED BY MRS. SHAW

Chicago Historical Society

Howard Van Doren Shaw.

Mr. Shaw's design, whether it be a suburban home or a church, a civic group or factory center, a multi-family city apartment or an office building, a club or a theater, always manifested an esthetic quality with an atmosphere and a degree of originality coupled with knowledge of precedent. His buildings command the interest and admiration of his fellow architects as well as the laymen, and carry a message, the significance of which will be valued more surely in the next generation.[1]

The son of a successful Chicago drygoods merchant, Howard Van Doren Shaw was born in 1869. After graduating from the Harvard School, he went east to Yale, matriculating with the class of 1890. For his architectural education he attended MIT in 1891–1992, combining the work of two years in one. After graduation he traveled extensively in Europe, making measured drawings and sketches in England, Italy, and Spain. His office experience included a period in the office of Jenney & Mundie, where he knew William Le Baron Jenney, the designer of America's first skyscraper, the famous Home Insurance Building (1884). He was not, however, much attracted to Jenney's version of the structural expressionism so characteristic of the first Chicago school. In 1895 he moved into a downtown office of his own and was almost immediately successful. In the words of his friend and biographer Thomas Tallmadge, he was "probably the most highly regarded architect in the sphere of domestic, ecclesiastical, and non-commercial architecture in the Middle West."[2]

The basis of Shaw's practice was a series of large country houses in the suburbs north of Chicago for the city's commercial elite. These were mostly in Lake Forest, for which Shaw also built an attractive shopping center. His clients included the Ryersons, the Swifts, the Donnelleys, and numerous other members of the second generation of Chicago millionaires. His houses were generally eclectic in character and often derived from English precedent, although the Ryerson place is obviously Italian in its origins. Shaw handled the imported styles with consummate skill. In the finesse of his compositions he may well be compared to the best of eastern practitioners in the eclectic mode. The Fourth Presbyterian Church on Michigan Avenue was done in collaboration with Ralph Adams Cram. Although he knew the work of Frank Lloyd Wright and was fond of him personally, he was never attracted to the ideas of the Prairie school.

Concerning Shaw's houses, his best-known work, we can make a few generalizations. They were beautifully composed and often quite formal

---

1 "Howard Van Doren Shaw—Address of Mr. [E. V.] Waid," *Proceedings of the Sixtieth Convention of the American Institute of Architects*, AIA, Washington, D.C., 1927, p. 131.

2 Thomas Tallmadge, "Howard Van Doren Shaw," in Dumas Malone (ed.), *Dictionary of American Biography*, Scribner's, New York, 1950.

in plan; Shaw was particularly fond of the English eighteenth century, and he may well have been at his best in neo-Georgian design. His city house for Mr. and Mrs. John P. Wilson (Chicago, 1924) was so polished a performance that it might well have been located in London or Bath. In accordance with American upper-class taste of the 1920s, the owners of Shaw's houses tended to furnish them with English antiques. All were immaculately detailed and exceptionally well-built. The Wilson House was framed in concrete, a material which Shaw also used in flat slab form for his large industrial buildings for the Donnelley Printing Company. Commercial work, however, was only a small part of his life. He was never much interested in it.

In Shaw, then, we have one of the most polished American eclectics. His contribution to the development of architecture in the United States is now more highly rated than in years past. He died in 1926 of pernicious anemia.

CONTRIBUTED BY LEONARD K. EATON

Howard Van Doren Shaw: John P. Wilson House, Chicago, 1924.

"Residence for Mr. John P. Wilson, Chicago." *Western Architect*, vol. 35, September 1926

GOLD MEDAL FOR 1929 **MILTON BENNETT MEDARY**

AWARDED ON APRIL 23, 1929
AT THE CORCORAN GALLERY
WASHINGTON, D.C.

Courtesy of Mrs. William Norris

Milton Bennett Medary.

No man who we have known in this generation has more of that discriminating quality in the judgement of his own work than Milton Medary. He combines qualities sometimes regarded as impossible of combination. His architecture in its great masses as in its smallest details bears witness to the sustained solicitude of its author.

He started with a love of beauty and soon developed a rare capacity of judgement in all the activities and responsibilities which rest upon the architect in carrying out great work. To these qualities he unites an unusual sympathy, an unusual gentleness, an unusual kindness in his judgements of others, with an absolute adherence to his artistic convictions. These qualities have been exemplified in his work, in his life, and in his administration of the responsibilities, architectural, educational, and governmental, which through the years have crowded upon him.[1]

Milton B. Medary, Jr., was born in Philadelphia in 1874 and educated in the Philadelphia public schools. He spent one year at the University of Pennsylvania's School of Architecture; but during his first vacation from the university in 1891, he began working in the office of architect Frank Miles Day, where he remained until the spring of 1895. In 1895, Medary joined Richard L. Field, an 1892 graduate of the University of Pennsylvania, in the firm of Field & Medary, an association which continued until Field's death in 1905. Medary then worked independently until 1911, when he joined Clarence Clark Zantzinger and Charles Louis Borie, Jr., in the firm of Zantzinger, Borie & Medary. It was with this firm that he was associated until his death at the age of 55 in 1929.

Medary's architectural career was marked by several notable and complex projects, including the Washington Memorial Chapel at Valley Forge, Pennsylvania, the Philadelphia Divinity School, the Foulke and Henry dormitories at Princeton University, and the Bok Singing Tower in Mountain Lake, Florida (Plate 6). Several of these projects show Medary's fondness for the Gothic or Tudor revival so popular for ecclesiastical and collegiate projects at the time; but he was equally at ease in the use of the Georgian revival, in each case fitting the style to the symbolic use of the building, while integrating function, siting, and the relation of the new building to others already present.

Equally important in Medary's career was his service to the public and to his profession. By 1918 he had been appointed to the first of many positions utilizing his organizational skills and abilities in urban planning. He was made chairman of the U.S. Housing Corporation during World War I, designing and supervising the rapid construction of workers' villages in Bethlehem, Pennsylvania, and on Neville Island, Pittsburgh, Pennsylvania. Successive appointments to the National Commission of Fine Arts, the National Capital Park and Planning Commission, and the Board of Architectural Consultants of the U.S. Treasury Department enabled Medary to affect conclusively the location of the Arlington Memorial Bridge and the development of the District of Columbia, particularly in the area of the Federal Triangle, where his firm designed the new Department of Justice Building.

These public activities did not cause him to neglect service to his profession, however. After serving as president of the T-Square Club and of the Philadelphia chapter of the AIA, he was elected president of the national AIA, retaining that office from 1926 until 1928. Respect from his colleagues in Philadelphia was evident in 1927 when he received

---

1   Address of James Monroe Hewlett, *Proceedings of the Sixty-second Annual Convention of the American Institute of Architects*, AIA, Washington, D.C., 1929, p. 64.

Field & Medary: Houston Hall, University of Pennsylvania, Philadelphia, 1895.

both an honorary doctorate in fine arts from the University of Pennsylvania and a Gold Medal from the Philadelphia Art Club.

CONTRIBUTED BY SANDRA L. TATMAN

GOLD MEDAL FOR 1933 **RAGNAR ÖSTBERG**

AWARDED ON MAY 16, 1934
IN THE EAST ROOM, THE WHITE HOUSE
WASHINGTON, D.C.

Courtesy of Elias Cornell

Ragnar Östberg.

The recognition of his artistic imagination, adaptiveness and wealth of ideas, uniting a fine sense of form and plasticity combined with firmness of design, as particularly manifest in the City Hall of Stockholm. The Institute also recognizes that Professor Östberg's contribution to the modern development in architecture, while being chiefly evidenced in his monumental and lesser creations in Sweden, must exert a beneficial influence far beyond the confines of that country.[1]

Ragnar Östberg was born in 1866 in Vaxholm to parents who were involved with the theater. He trained at the Institute of Technology and the Royal Academy of Arts in Stockholm and then worked with I. G. Clason on the designs of the Nordiska Museet. The consequence was an interest in Swedish building traditions and handicrafts that would emerge in his later architecture. In 1893, while traveling in the United States, he saw the Chicago World's Columbian Exposition. It was Sullivan's Transportation Building, rather than the classicism, that impressed him; he became one of the first Scandinavian admirers and publicists of Sullivan. In 1896 he began a three-year tour of Europe. Upon his return, Östberg acquired a reputation as an outstanding architect of villas. By 1900, Östberg and his friend Carl Westman had become two of the leading architects of their generation.

During the years 1901–1923, from the age of 35 to 56, most of Östberg's capacity and interest was centered on planning the Law Courts and the subsequent City Hall of Stockholm (Plate 7).

Nevertheless he had time and energy to spare for designing a succession of other buildings during those years. These were not only villas, but also included a school, the Swedish Patents Office Building, an Odd Fellows' House, etc.

Upon the completion of the Stockholm City Hall, Östberg acquired worldwide fame and was awarded the Royal Gold Medal of the RIBA in 1926.

Despite this recognition from abroad and a professorship of architecture at the Royal Academy of Arts, Östberg received few Swedish commissions. He built some villas, a crematorium in Hälsingborg, a school in Kalmar, and the Naval Museum in Stockholm, but much of his interest in his later years was concentrated on designs for the reshaping of central Stockholm. From 1918 to 1937 he produced one plan after another for the renewal of the government and parliamentary buildings. Little of this work was carried out, but even today consideration is given to Östberg's designs in discussions concerning Sweden's official center.

Östberg's work covers a period of transition in Scandinavian and European architecture. He started his career with an academy Gold Medal design for new buildings for the very academy he was then leaving. The drawings were in a heavy, ornamental, classical style derived from the École des Beaux-Arts. He abandoned this style upon settling down in 1899. His designs and buildings dating from the years prior to 1907 are art nouveau and arts and crafts, with the influence of Swedish idioms. Östberg and his generation, however, were not doctrinaire, and consequently his buildings show impressions from England, the United States, and other countries.

1   "The Gold Medal Presentation", *The Octagon*, vol. 6, May 1934, p. 28.

About 1907, when changing over from law-courts drawings to city-hall designing, Östberg manifestly changed his style toward traditional Swedish regionalism and handicraft. The deepest trend of his ambition, however, was toward an aesthetic simplification of architecture. This is clearly demonstrated in the Villa Elfviksudde of 1910–1911, designed for a Stockholm banker. Eventually the architect's interest was directed toward the purer, more classical elements in Swedish building heritage. For Östberg, the process ended in shaping the development of the Scandinavian neoclassicism of the 1920s.

With Gunnar Asplund's Stockholm Exhibition in 1930, the trend in modern architecture called functionalism emerged triumphant in Sweden. That same year Östberg built his one and only building in the new style, a center for the small industries in Stockholm. In principle, however, he never wanted to follow the functionalists. Perhaps he was not able to change his mind once again. He kept to neoclassicism for the rest of his life, thus ending his career more or less isolated from his colleagues.

The Stockholm City Hall, the source of his fame, nonetheless occupies a strange position in Östberg's development as an architect. The long period of its achievement caused him to change the drawings several times. On the other hand, he never departed entirely from earlier ideas in later drawings. Features from all the stages of its development linger in the final fabric. Reminiscences of art nouveau are integrated in a structure which in style is mainly of a national and handicraft character but also incorporates precursors of neoclassicism.

This is the most renowned monument of early twentieth-century Sweden and is indeed of importance. Paradoxically its architect's influence on his own time and nation was not exerted mainly through this building. Rather his importance lay in his rejection of nineteenth-century cosmopolitanism by simplifying building to accord with national and handicraft conditions, and in his work as an eminent—and accordingly disputed—architectural writer and educator.

CONTRIBUTED BY ELIAS CORNELL

Ragnar Östberg: Stockholm City
Hall, 1907–1923, plans.

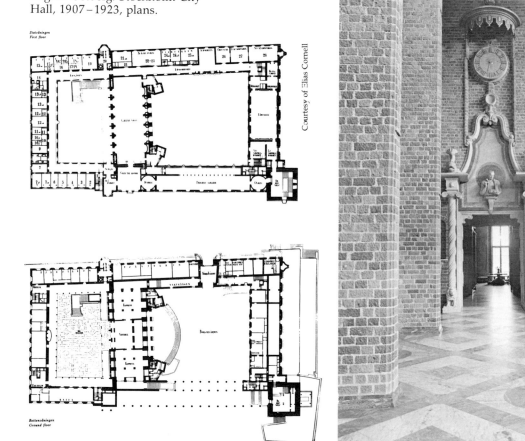

Stockholm City Hall, Blue Hall,
detail.

161

PAUL PHILIPPE CRET

AWARDED ON APRIL 20, 1938
AT THE DELGADO MUSEUM OF ART
NEW ORLEANS, LOUSIANA

National Academy of Design

Paul Philippe Cret. Portrait by
Adolphe Borie.

Architect — Teacher — Scholar. Increasingly honored by a professional recognition that distinguishes him even among his peers.

He has brought to the land of his adoption the sound sense, the clear logic, the discriminating taste that belong to the classic tradition of an older civilization. Thus armed he has met and mastered with outstanding skill those problems that are inherent in new materials in a new world.

As his designs are acclaimed for their beauty, order and character, so is he loved for his modesty and humor. Once again, as in the days of Washington, our architectural heritage is enriched by the presence among us of a distinguished Frenchman.[1]

Paul Philippe Cret was an architect of well-defined goals. Born in Lyons, France, in 1876, Cret worked for an architect uncle in that city before entering the École des Beaux-Arts Lyons in 1893. Winning the Prix de Paris in 1897, Cret entered the Paris École as the highest-ranked member of his class and chose to study in the atelier Pascal. Due to his popularity and high academic achievements he was recruited directly from the École in 1903 by the University of Pennsylvania. The École's ordered method of design was perpetuated by Cret in his teaching and throughout his work until his death in 1945. Cret eventually formed a partnership under his own name in Philadelphia with Harbeson, Hough, Livingston, and Larson (now H²L²) and executed a considerable number of designs, including locomotives, bridges, monuments, and college campuses.

Paul Cret expressed the complexity of his age by designing in a variety of styles. In this diversity he embraced modern technology but used it as an adjunct to what he considered to be his principal role as an architect: the expression of beauty. He held a strong conviction that architecture was a fine art which evolved slowly by individual effort. He did not feel bound stylistically, for he felt that there were no specialists in architecture. Every architectural problem should be handled in the same manner: using an analysis of the needs and functioning of a certain type of building, a knowledge of the methods of construction, and the ability to design a beautiful form. Cret's major contribution to American architecture was through the evolution and modernization of traditional classical forms. As his succession of forms matured, Cret's concept of beauty was influenced by the modernist movement.

Cret won an American competition in 1907 with the Pan American Union, his first major work. Although an excellent design, it is more closely linked to his student work, resembling his design for the Labarre Prize of 1897 and a *plan esquisse* of 1900–1902. One of the earliest designs which pointed to the later development of his modernized classical idiom in the 1920s was the Indianapolis Public Library, 1914.

Cret's modernized classical work matured in the 1930s with three prime examples in Washington, D.C.: the Folger Shakespeare Library, 1929–1931; the Federal Reserve Board Building, 1935–1937; and the National Naval Medical Center, 1939–1941. Each of these exhibited the basic characteristics which produced a strong, quiet, monumental tone of articulate simplicity: symmetrical, interconnecting, sharp-edged masses; a pilastrade forming the window-wall surface; recessed windows vertically joined by spandrels; smoothly finished volumetric planar surfaces; shallow or incised subsidiary decoration; and descriptive figurative sculpture. Chronologically, each of these three designs is

---

1   Citation.

Paul Cret and Albert Kingsley: Pan American Union, Washington, D.C., 1903–1907. Photograph by Abbie Rowe.

Paul Cret: National Naval Medical Center, Bethesda, Maryland, 1939–1941.

larger, more restrained in traditional decoration, more monumental, and more public in nature. The medical center was Cret's ultimate design, a tensile point of classical abstraction. The beaux-arts method of *parti* assured that each design would be individually suited for its function while the *esquisse*, or expression, enabled Cret to create a mod-ern statement within the continuity of history.

While relying on basic beaux-arts design methods, Paul Cret personally developed architectural forms which offered a middle-ground alternative in an era of contradictory and confusing contemporary currents.

CONTRIBUTED BY TRAVIS C. MCDONALD

GOLD MEDAL FOR 1944 **LOUIS HENRY SULLIVAN**

AWARDED ON MAY 9, 1946
AT THE TERRACE RESTAURANT
MIAMI BEACH, FLORIDA
ACCEPTED BY PAUL GERHARDT, JR.,
FOR GEORGE GRANT ELMSLIE

Louis Henry Sullivan.

Art Institute of Chicago

His profession of architecture was a lifetime dedication of all his energies of mind and spirit.

By esteeming practical requirements as aesthetic responsibilities he unfolded a new discipline of design.

He believed that the dimensions of American architecture are the dimensions of American life, and thus directed us to an art of, by, and for our own people.

He approached each task afresh, believing that each problem contains and suggests its own solution.

He demanded of himself an emotional and spiritual expenditure to endow each building with its own identity of beauty.

He attacked entrenched beliefs. He repudiated false standards. He scored the stylistic gods of the market-place.

He fought almost alone in his generation, lived unhappily, and died in poverty.

But because he fought, we today have a more valiant conception of our art. He helped to renew for all architects the freedom to originate and the responsibility to create. The standards he set have contributed much to the achievement of today and will augment the promise of tomorrow.[1]

Born in 1856 of immigrant parents in Boston, Louis Sullivan is one of the most complex figures in the history of American architecture. After graduating from the Boston English High School, he briefly attended MIT, worked for Frank Furness for a few months, and then in 1873, gravitated to Chicago. He was to be identified with that city for the remainder of his life. After gaining experience in the office of William Le Baron Jenney, he decided that he needed the kind of professional training which could then only be secured at the École des Beaux-Arts. Sullivan's attitude toward the École has been much misunderstood. He retained a profound respect for its method all his life. He simply believed that the problems with which it dealt were not those of nineteenth-century industrial civilization. Returning to Chicago in 1875, Sullivan worked for several different architects in the city and then, in 1879, formed his famous partnership with Dankmar Adler. The next sixteen years were the most successful of his life.

With Adler as engineer and man of business and Sullivan as designing partner, the firm flourished; the practice was devoted largely to commercial buildings and theatres. Their greatest triumph was undoubtedly the Auditorium Hotel and Opera House, in which Adler showed himself to be at least a generation ahead of his time in the difficult science of acoustics, and Sullivan's highly personalized ornament was at its very best. In the 1880s, Sullivan, like most of his contemporaries, was profoundly affected by the architecture of H. H. Richardson, and the Auditorium, like the Walker Warehouse and the Dooley Block in Salt Lake City, were variations on Richardsonian themes. In the Wainwright Building of St. Louis in 1891, he came into his own, and the first Sullivanion skyscraper emerged. While it was not as fine as some of his later work, it stated a theme with which he was to be preoccupied for the remainder of his life: the skyscraper should be "a proud and soaring thing."

For Sullivan the decade of the 1890s was filled with important projects. Probably most significant were the Prudential Guaranty Building of 1895 in Buffalo, the Transportation Building at the Chicago world's fair of 1893, and the Schlesinger-Mayer Building in Chicago of 1899–1904. In the last named, later the Carson, Pirie, Scott and Company Store, he achieved one of the finest expressions of the steel frame ever constructed. Also noteworthy

---

1   Citation.

was his development of a system of architectural ornament which gave a particular life and excitement to his structures. Sometimes this ornament was executed in metal and sometimes in terra cotta. He was undeniably the greatest master of ornament in the history of American architecture, and his treatment of this problem influenced a number of other designers who were to make important contributions. It profoundly affected Frank Lloyd Wright, who was in his office for six years and who always referred to him as "lieber meister."

The career of Louis Sullivan after the turn of the century is important for American architecture in an entirely different way. About 1902 he suffered a psychological collapse, the exact nature of which is still obscure. It is clear that he was profoundly affected by the breakup of his marriage, the dissolution of his partnership with Adler in 1895, and the increasing success of the academic revival. He became sorry for himself and began to drink heavily; his personality became extremely difficult. During the next two decades of his life he did only a hand-ful of small-town banks and commercial structures in the midwest. These, however, are among the gems of American architecture. Perhaps the finest is in Owatonna, Minnesota; it was done in cooperation with his former chief designer, George Elmslie. He also wrote extensively: *Kindergarten Chats* (1902) and *The Autobiography of an Idea* (1922) are his two most significant works. His few commissions and his publications were not, of course, sufficient to sustain him. When he died in 1924, he was living in a third-rate Chicago hotel on the charity of his friends.

Sullivan, then, is the architectural representative of a type familiar in American culture: the failed hero. He saw his career, and subsequent generations have perceived it in the same way, as a reproach to the failure of the democratic ideal. He achieved enormously. He suffered enormously. He deserves to be remembered.

CONTRIBUTED BY LEONARD K. EATON

Louis Sullivan: Carson, Pirie, Scott and Company Store, Chicago, Illinois, 1899–1904.

Carson, Pirie, Scott and Company Store, detail of entrance ornament.

ELIEL SAARINEN

AWARDED ON APRIL 30, 1947
AT THE PANTLIND HOTEL
GRAND RAPIDS, MICHIGAN

Cranbrook Academy of Art

Eliel Saarinen.

You have brought to your chosen profession of architecture a rich dower of understanding and talent. Through the individuality, logic and quiet beauty of your work, you have exerted a marked influence on the architecture of your day and have made a profound contribution to contemporary cultural enjoyment.

By precept and example, and by friendly counsel, you have instructed and inspired your fellow architects and the many students entrusted to your mentorship.

In recognition of your impressive accomplishments and your leadership in the field of architecture, education and civic design.[1]

Eliel Saarinen was born in 1873 and educated in Finland, although he spent eight childhood years in Russia. In Helsinki he studied painting at the university and architecture at the polytechnical institute. Saarinen, Herman Gesellius, and Armas Lindgren designed the Finnish Pavilion for the 1900 world's fair in Paris, and the Helsinki railway station in 1904. In that year Eliel married Gesellius's sister Louise (Loja) who assisted him in the preparation of *Munksnäs-Haga* (published in 1915), and many later projects. Eliel's second-prize award in the Chicago Tribune competition financed his family's emigration to the United States in 1923. While Saarinen was teaching at the University of Michigan (1924–1925), George Booth, the Detroit newspaperman, commissioned him to design schemes for Detroit's river front and for an educational complex for Cranbrook, his estate in Bloomfield Hills. After settling there permanently in 1925, Eliel, Loja, their son Eero, and their daughter Pipsan designed the Cranbrook (1925–1930) and Kingswood (1929–1930) schools, the Academy of Art (1926–1941), the Institute of Science (1932–1937), their furnishings, and their grounds. Eliel Saarinen died in 1950.

Saarinen's academic education led him to develop themes found in nineteenth-century beaux-arts city plans. His entire career focused on the expression of this formal issue: How can public and private, void and solid, exterior and interior be re-

lated and expressed as a totality? Thus, at Cranbrook the main theme was the juxtaposition and reconciliation of the informal landscape setting, the buildings, the urban spaces defined by the buildings, the interior spaces, and the handcrafted structural elements. The axes and cross-axes defined by the siting of the buildings related the various urbanistic, architectural, and landscape elements. The formal monumentality of the academy's museum (1940), its landscape gardens, and its fountains contrasted with the informality of picturesque faculty housing (1928–1929) and the continuous open space of the surrounding landscape; but the axes simultaneously united these contrasting elements and formed a single, unified composition.

Although it rejected the ornament of the past, Saarinen's architecture neither incorporated International-Style elements nor developed Wright's interpenetrating space, Le Corbusier's cubist space, or Mies van der Rohe's universal space. Instead, he remained tied to classical space and handicraft. Helsinki's utilitarian train shed was masked by a procession of classicizing spaces. Cross-axial symmetry and enfilades welded individual rooms into processional spaces in Saarinen's proposal for a Finnish parliament (1908) and in the Kingswood School.

In 1932, Booth, a devotee of the arts-and-crafts

1   Citation.

movement, stimulated Saarinen's role as an educator by establishing a postgraduate architectural and urban-design studio at Cranbrook. It emphasized the relationships between urban design, architecture, and handicrafts. Edmund Bacon's and Carl Feiss's advocacy of their teacher's ideals helped urbanism weather the antiurban polemics of modernism. The studio's cooperative atmosphere nurtured the innovative furniture design of Harry Bertoia, Charles Eames, Florence Knoll, and Eero Saarinen. The focus of the Saarinens' architectural activities shifted to their off-campus offices following the academy's accreditation in 1942.

Saarinen's ideology was disseminated in *The City* (1943). It used the vocabulary of the social sciences to modernize arguments Saarinen originally adapted from the work of Camillo Sitte and the English garden-city advocates for inclusion in *Munksnäs-Haga*.

CONTRIBUTED BY J. MACDOUGALL PRATT

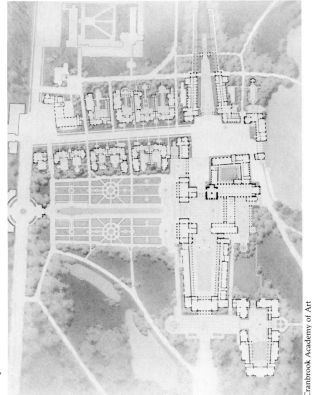

Cranbrook Academy of Art

Eliel Saarinen: Cranbrook Academy, preliminary study, aerial perspective, 1926.

Eliel Saarinen: Cranbrook Academy, Bloomfield Hills, Michigan, 1925, preliminary plan.

Cranbrook Academy of Art

AWARDED ON JUNE 24, 1948
AT THE HOTEL UTAH
SALT LAKE CITY, UTAH

Kennedy & Kennedy

Charles Donagh Maginnis.

He has, for more than half a century, enthusiastically dedicated his energies to the profession of Architecture. With inviolable fidelity to the lofty principles of his profession, he has inspired his contemporaries and has served as model and ideal to the generations that follow him. He had contributed notably to the architectural aspect of the American scene and by example and inspiration has influenced the artistic standards of an epoch. In the fields of ecclesiastical architecture particularly, he has set for his successors the highest standard of achievement.

The skill of his facile pen is no less a force in the drafting-room than it is vigorous and persuasive in the press; he is as revered for the clarity and beauty of his diction as for the brilliance of his Celtic wit. In the exercise of both, and in the charm of his personality, architecture has gained a truer appreciation of its position in the civic and artistic order of our society.

In his love of architecture, he is contemporary with its best interests. With knowledge born of creative experience, he is ever ready to recognize that the true fundamentals of design are as inviolate now as they were in the past. For him, names and declamation do not establish qualities of design.

For more than forty years a Fellow of The American Institute of Architects, he endowed with rare distinction the office of its Presidency. The genius that he would modestly disclaim has been recognized at home and abroad by universities, learned academies, his nation and his Church.[1]

Charles Donagh Maginnis was possibly the greatest architect of Catholic churches America has produced; he certainly was the most productive and influential of the twentieth century. His architectural approach ranged from the traditional to the conservative modern. He was apprehensive of the radical modern or the International-Style, which he considered sterile, arid, graceless, and lacking in the spiritual. While his own architecture was derived from ancient idioms, his feeling for the beauty in traditional architectural styles was so inherent that although most of his buildings owe allegiance to the past, they were never slavish copies or archaelogical reconstructions.

Charles Donagh Maginnis was born in Londonderry, Ireland, in 1867. He received his secondary education at Cusack's Academy in Dublin and then attended the South Kensington Museum School of Art in London, where he won the Queens Prize in mathematics. While he never received any formal training in architecture, "becoming an architect," he

later remembered, "was expected of me. Mother made up her mind when I was only seven that I was to be an architect."[2] In 1884 with his widowed mother and five brothers and sisters he left Ireland for Toronto before settling in Boston in 1885. There his natural ability to draw obtained him positions with several architects, including William P. Wentworth and Edmund M. Wheelwright. He became active in the Boston Architectural Club, exhibited his drawings, and in 1898 published *Pen Drawing*, which went through seven editions. Also in 1898, Maginnis joined with Timothy Walsh and Matthew Sullivan to form the firm of Maginnis, Walsh & Sullivan, which became in 1906 Maginnis & Walsh, and in 1954 Maginnis, Walsh & Kennedy.

Maginnis also began writing extensively, especially on the low estate of Catholic church art and

---

1   Citation.

2   Herbert A. Kenny, "Artist in Stone," *The Sign*, n.v., January 1944, p. 44.

architecture, and called for a new approach to ecclesiastical design.[3] The result was a commission for St. Patrick's Church, Whitinsville, Massachusetts, the first of a long line of commissions for Catholic churches, seminaries, schools, and other buildings. Maginnis was the Catholic church contemporary of Ralph Adams Cram, and whereas Cram liked to think of himself as the American Pugin, Maginnis was really the twentieth-century Pugin for American Catholicism. Yet Maginnis differed from Cram in that he was never bound by strict archaeological reconstruction; rather he was more akin to Bertram Goodhue, whom he greatly admired. Maginnis's designs owe a debt to the past, yet they were never slavish copies, but modern reinterpretations.

The National Shrine of the Immaculate Conception, 1922–1955, is certainly Maginnis's best-known work and illustrates his attempt to use the Lombardic Romanesque in a modern manner. An updated Gothic idiom was used at Boston College, Holy Cross College, and Notre Dame University. St. Thomas the Apostle Church in Los Angeles, 1905, uses the mission-revival style as its idiom. The Carmelite Convent in Santa Clara, California, 1925, uses the Spanish Churrigueresque idiom. The seminary for the Maryknoll Fathers at Maryknoll, New York, has Chinese roofs and native-fieldstone walls. As his work progressed, Maginnis gradually reduced the stylistic references, removing excess ornament and details. The Boston College Law School, 1949–1954, demonstrates this simpler mode.

Maginnis was also noted for his extensive writings on Catholic church architecture and the liturgical arts. He was the first president of the Liturgical Arts Society and also served as president of the American Institute of Architects. He held membership in the National Academy of Design and the National Institute of Arts and Letters. His awards included the Laetare Medal from Notre Dame University; the honorary degrees of L.L.D. from Boston College and Holy Cross College; Doctor of Humane Letters from Tufts University; Doctor of Arts from Harvard University. And his church honored him by making him a Knight of Malta.

He married Amy Brooks of Newton, Massachusetts, lived most of his married life in Brookline, Massachusetts, and had four children. He died in 1955.

CONTRIBUTED BY EUGENE F. KENNEDY, JR. AND RICHARD GUY WILSON

3   Charles D. Maginnis, "A Criticism of Catholic Church Architecture in the United States," *The Architectural Review,* vol. 8, 1901, pp. 111–115; "Catholic Church Architecture," *Architectural Forum,* vol. 15, 1906, pp. 23–26, 33–39; "Catholic Church Architecture," *Architectural Forum,* vol. 27, August 1917, pp. 33–38; "Architecture and Religious Tradition," *Architectural Record,* vol. 98, September 1944, pp. 89–91.

Maginnis & Walsh: Carmelite Convent, Santa Clara, California, 1922.

Maginnis & Walsh: Boston College Library, Newton, Massachusetts, 1927.

GOLD MEDAL FOR 1949 **FRANK LLOYD WRIGHT**

AWARDED ON MARCH 17, 1949
AT THE RICE HOTEL BALLROOM
HOUSTON, TEXAS

Frank Lloyd Wright.

Library of Congress

Prometheus brought fire from Olympus and endured the wrath of Zeus for his daring; but his torch lit other fires and men lived more fully by their warmth.

To see the beacon fire he has kindled is the greatest reward for one who has stolen fire from the gods.

Frank Lloyd Wright has moved men's minds. People all over the world believe in the inherent beauty of architecture which grows from the need, from the soil, from the nature of materials. He was and is a titanic force in making them so believe.

Frank Lloyd Wright has built buildings. Structure in his hands has thrown off stylistic fetters and taken its proper place as the dominant guiding force in the solution of man's creative physical problems.

Frank Lloyd Wright has kindled men's hearts. An eager generation of architects stands today as his living monument. By precept and example he has imparted to them the courage to live an architectural ideal. They are reaching leadership in our profession, themselves dedicated to creating order and beauty, not as imitators, but as servants of truth.

It is for that courage, that flame, that high-hearted hope, that contribution to the advancement of architectural thought.[1]

Frank Lloyd Wright represents best the attempt to create an American architecture. He was born in 1867 on a farm in southwest Wisconsin, near where he would later built Taliesin; his father was an itinerant preacher-musician, and his mother a Welsh immigrant who was determined that her son would be an architect. He studied briefly at the University of Wisconsin, but Chicago held out the richest hope of joining the American march of progress, and it was here that he made the crucial choice in 1887 to work for Louis H. Sullivan, the man he called *Lieber Meister.* The architectural practice Wright pursued in Oak Park after he left Sullivan in 1893 was a model of success combined with principle, but in less than fifteen years, frustrations of work and family led him to abandon them for a year in Europe in the company of a client's wife. Upon their return in 1910, Wright built his studio and home, which he called Taliesin, the name of a medieval Welsh bard. For the next twenty years, Wright took positions opposing American culture, which had gone wrong in his view. He worked in Japan and California but could not recapture the broad coherence of his earlier work. When he returned to Taliesin in 1928, he was accompanied by his third wife, who encouraged him to write his *Autobiography* (1932) and to open a fellowship for architectural apprentices.

Until his death in 1959, Wright cultivated the role of flamboyant American individualist, playing to audiences in person and in books. The relative continuity of his life during this time produced a second phase to his career whose varied buildings augmented the successes of his earlier ones in Oak Park.

Wright's outstanding achievement was to produce a comprehensive architectural expression without direct historical references. His swift assimilation of the complexities of various architectural traditions and his transformation of them into a coherent language is astonishing. He drew equally from formal, beaux-arts principles traceable back to Plato, as he explicitly does in his 1912 essay on the Japanese print, and the freer, individual expression of picturesque composition. Together these form an identifiable core to his ideal of organic architecture.

The Winslow House of 1893–1894, Wright's first independent work after leaving Sullivan, previewed these two approaches with the symmetrical front and the freely disposed elements of a back. If their conjunction was not completely resolved, this remarkable early house signals important future architectural developments. By the time of the design for Unity Temple, 1904, Wright had clarified

---

1   Citation.

170

the interrelationship of symmetry, formal community setting, and structural rationality for poured concrete. For the Robie family he celebrated the expansiveness of individual life, even on a city lot, through banks of windows and sheltered terraces. The mutual adjustments of site, climatic comfort, structure, symbolic image, and formal coherence produced not awkward compromises but powerful consistency. The principle of continuity which correlated structure, space, and materials received its ultimate refinement in ornament as exemplified by Midway Gardens (1914) and the Millard House (1923).

Wright's responsiveness to the America around him resulted in domestic settings that satisfied needs in the American family as it evolved from turn-of-the-century formality to midcentury informality embodied in his Usonian houses of the 1930s and 1940s. His Broadacre City proposal of 1934 is so close to suburban growth of twenty years later as to seem prophetic. Both the Kaufmann House (Falling Water) over the waterfall (1936) and the Johnson Wax Company building (1936) show Wright at his dramatic best.

The Guggenheim Museum, a project begun during World War II and only completed in 1959, is seen by many as Wright's most complete embodiment of spatial continuity (Plate 14). A sense of infinite expansion is dramatized by light, structure of poured concrete, and human movement. In this and other late work, the grand gesture may have overwhelmed the tighter conceptions of earlier work. The parts of both the program and the building seem more separable in later work, but this less well understood phase of Wright's career may signal a more complex interpretation of architectural composition than the earlier polarity of formality and freedom.

Although his last years were characterized by creeping repetitiveness as followers sought to enshrine his legacy, Wright's 500 buildings will remain fascinating expressions of a fertile imagination and a comprehensive view of architecture.

CONTRIBUTED BY SIDNEY K. ROBINSON

Ausgeführte Bauten und Entwürfe von Frank Lloyd Wright, Ernst Wasmuth, Berlin, 1910

Frank Lloyd Wright: Unity Temple, Oak Park, Illinois, 1904.

Frank Lloyd Wright: Solomon R. Guggenheim Museum, New York City, 1943–1945, 1956–1959, interior.

Frank Lloyd Wright: William H. Winslow House, River Forest, Illinois, 1893–1894.

Library of Congress

Robert E. Mates, photographer; Guggenheim Museum

AWARDED ON MAY 12, 1950
IN THE MAYFLOWER HOTEL BALLROOM
WASHINGTON, D.C.

Courtesy of Gerald Dix

Sir Patrick Abercrombie.

Master planner of cities, well loved leader in the world of education, author of influence. Early in the century he gained direction and stature as the planner of a New Dublin: now noted throughout the world for the replanning of London, Edinburgh, as well as many other of the old cities in the war torn isles of Britain. A designer of humble villages, an honored consultant to lands far across the many seas, an early advocate of the preservation of the countryside of England, his surveys and reports are moving tributes to England's beauty. Firm believer in humanity and inspired interpreter of humanity's needs, his every plan, his well founded principles bring faith and hope to the possibilities of an urban order and are pointers to a democratic scale in our time. The works of his creative life, his numerous thoughtful plans are long spans over which mankind may move to responsible happiness.[1]

Patrick Abercrombie (1879–1957) pioneer planner, author of proposals for the postwar rebuilding of many towns and regions, and joint founder of the Council for the Preservation of Rural England and of the Union International des Architects, enjoyed a professional career of extraordinary duration and enduring ability which coincided with the first fifty years of statutory planning in Britain.

Leslie Patrick Abercrombie was born in Ashton-on-Mersey, Cheshire, in 1879, the ninth child of a middle-class Manchester family. He was educated at Uppingham and on the continent before being articled in May 1897 for four years, at a premium of £300, to a Manchester architect. When his apprenticeship ended he moved first to Merseyside, then to an architect's office in Chester, but he was only there for a year before accepting an invitation to a lectureship in the Liverpool School of Architecture, under C. H. Reilly. Quickly transferring to the Department of Civic Design when it was established in 1909, Abercrombie was first a research assistant and then for twenty years, from 1915, Lever Professor of Civic Design. In this first British planning school he was able to lay down a pattern that others were to follow, feeding the results of his extensive practice into his teaching, for it was Abercrombie's ambition to produce students endowed with a breadth of outlook and with technical skill, adopting Patrick Geddes's fundamental triad of "place, folk, work" as the basis of his teaching. By his policy as founder editor of the *Town Planning Review* he was able to

establish the reputation of the young journal, the early volumes of which contained important and authoritative reviews, describing planning as it was developing in Europe and America.

Abercrombie's private practice began modestly enough with the occasional commission to design housing schemes and cottages, as at Chester and Mouldsworth, or a country house, such as Hownhall, Ross-on-Wye. He said that this early work enabled him to develop the ability to consider concurrently and then master a range of functional and aesthetic requirements. It was his success in association with Sydney and Arthur Kelly in the Dublin Town Planning Competition of 1914 that marked Abercrombie's entry into the leading ranks of the young planning profession. The principles of this plan, in which the town was studied in relation to its regional function and its setting further developed in his regional plans for Doncaster (1920) and East Kent (1925) and in the Sheffield Civic Survey of 1924, which Abercrombie regarded as the foundation of his planning work.

In addition to being the first real regional plan in Britain, the Doncaster plan contained ideas of continuing significance, including proposals for new towns, for limiting the size of the main center, and for siting the principal road routes between settlements. More importantly, Abercrombie and his

---

1   Citation.

partner Henry Johnson of Doncaster—he always worked with a locally based planner—were careful to distinguish between elements of dynamic regional significance and more static local matters which would later be amplified by the district councils concerned. In each of his plans—for Bath and Bristol, where villages and scenery were a major concern, for Cumbria with its superb mountain and lakeland scenery, for East Suffolk, with its marshlands, narrow estuaries, and pink pargetted houses, and for many others as well—Abercrombie developed further the techniques of regional planning.

During World War I Abercrombie had called for a national plan in the *Town Planning Review,* and in 1926 there followed a campaign for the establishment of the Council for the Preservation of Rural England. Service from 1937–1940 on the (Barlow) Royal Commission on the Distribution of the Industrial Population led to his minority report on the problems and requirements of national planning: flexible and continually evolving, based on research surveys and experience—a policy rather than a plan.

Plans for the County of London (1943) and for Greater London (1944), and a few years later for the Clyde Valley and for the West Midlands, were the high watermarks in a long and influential career. In these great works he put all the pieces together: precincts and traffic segregation in town centers, reduced densities and proper community structures, open spaces, greenbelts, and new towns.

As a young architect, Patrick Abercrombie was to show equal proficiency in the vernacular style and the determinedly classical studies. His design work combined the French spirit with the English tradition: Dublin in 1914 and Plymouth in 1944 both demonstrate his wariness of adventures into the picturesque: While he would always plan to suit topography and orientation, he clearly disliked forced informality, with its constant search for undisciplined order. Plans for residential development at Prestatyn, Dormanstown, and Aylesham show a nice blend of topographically guided informality and geometric regularity.

After the war Abercrombie—widowed, retired from the chair of town planning at London where he had worked for ten years after leaving Liverpool, most of the major consultant plans completed—devoted much of his time to planning and architecture. He reported on planning in Addis Ababa, in Cyprus—where he was following in the footsteps of his mentor, Geddes—and in Hong Kong, always with that same infectious enthusiasm that characterised his work. He traveled extensively, often in connection with the affairs of the Union Internationale des Architects, of which he was president and, later, honorary president. In Britain he retained his association with the Town and Country Planning Association, with the Housing Centre, and, above all, with his creations, and Councils for the Preservation of Rural England and Rural Wales.

Patrick Abercrombie came to epitomize planning, and this always seemed both to surprise him and give him pleasure. He never had a large office but always worked with a team of planners, usually much younger than himself. He was a firm but kindly leader to his colleagues and his profession, being president of the Town Planning Institute in 1925 and later its second Gold Medalist. He was awarded the Royal Gold Medal of the RIBA and knighted for his services to planning. Although not primarily a theorist, Abercrombie had a clear idea of the place of town and regional planning in society and was convinced of the indivisibility of the factors influencing development. He had a remarkably wide range of expertise and ability and considerable gifts as a draftsman and an expositer of planning. He was perceptive and sensitive, optimistic (as planners need to be) and realistic (as they should be), hard-headed and at the same time compassionate; in the words of a contemporary, he was "a genial wizard."

CONTRIBUTED BY GERALD DIX

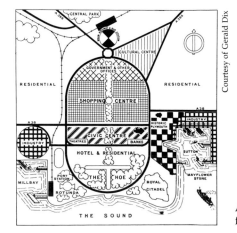

Courtesy of Gerald Dix

Abercrombie & Watson: Plymouth, function diagram of City Centre.

GOLD MEDAL FOR 1951 **BERNARD RALPH MAYBECK**

AWARDED ON MAY 10, 1951
AT THE NAVY PIER
CHICAGO, ILLINOIS
ACCEPTED BY MAJOR MAYBECK

Bernard Ralph Maybeck.

In our times great pioneers have courageously steered their way to the four corners of the spirit coursing ever on with free wills their souls — in adventurous paths, over seas, over the vast plains, the high mountains, hewing the great forests — have found new beauty and further understandings of human aspirations. While casting loose the anchor chains of tradition, they have guarded human hopes as precious cargoes. . . . Ever free in spirit: "Ever seeking a sad feeling, a hunger of an artist after beauty, a hunger that is never satisfied",—he has created the sturdy beginnings of an architecture truly representative of American life in a civilization, we hope, to be ever pioneering. Inspired to further seekings "we too take ship, O soul!"[1]

Among California architects at the turn of the century Bernard Ralph Maybeck stands out as a unique creative individual whose work contained the seeds of a new architecture which later flowered as a modern movement. Maybeck was not a revolutionary, nor a pioneer of modern design advocating a complete break with the building traditions of the past. He was an eclectic architect seeking principles in the designs of the past, which, with the techniques and materials of the present, would create the form of the architecture of tomorrow. In all of his work he never lost touch with the humane element of architecture. To Maybeck, a house could never be a "machine for living"; a house was always a shell and only gained interest from those who would live in it. He was an architect who, like Richardson, Sullivan, or Wright, made a distinctly American contribution to the art of architecture.

Maybeck's greatest influence has been in the field of domestic architecture. His inventive and novel planning of the small house set the example for a generation of California architects. In 1947, Lewis Mumford described the domestic architecture of the San Francisco Bay region as a "free yet unobtrusive expression of the terrain, the climate, and the way of life on the coast" and saw in the work of Wurster and others the continuity of principles of architectural expression initiated by Maybeck and his contemporaries.[2] Maybeck's contributions to the regional expression were his use of ordinary materials and simple carpentry techniques to achieve diverse structural and spatial arrangements responsive to human needs. His starting point was the human relation to a building, and he was convinced that each client's architectural problem was unique and demanded an individual solution.

Bernard Maybeck was born in the heart of what is now Greenwich Village in 1862. His father was a wood-carver who had initially studied in Vienna to become a sculptor. His mother, Elisa Kern, died when he was 3 years old, and he was the only child of her marriage. She remained in his memory as "a lively lady who wanted her son to be an artist." Maybeck's maternal grandfather, Christian Kern, and his father, Bernhardt Maybeck, were both emigrants from Germany, victims of the revolutionary events of 1848. They imbued young Bernard with a strong sense of democratic values, which resulted in Maybeck's idealism and respect of the individual society. His aesthetic belief, that an artist works for an expression of the spiritual meaning behind the visible, can also be attributed to his early exposure to German philosophy.

Maybeck studied architecture at the École des Beaux-Arts, Paris, with Jules-Louis André who carried on the traditions of Henri Labrouste's free atelier. Maybeck's emphasis on inventive structure and ready acceptance of new materials and technological developments, as well as his medievalism, are a result of his schooling. In 1886, Maybeck returned to New York to work with John M. Carrere and Thomas Hastings on the Ponce de Leon and Alcazar hotels in St. Augustine, Florida. Maybeck supervised the construction of the buildings, but by 1888 he had decided to start an independent practice. He spent an unproductive year in Kansas City and

---

1   Citation.

2   Lewis Mumford, "The Skyline," *The New Yorker*, October 11, 1947, p. 110.

moved to San Francisco in 1890 where he eventually found work in the office of A. Page Brown. The young men of the office—Willis Polk, A. C. Schweinfurth, and Maybeck—are credited with introducing an unpretentious style of residential architecture, expressive of its wooden construction.

The designs of the early years of Maybeck's career reveal a strong interest in structure and the craft of building. His design for Hearst Hall (1899), a large demountable structure employing laminated wooden arches, demonstrated skillful integration of materials, function, and structure, which resulted in a distinguished concert pavillion. In the latter part of his career, Maybeck's designs were dominated by his concern for mood and feeling in architecture. In the Palace of Fine Arts (1913), a transitory structure, Maybeck convincingly set a mood likened to sorrow, which he felt was akin to the feeling created upon seeing beautiful works of art (Plate 12). However, it is the First Church of Christ Scientist, Berkeley (1910) designed at the midpoint of his career, that has rightfully won recognition from lay and professional viewers for his imaginative architectural genius. In its design, structure and materials are balanced with feeling and form to create a beautiful building. It is apparent that Maybeck found the principles which he felt lay behind the beauty of all architecture. He died in 1957.

CONTRIBUTED BY KENNETH H. CARDWELL

First Church of Christ Scientist, interior.

Bernard Ralph Maybeck: First Church of Christ Scientist, Berkeley, California, 1910.

GOLD MEDAL FOR 1952 **AUGUSTE PERRET**

AWARDED ON OCTOBER 21, 1952
AT THE AMERICAN EMBASSY
PARIS, FRANCE

Studio Chevojan.

Auguste Perret.

Great master of architecture whose resounding fame echoes to honor all members of our profession; firm disciple of the creed of truth to materials, honesty of structure, sincerity of form; creative spirit whose career in architecture has ascended to ever higher levels, like one of your own staircases, the American Institute of Architects is privileged to recognize and award its Gold Medal of Honor to you, Auguste Perret of France. Forces in the world today are leading building to new patterns of integration, allowing us to satisfy better man's immemorial but never more diverse needs for shelter. You have stepped forward to grasp this architecture of the future, and where you have walked other architects will follow with gratitude.[1]

Auguste Perret's name became almost synonymous with reinforced-concrete structure; he gave a distinct aesthetic interpretation to the usage of reinforced concrete that dominated the first half of the twentieth century. Perret was one of the most honoured of twentieth-century French architects, receiving not only the AIA Gold Medal, but also the RIBA Gold Medal, 1948, the Medal of Honour of the Académie des Beaux-Arts, Denmark, 1949, and honors and awards from Finland, Czechoslovakia, and Luxembourg. At home he was an officer of the Légion d'Honneur, and president of the Conseil Supérieur de l'Ordre des Architectes, Cercle d'Études Architecturales, and Salon des Tuileries.

He was born in 1874 in Brussels, Belgium; his parents were French refugees from the Paris Commune of 1871. His architectural leanings betray his father's background as a building contractor: Perret always defined the architectural problem in terms of building and structure. The family returned to Paris, and Perret entered the École des Beaux-Arts in 1891. His atelier-*patron*, Julien Guadet, was one of the most important French architectural theorists and reinforced Perret's family teachings with statements such as "Truth is indispensable to architecture, and every architectural lie corrupts," and "No construction: no architecture." Perret joined his father's construction company in 1897, and with the death of the elder Perret in 1905, the firm was renamed Perret Frères.

His particular aesthetic emerged first in 1903, when he designed an apartment building in the rue Franklin, Paris, utilizing the Hennebique reinforced-concrete system. He wanted to drastically lighten and open the façade on a very confined site. The Hennebique construction had been patented in 1892 and was basically a structural system hidden behind an applied façade of masonry. Perret's particular contribution in the rue Franklin apartment block would be to express the frame as an element, distinct from the infill panels used for carrying glazing. In this case though, the frame was covered by faience tiles. Another innovation not normally noticed was that Perret inset the façade from the street and reversed the usual French light court at the rear of apartment buildings.

In the next several years Perret refined the reinforced-concrete frame as an architectural element worthy of expression in its own right, a unique concept at the time. His solution was basically a classical trabeated system, with reinforced-concrete piers and beams replacing wooden or masonry posts and lintels. The rue Ponthieu Garage, 1906, is a classical solution, though lacking the usual historicizing ornament. Perret gained a reputation as an architectural revolutionary in the years prior to World War I, with designs such as the Théâtre des Champs-Élysées (in collaboration with Henry van de Velde), where the building was considerably stripped of ornament — though neoclassical bas-reliefs still appeared. In 1910, Charles Édouard Jeanneret (Le Corbusier) spent some time in his office. While Perret's architectural composition always re-

1   Citation.

176

mained within an essentially classical system, he did advance the usage of reinforced concrete not simply as basic structure but as a total system encompassing precast window frames, door frames, wall panels, and nearly the entire building except for glazing. All were to be carefully manufactured within an exact tolerance, and consequently his buildings were far from inexpensive. Special attention was always paid to the moldings and profiles of the structure. Notre Dame du Raincy, Paris, 1922–1923 can be taken as representing the peak of Perret's development: a symbolic and traditional building brought up to date in materials—a cross between the structural armature of the Gothic cathedral and the architectural order of classicism. With Le Raincy, Perret lost the allegiance of the architectural avante garde (that is, Le Corbusier). While considered a modern, he was a conservative modern, his approach being analogous with that of his beaux-arts contemporary, Paul Cret. In 1932,

Perret joined the faculty at the École Spéciale d'Architecture du Boulevard Raspail, and in 1940 he joined the faculty of the École des Beaux-Arts.

Perret's growth in stature was accompanied by large commissions, and during the interwar years he designed a number of public buildings and expensive villas, all in reinforced concrete. Such was his prestige that he was appointed architect-in-chief for the reconstruction of Le Havre, the French seaport flattened by Allied bombardment in 1944. His approach did not change and in fact became more rigid, essentially an unvarying modular grid of reinforced-concrete prefabricated buildings—classicism reborn. Perret became honored for both the scale of his undertakings and his determination and single-mindedness. His concept of reinforced concrete as a trabeated system dominated architectural thinking from the 1910s into the 1950s.[2]

2   I am indebted to the late Peter Collins for much of the material in this biography.

Auguste Perret: Notre Dame du Raincy, Paris, 1922–1923, drawing by Perret Frères office.

Auguste Perret: Apartment Building 25 rue Franklin, Paris, 1903.

L'Architecture vivante, Fall/Winter 1923

L'Architecture vivante, Fall/Winter 1926

WILLIAM ADAMS DELANO

AWARDED ON JUNE 18, 1953
IN THE OLYMPIC HOTEL
SEATTLE, WASHINGTON
ACCEPTED BY EDGAR I. WILLIAMS

National Academy of Design

William Adams Delano. Portrait by
Dunbar Beck.

There are among us those who have created one or two or three brilliant works to accent the architectural record of our times. But to you, William Adams Delano, has been vouchsafed a half-century of professional activity. Filled with services to your fellows. And resulting in countless works of architecture in which the day-by-day achievement has not deviated from the high plateau established by your vision, skill and distinguished taste.[1]

William Adams Delano was born in the parsonage of the Madison Square Presbyterian Church, New York City, on January 21, 1874. His background was "pure New England ancestry — parsons, shipbuilders and shipowners, schoolmasters, bankers, and so forth."[2] At age 12 he decided on an architectural career after observing the construction of a family home under the direction of the Philadelphia architect Theophilus P. Chandler. Delano took his Bachelor of Arts from Yale in 1895, then attended the Columbia School of Architecture for two years, after which he joined Carrere & Hastings as a draftsman during the time when they were competing successfully for the New York Public Library and National Academy of Design buildings. Hastings convinced Delano's "very reluctant Presbyterian family" to send him to the École des Beaux-Arts for one year, although they feared that "Paris was the road to Hell." He entered the atelier of Victor Laloux and graduated in 1902. In 1903 he went into a partnership with Chester Holmes Aldrich that lasted until the latter's death in 1940. From 1903 to 1910, in addition to his practice, he served as a professor of design at Columbia.

Delano was to receive many professional honors throughout his career. He was made a fellow of the American Institute of Architects in 1912, and in 1923 he was made a Chevalier of the Legion of Honor. He served as president of the Society of Beaux-Arts Architects from 1927 to 1929 and president of the New York chapter of the AIA from 1928 to 1930. In 1940 he received the Gold Medal of the National Institute of Arts and Letters for "distinction in architecture." He was elected an honorary corresponding member of the Royal Institute of British Architects in 1948 and was made a corresponding member of the Académie des Beaux-Arts of the Institut de France. He died in 1960.

The work of William Adams Delano illuminates many of the vicissitudes that occurred in the career of the Beaux-Arts-trained American architect in the first half of the twentieth century. While Delano was always a spokesman, both in print and as a speaker, for the conservative or traditionalist viewpoint, the designs of his firm spanned a large gamut. Beaux-arts classicism can be seen in the first major design, the Walters Art Gallery, Baltimore, 1910, and later in the United States Chancellery, Paris, 1934. Adamesque, Palladian, Jeffersonian, and French provincial precedent is observable as the controlling grammar in the large country and city houses and New York clubs that the firm designed. For the Stirling Divinity Quadrangle at Yale University, New Haven, 1932, Delano drew upon Jefferson's University of Virginia *parti*; it is one of the most successful replicas of that design. Yet for more commercial work, such as the original La Guardia Airport Terminal and the Marine Air Terminal, 1939, Delano chose the art deco mode of smooth surfaces, setbacks, and "moderne" French-styled ornament. They did extremely functional air stations for Pan American airways at Miami, Florida, and Midway, Wake, and Guam islands. The extensions the firm did for the United States Military

---

1 Citation.

2 This and all subsequent quotations are from "Architect," *The New Yorker*, April 5, 1958, p. 23–24.

Academy at West Point, 1945, are a modern hybrid of the stripped classical and Gothic idioms. From 1949 to 1952, Delano was the architect in charge of the restorations of the White House. Of the experience and especially the addition of the controversial second-story balcony, Delano remembered: "I loved Truman. He knew exactly what he wanted."

Delano and Aldrich's best-known work is the extensive series of huge country places they designed in the halcyon days before October 1929. In this type of practice they were the successors to earlier firms, such as McKim, Mead & White, Carrere & Hastings, and Charles Adams Platt. An outstanding example is the house for B. G. Work, the president of B. F. Goodrich Company. "One day my telephone rang," Delano explained, "and a voice said, 'I'm Mr. B. W. Work, of Akron, Ohio; you've never heard of me. I've bought a piece of land at Oyster Bay, Long Island. May I see you? You're the only architect in New York who hasn't asked to build my house.' . . . He said he wanted a small but perfect house. 'And I want to build it out of income—not a cent of capital,' he added. He must have had a huge income, for the house, garage, and gardens cost nearly a million dollars by the time they were finished." Named as Oak Knoll, the site is very complicated, on a hilltop overlooking Oyster Bay. Delano solved it by placing a skillfully designed classical courtyard off the road, with handsome paving and niches enriched with sculpture and wrought iron. From this court, the visitor winds up the hill via a curving road to a second paved court with a fountain on one side and the façade of the house at the other. As was usual with his houses, the gardens were also of Delano's design— beyond the house court a great, square formal garden, surrounded by an arbor of trees, is provided with a central gazebo and secluded from the water view. The back of the house overlooks the bay; from a board terrace one can look down the steep hillside toward the distant water. The façade is a formal expression in stucco and stone, with a circular portico set into a niche. The entrance is approached via a pair of semicircular stairs bordered by an exquisite wrought-iron railing. The ironwork is carefully designed and of superb quality, based upon the innate function of wrought iron, following both the rods and flat-hammered surfaces of the material. Like the remainder of the house, the motif in the ironwork, cornices, and interior is based upon the sea: that is, shells, flying fish, and turtles.

In Washington, D.C., in addition to being responsible for the restoration of the White House, Delano designed the Post Office complex in the Federal Triangle. Among his more well known and interesting designs, this graceful series of buildings is superbly detailed. This neoclassical design was intended to form a circus which was never completed. Unfortunately, this grand urban composition was bordered on one side by the Old Romanesque-revival Post Office, which Delano and the Planning Commission had decided would be demolished. However, with the recent rise of interest in preservation, it was decided that the old building would be used for adaptive purposes and the brilliant circus will probably never be completed. Delano also constructed the Japanese Embassy in Washington (now the Chancellery), where he achieved a notable success, with large-scale rooms and elegant detailing. The entrance opens onto a long cross hall, from which a series of public rooms in turn open onto a terrace overlooking Rock Creek Park, in a plan reminiscent of Oak Knoll.

With renewed interest in the American revivals of the early twentieth century and in the work of the beaux-arts architects, Delano's work is being reappraised as one of the important traditional architects of this period.

CONTRIBUTED BY FREDERICK DOVETON NICHOLS

Delano & Aldrich: Oak Knoll, Bertram G. Work House, Oyster Bay, Long Island, New York, 1920.

Oak Knoll, garden front.

GOLD MEDAL FOR 1955 WILLEM MARINUS DUDOK

AWARDED ON JUNE 23, 1955
IN THE RADISSON HOTEL BALLROOM
MINNEAPOLIS, MINNESOTA

Courtesy of Hans van Grieken

Willem Marinus Dudok.

Your contribution has been, not in slogan or manifesto, not in establishing a school or striving to win disciples, but rather in works of architecture which speak for you, and in language of humanism.

Disdaining the easy way of building to amaze, you have chosen to satisfy man's inherent longing for a more lovely environment. To construction, functionalism and the economy of austerity—these demigods of our brief day—you have shown respect but not worship. Aided by your joy in color, you have preserved in a quest of ways to enclose and divide space and endow it with more gracious appeal, in the hope that space may sing again. Your individuality as an artist and the work of your mind, heart and hand have placed our world in your debt.[1]

Willem Marinus Dudok represented the particular strain of modernism: simplified yet traditional forms, plastic modeling, ornament, and texture. Best-known for his works of the 1920s and 1930s in Hilversum, the Netherlands, such as the Hilversum Town Hall, 1924 (constructed 1928–1931), Dudok never fully came to grips with the radical-modernist aesthetic of bare-bones functionalism and the machine (Plate 20). His position is summed up in a 1954 statement: "Why only visible construction should be considered as honest work has never become clear to me. . . . I fully appreciate reinforced concrete but I don't like the colour and I don't see why I should not be allowed to cover a good concrete construction with a material of finer colour and texture."[2]

Dudok was born on July 6, 1884 in Amsterdam and grew up in a musical family. He would always claim that music was his greatest source of inspiration. Trained as a military engineer, not as an architect, he spent his early years designing fortifications and barracks. He left the army in 1913 and established a private architectural practice. In 1915 he was appointed director of the Municipal Works for the garden city of Hilversum. In 1927 he became municipal architect, a title that he retained until 1949. Dutch law required that all municipalities of over 10,000 population have a comprehensive plan, and a 1901 housing law mandated all municipalities to provide decent housing. In addition to over 100 designs for Hilversum and over 75 completions,

Dudok became the town planner of the Hague in 1933 and designed many buildings for other locations in Holland and abroad. He was easily the most-honored Dutch architect of the first half of the twentieth century, receiving many awards including the Gold Medal of the Royal Institute of British Architects in 1935. He never cared much for public speaking or writing, though he did come to the United States for the first time in 1953 on an AIA-sponsored speaking tour.[3]

Dudok's architecture represents a creative intermingling of several different influences, along with his own consummate sense of plastic form and detail. His earliest work combines an English arts-and-crafts approach with the native Dutch art nouveau, or *Jugenstil*, of Hendrikus Petrus Berlage. Berlage, in particular, stood for the Dutch tradition of brickwork, as in his Amsterdam Exchange of 1898–1903. Brick, as a material, would remain with Dudok, as he was successively influenced by the stripped Gothic mode of Eliel Saarinen and Bertram Goodhue, the Amsterdam expressionists, and then the de Stijl movement and Frank Lloyd Wright. Wright, through the *Wasmuth* portfolio and later

---

1 Citation.

2 R. M. H. Magnee (ed.), *Willem M. Dudok*, G. van Sanne, Amsterdam, 1954, p. 136.

3 The *AIA Journal* reprinted two of his talks: "To Live and to Build," vol. 21, March 1954, pp. 99–105; "Town Planning," vol. 21, April 1954, pp. 152–158.

publication in the Amsterdam periodical, *Wendigen*, made a particular impact upon Dudok. However, Dudok's work, such as the Dr. H. Bavinck School, 1921, Hilversum, is not particularly Wrightian. The basis of Dudok's work is the elaboration of planes and volumes, not structure, as in Wright's. Characteristic elements which Dudok manipulates are recessions and projections of the façade and a dynamic balance between a strong horizontal tendency and verticle accents. The horizontal element is reinforced by use of a special long, narrow brick that came to be called the "Hilversum brick." Dudok always remained tied to traditional imagery, and towers and *Groois*, or thatched roofs, appear in many designs of the 1920s.

The Hilversum Townhall represents Dudok's peak of accomplishment. He totally controlled the design of the building down to the most minute detail.

The plan is pinwheel in form. Linear single-loaded corridor units enclose an inner courtyard and an auto court. The entire composition is conceived in rotation, with the focal point, the tower, at one edge marking the major entrance. The approach is around the building on a series of short, right-angled paths that skirt the lake and fountain and ultimately bring the visitor parallel along the façade to the entrance. Volumetric forms revealing inner spaces are plasticly deployed and create a staccato rhythm.

In the 1930s, Dudok simplified his compositions and employed large, uninterpreted surfaces. A certain blandness crept over his work, especially after World War II. At the same time a historicizing element appeared. The anonymous character of his architecture drew frequent criticism at home, though his foreign reputation, fueled by memories of his earlier work, increased. When he died in 1974, many assumed he had been dead for years.

CONTRIBUTED BY HANS VAN GRIEKEN, MAX CRAMER, AND RICHARD GUY WILSON

Willem Marinus Dudok: Doctor H. Bavinck School, Hilversum, 1921.

CLARENCE S. STEIN

Clarence Samuel Stein.

Courtesy of Aline MacMahon Stein

Architect of Neighborhoods, Communities, Cities—in a lifetime of active practice your vision of the architect's responsibility early burst the limitations imposed by the design of an individual structure. That vision embraced the wider aim of designing for mankind's environment rather than for mere shelter—for a way of life rather than for walls and a roof. This measure of the architect's opportunity of serving society more effectively, given clearer form by your own achievements over the years, enriches our conception of architecture as the mother of the arts. All who march under her banner, now and henceforward, will be the better for your example.[1]

Clarence Stein is known internationally for the planning and design of Radburn, the new community built in 1929–1933, following the concepts of the English garden-city movement. The planning concepts demonstrated at Radburn—particularly the separation of people and cars, the use of the superblock, and the use of parks and open space as a focus of the plan—continue to influence new town development in the United States and throughout the world (Plate 13).

In addition to Radburn, Stein is probably best-known for his book, *Toward New Towns for America.* TNTFA documents Stein's own new community work beginning with Sunnyside, New York (1925), and including Chatham Village, Pittsburgh (1932), Baldwin Hills, California (1941), as well as the development of the greenbelt new towns in the 1930s. All of Stein's work presented in TNTFA was essentially undertaken between 1922 and 1935. While it has always been recognized as a remarkable professional accomplishment, the work becomes even more impressive when seen in the fuller context of Stein's life and career.

Clarence Stein was born in Rochester. He moved to New York City at the age of 8 when his father was placed in charge of the Hoboken office of the National Casket Company. Stein's childhood was strongly influenced by his mother's activities. She was a founder of the Ethical Culture Society in New York and active in the Hudson Guild Settlement House. Stein attended the Ethical Culture Society schools, where he was a pupil of Dr. John Elliott. He accompanied his mother to the Hudson Guild and developed an association with the settlement that lasted for his entire life.

Stein never finished high school. He left at age 16 when he lost his eyesight following an appendectomy. After his sight returned, he worked for four years at the National Casket Company. For his twenty-first birthday, his father took him on a trip to Europe. This trip reinforced his developing interest in interior design. On his return, he entered the Columbia School of Architecture but left after one year to go to Paris to attend the École des Beaux-Arts. He stayed in Paris seven years, studying and traveling in Europe and England.

By the time he returned home at the age of 29, Stein's interests had shifted to architecture. He obtained a position in the office of Bertram Goodhue, primarily because of sketches he made while traveling in Spain. Goodhue put him to work on the buildings for the San Diego fair. Stein remained in the office for seven years and also worked on St. Bartholomew's Church in New York and the Village of Tyronne, New Mexico. He left Goodhue in 1918 to serve as a first lieutenant in the U.S. Army Engineers.

After the war, Stein opened his own architectural office, which he maintained until about 1940. Most of his work was done in collaboration with Robert Kohn, Charles Butler, and Frank Vitolo. Although not known primarily for his architecture, Stein considered himself a designer first, a planner second. Among his most important architectural projects were the Temple Emanu-El, New York (1930), Phipps Garden Apartments, New York (1931 and 1936), the Wichita Art Institute, Kansas (1938), and the Hillside Home Apartments, New York (1935).

At this time Stein began to turn his attention to housing and community planning. He developed

---

1   Citation.

an association with Frederick Ackerman, Lewis Mumford, Henry Wright, and Benton MacKaye that led to the establishment of the Regional Planning Association of America in 1923. Stein brought the concepts of the RPAA to public attention in his position as chairman of the AIA Committee on Housing, as secretary of the Committee on Housing of the Reconstruction Commission of New York State, and later as chairman of the State Committee on Housing and Regional Planning. He also organized the special regional planning member of the Survey Graphic (1925) devoted to articles by RPAA members.

In 1922, Stein began a professional association with Henry Wright that lasted twelve years. Together they produced three housing and new community plans that had international influence: Sunnyside Gardens (1924), Radburn (1929), and Chatham Village (1932).

In the midst of this highly productive period, Stein married Aline MacMahon. He was 46, and she was 29. Aline was an actress whose career in the films took off immediately after their marriage. For most of the 1930s, she lived the better part of the year in Hollywood. Aline and Clarence corresponded daily and, in spite of the separation, their marriage—and careers—prospered. Aline appeared in twenty films during the 1930s, including *Five Star Final, Babbitt, Ah, Wilderness* and *Kind Lady.* She continued her career in films and on the stage up until the late 1970s. In between Aline's films, she and Clarence traveled extensively, including trips to China, India, and Bali and later Peru, Israel, and Holland.

The mid-1930s were a turning point in Stein's life and career. In 1934, he separated from Henry Wright. At the same time, he had great difficulties in obtaining support for his ambitious Hillside Homes in the Bronx. In 1935, he and Aline spent the year in China. He served as a consultant to the greenbelt new-town program of the Resettlement Administration, but in spite of his previous work and friends in the Roosevelt administration, he never received a significant independent commission for planning or architectural work. At the age of 59, he worked on plans for the new community of Baldwin Hills, California. Although he continued to serve as a consultant after that, Baldwin Hills marked the close of his professional career.

Clarence Stein lived for thirty-four years after completing his work on Baldwin Hills. During that time, he suffered periodic nervous breakdowns, but in between he wrote, traveled, provided consultant services, and advised planners from around the world. He worked on several projects with Matthew Nowicki, assisted Gorden Stephenson at Stevenage, and advised on the preliminary plans for the new town of Kitimat, British Columbia (1951). In 1951, at the age of 69 he wrote *Toward New Towns for America* still the best documentation of his own work and the related greenbelt towns. In 1960, he was awarded the Ebenezer Howard Medal of the Town and Country Planning Association of England.

Clarence Stein's life is one of both great accomplishment and tragedy. In the fifteen years from 1921 to 1936, he generated a series of ideas about housing, community planning, and regional development that are as important today as they were in the 1930s. Radburn and Chatham Village remain among the best examples of residential development in the United States, and there is increasing interest in the work of the RPAA. On the other hand, Stein's sickness and lack of support from certain professional associates denied him an important role in the greenbelt town movement to which he was ideally suited to make an important contribution. He could also have contributed to the development of federal urban policy after World War II. But these lost opportunities never bothered Stein: He felt, correctly, that he had established an important foundation for others to build upon.

CONTRIBUTED BY JOHN ANDREW GALLERY

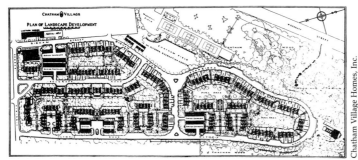

Wright & Stein, planners: Chatham Village, Pittsburg, Pennsylvania, 1930 plan.

Wright & Stein, planners; Ingham and Boyd, architects; Griswold and Kohandie, landscape architects: Chatham Village, 1930, 1932–1936.

AWARDED ON MAY 16, 1957
AT THE SHERATON HOTEL
WASHINGTON, D.C.

Katherine Young, photographer; Haines, Lundberg & Waehler

Ralph Walker.

In this year when the Institute feels entitled, through reaching an established maturity, to express unashamedly its affection for a favorite and gifted son, this token of its pride needs no further warrant.

It is offered to one whose path through the years, in tireless devotion to the ideals of his profession has led always in the direction of greater service to his fellow artists and to a fuller life for that portion of mankind that his wide range of travel and thought could reach.

The brilliance of his contribution to the Institute, in its presidency and in its ranks, will brighten a long span of the century that beckons.[1]

Ralph Walker was born in 1889 and grew up in Providence, Rhode Island, where his father managed a General Electric plant. His initial architectural experience was with the Providence firm of Hilton & Jackson, prior to training at the Massachusetts Institute of Technology, from which he graduated in 1911. Thereafter he worked in New York, successively for the firms of Warren & Wetmore, York & Sawyer, and Bertram Goodhue, interrupted by a Rotch Travelling Scholarship spent mostly in an extensive tour of Italy. He left Goodhue to join the camouflage detachment of the Army Engineers as a second lieutenant during World War I.

On his discharge, he found employment with McKenzie, Voorhees & Gmelin as they were about to begin work on a skyscraper for the New York Telephone Company at Barclay and Vesey streets in lower Manhattan: Walker had found the firm with which he was to be associated for life, and an initial commission which gave him instant stature among young New York architects.

When it was built, the Barclay-Vesey Telephone Building (1920–1926) rose thirty-two stories in an entire block above its neighborhoods and was therefore exceptionally visible. Its Gothic-moderne massing, in which pier and spandrel walls enclosed a stepped mass so that the uncorniced, serrated edges of the tier below opened visually to the continued verticals of the tier above, became a norm for progressive-skyscraper design in the late 1920s and early 1930s. It was, moreover, lavishly and unconventionally ornamented with floral motifs, stylized

from seed catalogs, incised at places on the walls to relieve their planarity, and accentuating entrances and lobbies. Hence Barclay-Vesey also became a bellweather of what has come to be known as the art deco movement in New York architectural design. On completion of the building, the firm became Voorhees, Gmelin & Walker.

Under Walker's aegis his firm quickly provided a series of skyscrapers which are today viewed as key monuments of art deco: the Western Union Building in the block bounded by West Broadway, Thomas, Worth, and Hudson streets (1928–1932), the Irving Trust Building at Broadway and Wall Street (1929–1932, with Henry Coke Smith as much responsible as Walker for the design), together with telephone buildings in Syracuse (1926–1928) and Brooklyn (1931). The rather folkish floral inspiration from the seed catalog in the early buildings tended toward more abstract, angular effects in the later ones. During this period, too, Walker began his active career as committeeman, officer, and enthusiastic supporter of professional organizations and causes, especially in the Architectural League and the Beaux-Arts Institute, which were, at that time, as he himself stated, more influential in New York than the local chapter of the AIA. Among his closest professional friends were Raymond Hood and Ely Jacques Kahn. All were noticeably short, energetic, and a bit peppery on occasion. Collectively they earned the sobriquet of the Three Little Napoleons.

---

1   Citation.

Together with another close friend, Joseph Urban, they could well be considered the Napoleonic core of Manhattan art deco.

The brief fireworks of art deco had its final appropriate salvo in Walker's career, with his appointment to the architects board of the Chicago world's fair of 1933–1934, for which he did several exhibition buildings. But the 1930s saw Walker's work increasingly turn to a classicized modernism in tune with the times. Much of his work was for corporate clients; among those executed were the George Eastman Memorial in Rochester (1933–1935), the General Foods Office Building in White Plains (1952–1954), and a series of laboratory buildings which became something of a specialty of the firm, like the IBM Research Center in Poughkeepsie, the Bell Telephone Laboratories in Summit, New Jersey, and the Argonne National Laboratories in Chicago (1948–1952). Among executed institutional and governmental commissions were buildings for the Belgian Chancellery (1956–1957) and the American Federation of Labor (1953–1956) in Washington, and the Hayden Library for his alma mater (1949–1950). Inevitably, he played a conspicuous role as architect and advisor for the New York world's fair of 1939–1940. Increasingly, however, he became less directly active in design as he became more involved with service in various consultative capacities on planning commissions, in civic activities, and in housing problems (the latter resulting in his firm's outstanding Fresh Meadows Housing Project in Queens of 1946–1949 for the New York Life Insurance Company). He lectured widely and diversely on architecture and planning topics and wrote frequent articles, among them repetitive attacks on the "functionalist materialism" of such "extreme" modernists as Le Corbusier and Gropius.

During a long quasi retirement he continued his activities as consultant, speaker, and writer. He was interested in modern poetry and gathered a fine collection of first and rare editions of modern American poets. In the final decades of his life he had time for his own poetry, which he privately printed in editions handsomely designed by himself. *The Fly in the Amber* (1957) distills his distaste for the International Style of modern architecture: "like a fly in amber . . . imprisoned within its dogma of skeleton and glass." He continued to garner honors, among them an honorary degree from Syracuse University in 1965.

He married Stella Forbes in 1913, but remained childless; after her death in 1972, he married Christine Foulds. He died a year later, in 1973, at his beloved Walkerburn, a rundown farm house discovered in suburban Chappaqua in 1923 when it was still substantially rural. He extensively remodeled it into the kind of pitched-roof, traditionally furnished, vernacularized modern that represented his middle-of-the-road style. It was all set down in an exquisite garden. As early as the 1930s, in repeated talks and writings, he had long ago concluded that the skyscraper was a mistake.

CONTRIBUTED BY WILLIAM H. JORDY

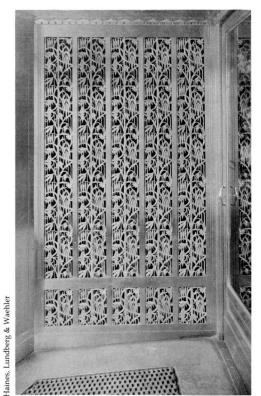

Ralph Walker, for McKenzie, Voorhees & Gmelin: New York Telephone Company Building, interior bronze grill.

Ralph Walker, for McKenzie, Voorhees & Walker: Irving Trust Company Building.

185

LOUIS SKIDMORE

AWARDED ON MAY 16, 1957
AT THE SHERATON HOTEL
WASHINGTON, D.C.

Skidmore, Owings & Merrill

Louis Skidmore.

Architect in a new technology pioneering new paths in a profession depending hitherto largely upon individual service. You have built an organization with the name of Skidmore, Owings & Merrill, in which you have united in singleness of purpose the manifold skills, imagination and judgment fitted to serve, with marked distinction, a wider and more diverse clientele than had been thought possible. In giving architectural service to the needs of an era of vast building activity, you and your collaborators have won for the profession a wider understanding and appreciation.[1]

Louis Skidmore cofounded one of the most successful and highly regarded architectural practices of the mid- and late twentieth century, Skidmore, Owings & Merrill. It is fair to say that this firm has dominated the large-scale corporate practice of architecture since 1950. Through their designs, which have been erected in nearly every corner of the globe, the radical European modern style of the early twentieth century was transformed into the image of capitalism and government. Louis Skidmore's contribution to this transformation was fundamental, and while he was never known as an outstanding designer, his salesmanship and organizational methods were fundamental; from his office issued some of the most electrifying images of the 1950s.

Skidmore was born in 1897 in Lawrenceberg, Indiana, and educated at Bradley University, Peoria, Illinois. He served with the U.S. Air Corps in Great Britain during World War I. He returned to attend the MIT School of Architecture and then worked for two years for Charles D. Maginnis in Boston before winning the Rotch Travelling Scholarship in 1926. He spent three years in Europe, including a year at the American Academy in Rome. Known for his sketching talents, he provided illustrations for Richard Chamberlain's *Tudor in Architecture* (1929). He returned from Europe in 1929 to marry Eloise Owings, the sister of his future partner, Nathaniel Owings. Also in 1929, Skidmore became the chief of design for the Century of Progress

Exposition to be held in Chicago in 1933. Owings was his assistant. Skidmore was a dapper and engaging young man whose enthusiasm and persuasiveness could charm the most recalcitrant client or architect. Planned during the halcyon days prior to the stock market crash of October 1929, the Chicago exposition had a nine-member architectural board that included Paul Cret, Raymond Hood, Ralph Walker, and John Root. Skidmore adjudicated between the conflicting talents and produced a stylized art moderne extravaganza that introduced the American public to modern architecture. His European sojourn of the late 1920s was crucial, and the Chicago fair in many ways prefigures his later success in making the images of modern architecture acceptable for Americans. The position of Skidmore and Owings can be likened to that of Daniel Burnham at the 1893 World's Columbian Exposition: They gained expertise in management, construction, working against tight deadlines, and the friendship of the elite of the American architectural and business community. And their subsequent practice followed Burnham's lead in many ways, the large competent architectural office renowned for producing quality work that fit the image and cost-conscious business world.

On January 1, 1936, the firm of Skidmore & Owings was founded in Chicago. Subsequently, John Merrill, an engineer, joined in 1939. His inclu-

---

1   Citation.

sion indicated the direction of the firm, first in design toward a close relationship between structure and architecture, and second the idea of comprehensive services, design, engineering, and, ultimately, planning, interiors, landscaping, and programming. During World War II the firm handled a number of large government contracts, perhaps the most notable being the design of Oak Ridge, Tennessee, the site of the construction of the first atom bomb. In 1937, Skidmore opened a New York office and subsequently hired a talented team of Gordon Bunshaft, Walter Severinghaus, Robert Culter, and William Brown.

With Skidmore in charge, the New York office rose to the top of the American architectural community in the 1940s and 1950s. In 1950 the prestigious Museum of Modern Art accorded Skidmore, Owings & Merrill an exhibition, the first ever devoted to the work of a firm, rather than an individual architect. A model of Lever House was the central object, and the catalog stated that the members of the firm were "animated by two disciplines, which they all share . . . the discipline of modern architecture and the discipline of American organizational methods."[2] The firm's organization called for a designer to be a leading member of a team, supported by the partner-in-chief to deal with the client and a project manager to deal with the business side. The centrality and importance of the designer was a key to Skidmore, Owings & Merrill.

The tremendous building boom and prosperity of the post-World War II years helped fuel the firm's success in producing a modern image of corporate America. The major buildings produced by Skidmore's New York office with Bunshaft as the chief designer defined in many ways the parameters of American architecture: Lever House (1949–1952), Manufacturers Hanover Trust (1953–1954), both in New York, and Connecticut General Life Insurance (1954–1957), near Hartford, Connecticut (Plate 15). Each was a refinement of a particular modernist ideal: the slab-shaped glass tower (Lever House), the low glass pavilion (Manufacturers Hanover Trust), and the machine in the landscape (Connecticut General Life Insurance). The exquisiteness of the detailing, the self-consciousness, perpetual newness, the modern materials, and the insertion of modern painting, sculpture, and decorative objects dazzled critics, architects, the public, and the business world. Later Skidmore, Owings & Merrill would explore other architectural idioms and adopt other images, and other branch offices with other designers in Chicago, San Francisco, Portland, Houston, and so on would succeed as well. Yet it is perhaps the 1950s New York-designed buildings that remain the seminal images. Certainly the other founding partners, Owings and Merrill, made contributions, and Gordon Bunshaft was the unmistakable designer, yet without Skidmore, none of it would have been possible. Skidmore retired from the firm in 1955 and died in 1962.

2 "Skidmore, Owings & Merrill Architects, U.S.A.," *Museum of Modern Art Bulletin*, vol. 18, Fall 1950, p. 5.

Skidmore, Owings & Merrill: Connecticut General Life Insurance Company, Bloomfield, Connecticut, 1954–1957.

Ezra Stoller © ESTO, photographer; Skidmore, Owings & Merrill

GOLD MEDAL FOR 1958 JOHN WELLBORN ROOT II

AWARDED ON JULY 10, 1958
IN THE STATLER HOTEL BALLROOM
CLEVELAND, OHIO

John Wellborn Root II.

Distinguished son of a distinguished father, it has been your good fortune to live and practise in a time of abrupt change, when architecture opened a new chapter in its history.

Though many scorned the lessons of the past, you held resolutely to its basic truths and built afresh upon a tested foundation.

For your examples over a wide range of function and geography, your contemporaries raise a paean of thanksgiving.

You have demonstrated that the broad path of architecture need not become a dead-end street.[1]

John Wellborn Root II was born in 1887, the son of John Wellborn Root, partner in the famous firm of Burnham & Root, and of Dora Louise (née Monroe) Root, sister of Chicago author Harriet Monroe. After the death of his father in 1892, Root was raised by his mother and aunt in Chicago and Europe. After graduating from Cornell with a degree in architecture in 1909, Root went on to Paris to enter the École des Beaux-Arts, where he formed a friendship with John A. Holabird, son of the founding partner of Holabird & Roche. After receiving his diploma in 1914, Root returned to Chicago and rejoined Holabird. Both men left for France in 1917 to serve in the army, and both returned to Chicago in 1919 where they became partners in Holabird & Roche. The two men took over complete control of the office at the death of Martin Roche in 1927 and changed the name to Holabird & Root in the following year.

A partner from 1919 until his retirement in 1959, Root spent his entire career in this firm, one of the largest and most versatile in the country. Because the office was so large and because it emphasized a consistently high level of design competence rather than individual brilliance, it is difficult to estimate the exact contribution of Root, but it is clear that both he and Holabird were closely involved with most major designs. In general, Root was most in-terested in the aesthetic aspects of the firm's practice and concentrated on design, leaving to Holabird the running of the office.

A good example of the firm's production soon after Root became a partner is the Palmer House Hotel in Chicago, a well-planned building, executed lavishly but in a conventional classical vocabulary. In the late 1920s, especially after Holabird and Root took over full control, the designs for large buildings became simpler and the classical detailing became more abstract. The firm reached a pinnacle of success in the last years of the 1920s with such great set-back skyscrapers as the Palmolive (now Playboy), Old Daily News (now Riverside Plaza), and the Chicago Board of Trade buildings. These won national acclaim and several major awards for the firm, notably the Gold Medal of the Architectural League of New York in 1930. During the 1930s the firm had a smaller output but did produce the Chrysler Motors Building at the 1933 Chicago world's fair, as well as several buildings in Washington, D.C. The Research and Engineering Building for the A. O. Smith Company of Milwaukee, 1929–1931, was a highly publicized design, notable for its structure, clear-span space, and extensive glazing.

---

1   Citation.

Holabird & Root: Chicago Board of
Trade, Chicago, Illinois, 1929–1930.

After the death of John Holabird in 1945, Root
continued to run the large organization with increasing help from new partners. The name remained Holabird & Root, except between 1948 and
1956 when it was changed to Holabird & Root &
Burgee. During this last period the firm turned increasingly from its stripped classicism of the 1920s
and 1930s to the International Style. Urbane and
stylish, Root was active throughout his career with
civic functions in Chicago and participated in activities of the city's artistic community. He died in 1963.

CONTRIBUTED BY ROBERT BRUEGMANN

GOLD MEDAL FOR 1959 WALTER ADOLPH GROPIUS

AWARDED ON JUNE 24, 1959
AT THE DELGADO MUSEUM OF ART
NEW ORLEANS, LOUISIANA

Walter Adolph Gropius.

Architect, Philosopher, Teacher—during the greater part of a half century you have held steadfastly to one purpose, the reunification of art and science. You would have the connoisseur in design become once again the creator. You would restore to primacy the nature of materials and the march of technology, displacing a blind dependence on historical patterns.

This turning from the role of scholar to the role of master builder has not been brought about without struggle—in Germany, in England, in America. To you as pioneer have come the usual rejection, ridicule, refusal to understand, but your singleness of purpose, your patience, your weaving together of principle and practice—all these have proven invincible and triumphant. After centuries of timidly marking time, architecture has been aroused by your vision, and by those you have inspired, to take again the straight road ahead.[1]

Walter Gropius was born on May 18, 1883, into a prosperous Berlin family and died internationally famous in Cambridge, Massachusetts, on July 5, 1969. In recognition of his long and prestigious career, he was awarded the Gold Medal of the American Institute of Architects in 1959. But Gropius's professional life did not have the symmetry of most AIA medallists: It was fractured by historical forces beyond his control. His career had begun conventionally enough. He had studied architecture at the universities of Charlottenburg and Munich in the first years of the twentieth century, with the usual interruptions of a *Wanderjarh* in Spain (1904–1905) and a year's stint in the Imperial Army (1905–1906). He apprenticed in the office of Peter Behrens for three years, and then in 1910 he began his own practice in Berlin.

But this normal career was marked by two brutal interruptions: First, five years military service in the army (1914–1919), and then self-imposed exile from Nazi Germany after 1934. These cataclysmic events explain the discontinuous quality of his career. Thus, he was a full-time practicing architect for three distinct periods of his life: in Berlin from 1910 to 1914 and again from 1928 to 1934, in England, 1934–1937, and in the United States, 1952–1969. But sandwiched in between these periods were those when he was primarily an architectural educator: at the Bauhaus (1919–1927) and at Harvard's Graduate School of Design (1937–1952).

Gropius's work as an architect would alone have established him as one of the "great makers" of modern architecture. Long before he came to the

United States he had completed a number of seminal buildings: the Fagus Factory at Alfeld (1911); the pavilions for the 1914 Werkbund Exhibition at Cologne (1914); the Bauhaus campus at Dessau (1925–1926); the Siemenstadt Housing Project (1929). His unrealized projects were even more prestigious: the Chicago Tribune Tower (1922), the Total Theater (1927), and the Palace of the Soviets (1931). Finally, he had demonstrated his great ability as an industrial designer in a wide range of projects: locomotives (1913) and sleeping cars (1914) for the German State Railways; a luxury convertible for the Adler motor car manufacturer (1930); experimental prefabricated houses (1926–1927); and a wide range of furniture in the period 1925–1931.

As a matter of fact, much of Gropius's architectural work in the United States as a senior member of The Architects' Collaborative was to come after his receipt of the AIA Gold Medal. This body of work would alone have established him as a foremost figure in the modern movement, just as his work after 1959 would have qualified him for the medal. But it was his twenty-five years at the Bauhaus and later at Harvard which made him, quite simply, the most influential educator and theoretician in the world. And it is on this part of his career that the award is based. The specific principles embodied in Gropius's teaching are not easily encapsulated. Gropius himself found it necessary to amplify and develop them repeatedly after the

---

1   Citation.

publication of the first manifesto, but in essence they were these:

1. "The Bauhaus believes the machine to be our modern medium of design and seeks to come to terms with it."[2]
2. All design must recognize this fact of life and distil a new set of aesthetic criteria from it. Such a process would, for architecture, lead to "clear, organic [form] whose inner logic will be radiant and naked, unencumbered by lying facades and trickeries."[3]
3. The Bauhaus teaches "the common citizenship of all forms of creative work and their logical interdependence upon one another."[4]
4. The scale and complexity of modern problems necessitates collaborative design. "Any industrially produced object is the result of countless experiments, of long, systematic research."[5] The design school must recognize this and equip the student with "the common basis on which many individuals are able to create together a superior unit of work."[6]
5. The education of the designer "must include a thorough, practical manual training in workshops actively engaged in production, coupled with sound theoretical instruction in the laws of design."[7]

This was the program which catapulted the Bauhaus into international prominence, making it the most important single force in the design world for the next half-century. Every field of design registered its influence: architecture, product design, furniture; fabrics, silverware and pottery; graphics, typography, painting, advertising; photography, movies, stagecraft, even ballet. As a program, its capacity to regenerate design derived from its essentially correct analysis of the relation between design and production in an industrialized world.

The very ferocity with which the whole conceptual apparatus of the Bauhaus is currently being attacked is, in its own ironic way, a measure of its own continuing power. For, like all major revolutions, it altered the intellectual and aesthetic trajectories of its time. Whatever its initial deficiencies or subsequent mistakes, the movement in which the Bauhaus played such a dominant role did indeed remake the world, physically and conceptually. That impact cannot be expunged from the historical record, nor can its momentum be reversed.

2 Herbert Bayer, Ise Gropius, and Walter Gropius, *Bauhaus: 1919–1928*, Museum of Modern Art, New York, 1938, p. 27.

3 Ibid., p. 29.

4 Ibid., p. 127.

5 Ibid., p. 30.

6 Ibid., p. 28.

7 Ibid., p. 24.

CONTRIBUTED BY JAMES MARSTON FITCH

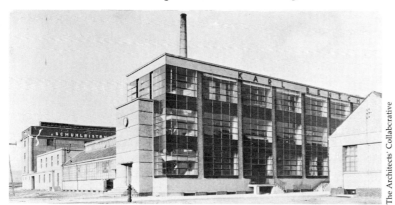

Walter Gropius and Adolf Meyer: Fagus Factory, Alfeld-an-der-Leine, Germany, 1911.

Walter Gropius: Bauhaus, Dessau, Germany, 1925–1926.

LUDWIG MIES VAN DER ROHE

AWARDED ON APRIL 21, 1960
IN THE PALACE HOTEL
SAN FRANCISCO, CALIFORNIA

Fujikawa, Conterato, Lohan & Associates

Ludwig Mies van der Rohe.

Son of a master mason; working for a time with an architect who built of wood; later associated with Bruno Paul and his design of furniture; then attracted by the brickwork of Holland, you have built knowingly in stone, wood and brick, and have a deep respect for the individuality of materials.

In steel and glass you have designed with more joy, more conviction, but throughout a busy life you have persevered in a quest for a technique of structure that would obviate the need of embellishing architecture, that would in itself be architecture, exemplifying the words of St. Augustine, "Beauty is the splendor of truth."[1]

Maria Ludwig Michael Mies was born in Aachen, Germany, March 27, 1886, one of four children of Michael and Amalie, née Rohe, Mies. His father was a stonemason, and the younger Mies first learned the nature and use of materials in his father's stone yard. He attended the Cathedral School of Aachen until he was 16. On leaving school he worked in his father's yard and achieved the status of journeyman brickmason. Working also as a draftsman in local architectural offices, he chose not to take academic training in architecture. In 1905 he went to Berlin, where he worked for the furniture designer Bruno Paul. He executed his first commission, the Riehl House, in 1907 and saw it published in 1910. In that year he went to work for Peter Behrens. Here he met Walter Gropius, Le Corbusier, and in the Wasmuth Edition, the work of Frank Lloyd Wright. He was influenced further by the integrity in the use of materials of H. P. Berlage, and the elegance and proportion of K. F. Schinkel. Also during these years he married Ada Bruhn. They had three daughters: Dorothea (known as Georgia), Waltraut, and Marianna.

Following the outbreak of World War I, Mies entered the German Army, serving in an engineering unit. At the war's end he returned to private practice, and he also initiated activity in professional associations, publications, and exhibitions. At first Mies attempted to resume his prewar manner, but then, in a series of five projects executed in the years 1919–1923, Mies sought an appropriate new architecture, faithful to the imperatives of modern materials, the spirit of the age, and human aspiration.

As an officer in the Deutsche Werkbund, he orga-
nized the 1927 Stuttgart Weissenhofsiedlung exhibition. The German Pavilion at the Barcelona International Exposition of 1929, and the Tugendhat House in Brno, Czechoslovakia, of 1930, were the buildings by Mies which achieved the greatest notice, criticism, and fame. He also designed furniture of great elegance during these years. He became the director of the Bauhaus in 1930, overseeing its move from Dessau to Berlin. He supervised its closing in 1933.

With his practice diminishing during the 1930s, Mies visited the United States in 1937, and this led to his becoming the director of the architecture program at Armour (later Illinois) Institute of Technology. The architectural curriculum he introduced at the Bauhaus was further developed and became the basis for the program, which remains to the present, at IIT. He began teaching in Chicago in the fall of 1938, continuing until his retirement in 1958. He became an American citizen in 1944. Mies's career in Chicago was marked by a substantial practice of exceptional influence. Among the notable buildings of his career in the United States are the IIT campus plan and numerous buildings, including Crown Hall, 1950–1956, the 860–880 Lake Shore Drive Apartments, 1948–1951, and the Federal Center, 1959–1976, all in Chicago; the Farnsworth House, 1945–1950, in Plano, Illinois; the Seagram Building, 1954–1958, in Manhattan; the Lafayette Park Housing Development, with his planning and landscape colleagues Ludwig Hilberseimer and Alfred Caldwell, 1955–1963, in Detroit; and the New National Gallery, 1962–1968, in Berlin. Mies died in Chicago on August 17, 1969.

1   Citation.

192

When accepting the Gold Medal of the AIA in 1960, Mies spoke of the "clarity of thought and action" necessary for good work. Clarity, as fact and idea, is central to his work. When he published a pair of glass-sheathed, steel-framed skyscrapers in 1922, the first of his five projects which helped to define modern architecture and set its agenda for half a century, Mies recorded his observations of the steel-frame building and of the model he had hung outside his window.

> Skyscrapers reveal their bold structural pattern during construction. Only then does the gigantic steel web seem impressive.
>
> I discovered by working with actual glass models that the important thing is the play of reflections and not the effect of light and shadow as in ordinary buildings.[2]

The special qualities of steel, glass, light, and space, and their interrelationships, were to continue as fundamental concerns. In his continuing study of Augustine and Aquinas, Mies gave attention to symbolic as well as tangible qualities of material, the need to discover order and relation, and, through them, significance. Others shared similar, but not identical interests. In the imagery of glass, there is clearly a difference between the crystalline, prismatic, and volumetric character of the work of his contemporary, the architect Bruno Taut, and the transparent, neutral, and planar quality of glass Mies recognized and sought to express.

Mies devoted much attention to the transcendant in the actual. As he liked to say, "Architecture begins when two bricks are brought together, carefully."[3] The thing and the idea, the significance of things, or the idea signified by things, was of very great importance to him. In the dialectic of gridded frame and free space, Mies sought to provide a synthesis.

For Mies, space and light were a central and powerful metaphor of chaos and order, and he sought an architecture in which the metaphor might be made explicit. He had written that "creative work has only a single goal: to create order out of the desperate confusion of our time."[4] In this effort to aid the *Zeitgeist*, glass and steel were symbolic of the order that the modern age could create from the most common and chaotic of materials. Natural space and light were likewise ubiquitous but unformed. Thus his work is literally, not phenomenally, transparent, because space is understood as a powerful presence in its own right, not a neutral medium to be shaped by a volumetric mass. Space is defined but not formed by precisely placed planes that are tangent to but not part of the space they punctuate. No space is displaced by these planes, and the material which defined such space was preferably rich in sheen or pattern, befitting its important role in indicating the significance of space.

As he wrote, "Architecture depends on facts, but its real field of activity lies in the realm of significance."[5] If structure is fact, then space is significance, and that significance is heightened as the space becomes less tangible and approaches idea. Mies was likewise interested in transforming the fact of the frame into the idea. In seeking to achieve the idea beyond the thing, Mies seems to have believed that if he could refine the architectural space and frame thoroughly enough, he might ultimately reach a point where architecture and his idea of it became one.

CONTRIBUTED BY KEVIN HARRINGTON

2   Mies van der Rohe, in *Fruhlicht*, 1922; reprinted in Peter Carter, *Mies Van Der Rohe at Work*, Praeger, New York, 1974, p. 12.

3   Ibid., p. 7.

4   Werner Blaser, *After Mies*, Van Nostrand Reinhold, New York, 1977, p. 30.

5   Philip Johnson, *Mies van der Rohe* (3d ed.), Museum of Modern Art, New York, 1978, p. 203.

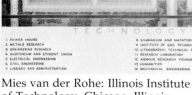

Mies van der Rohe: Illinois Institute of Technology, Chicago, Illinois, site plan, ca 1940.

Mies van der Rohe: 860–880 Lake Shore Drive, Chicago, Illinois, 1948–1951.

GOLD MEDAL FOR 1961 LE CORBUSIER

AWARDED ON APRIL 27, 1961
IN THE BELLEVUE-STRATFORD HOTEL
PHILADELPHIA, PENNSYLVANIA

© SPADEM, Paris/VAGA, New York, 1982

Le Corbusier.

Architect, Planner, Sculptor, Painter, Author, Poet, Teacher, Visionary, and, most of all, man of principle, who, often misunderstood but always respected, has by his tenacious insistence on seeking truth and beauty for the human environment, by his great works, by his discoveries, and by his motto that "Creation is a patient search" led and inspired the dawn of a new architecture.[1]

One of the most influential architectural talents of the twentieth century, Charles Édouard Jeanneret described himself as being an architect, urbanist, painter, poet, and philosopher. Born in the mountainous Jura region of Switzerland of a middle-class family in 1887, he was proud to include among his French and Swiss ancestry some local nobility, a painter, and a revolutionary. Entering school early at the age of 4, in 1900, at age 13, he was apprenticed to the local art school of La Chaux-de-Fonds to continue in the family tradition of watch enameling and engraving. Quickly demonstrating his design aptitude, he was encouraged to study architecture by his teacher l'Eplattenier, although claiming a horror of 'architects and architecture.'

In 1905, at age 17, he received his first commission for a house, and two years later, with the profits, he traveled to Italy, then Vienna, finally arriving in Paris in the spring of 1908. Working part-time for the Perret brothers, he was able to attend theory courses in architecture at the École des Beaux-Arts, study mathematics on his own, and copy drawings in various library collections. Returning home briefly, he then went to Germany and worked five months for Peter Behrens in Berlin. In 1911 he set out to tour the countries of the Mediterranean basin — Italy, Greece, and Turkey.

He returned home again to teach a design studio at his old school and to construct a series of houses. In 1914 he started work on his first major architectural invention — the *maison domino* structural system, a proposal for rebuilding housing being destroyed by the war. From this proposal he derived his five points for the creation of a new architecture:

the free plan, the roof garden, free façade, horizontal ribbon windows, and *pilotis*. In 1917, at the age of 31, he left for the last time to open an office in Paris, also becoming the owner of a brick factory, which he managed until 1921.

Introduced to the painter Amédée Ozenfant in 1918, Jeanneret was encouraged to begin painting full-time. Together they published manifestos and exhibited their paintings, conceived in a postcubist style which they call purism. From 1920 to 1925 they also published a review of contemporary culture called *l'Esprit Nouveau*, whose articles are the basis for a series of books, most notably *Vers une architecture* (*Towards a New Architecture*) published in 1923. It is signed with the pseudonym "Le Corbusier," a name derived from an extinct family branch chosen by Jeanneret in order to distinguish his work as an architect from that of his painting.

From 1922 to 1940, in association with his cousin Pierre Jeanneret, he begins the period of his mature architectural production, both real and theoretical: urban schemes for Paris, furniture, exhibits, and elegant villas culminating in the masterpieces, the Villa de Monzie-Stein at Garches, 1926–1927, and the Villa Savoye at Poissy, 1928–1931. In 1930 he married Yvonne Gallis and became a naturalized French citizen.

There can be no question of the influence that Le Corbusier working as architect, urbanist, and painter has had on twentieth-century aesthetics. Purism, the Radiant City, *pilotis*, roof gardens, ribbon windows, the free plan, and *brises-soleil* have

---

1   Citation.

194

all become visual and cultural clichés. His slogan of the house as a "machine to live in" was not, as often interpreted, a demand that architecture look like a machine, but rather that it should perform as logically and well as a machine. With his deep-rooted sense of order and logic and acute visual sensitivity, coupled with an idealist optimism in modern culture as expressed by technological progress, he attempted to link the visual products and intellectual qualities of the industrial revolution with the classical humanist tradition.

A concern for paradox and juxtaposition dominates much of his work. He attempted a modern reconciliation of individual choice or freedom with the necessity of collective responsibility by combining the virtues of monastic life with the formal and programmatic organization of the steamship. The result are projects like the housing block at Marseilles and the Salvation Army Hostel in Paris, projects that are self-contained and isolated, yet foster social interaction by means of shared facilities.

Increasingly his work of the 1930s abandoned the classic shell of the earlier houses for a vernacular and topographic response. The chapel of Notre-Dame-du-Haut, 1950–1955, at Ronchamp appears as a pulsating, primitive form, a sculpturally active object in the landscape that conversely encompasses and encloses the viewer. The building imitates vernacular construction; the rough-rendered white walls conceal not simply fieldstone but a reinforced-concrete frame.

He was without peer as a propagandist for modern architecture—continually lecturing, writing, and publishing including eight volumes of his own work: *Oeuvres Completes* (1929–1970), *Urbanisme* (*The City of Tomorrow*), 1925, and *La Ville radieuse* (*The Radiant City*), 1933.

As a cofounder of CIAM (International Congress for Modern Architecture) and active propagandist about urban problems, he became the proponent of our urban vision that, for better or worse, has become the dominant reality of the present—albeit for reasons he despised. Chandigarh, started in 1951 as the new capitol of the Punjab in India, represents in its unfinished and politically divided condition a telling statement regarding his aspirations and frustrations. In his acceptance speech to the AIA in Philadelphia, he said, "I've only a list in my pocket of all the defeats in my life, since that represents the bulk of my life's work."[2] He died while swimming in the Mediterranean in 1965.

CONTRIBUTED BY BRUCE ABBEY

---

2   Le Corbusier. "Remarks," *AIA Journal*, vol. 35, June 1961, p. 97.

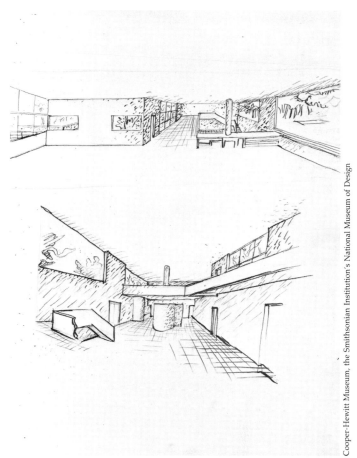

Le Corbusier and Pierre Jeanneret: Villa de Monzie-Stein, Garches, 1926–1927, interior drawings.

Le Corbusier: Notre-Dame-du-Haut, interior.

GOLD MEDAL FOR 1962 EERO SAARINEN

AWARDED ON MAY 10, 1962
AT THE STATLER-HILTON HOTEL
DALLAS, TEXAS
ACCEPTED BY ALINE B. SAARINEN

Eero Saarinen.

An illustrious son of an illustrious father, his years were few, his accomplishments many. The inner fervor impelling him to produce fresh, inventive and appropriate architecture knew no respite. Generous in his frequent association with others, the fundamental ideas controlling the design were generally acknowledged to be his.

Whatever Eero Saarinen touched — a design for a chair or a design for a great airport — his creative thought extended to each minor detail. Never fully satisfied with his achievement, only a new and challenging problem could bring him to write 'finis' to a preceding task. His life of fifty-one years was dominated by his passion to create beauty and usefulness. The world is, and will increasingly become, a richer and more beautiful place in which to live because of what he did and what he was.[1]

Eero Saarinen was a Finnish-born (1910) naturalized U.S. citizen who came to this country in 1923. He graduated from Yale University in 1934 with a B.F.A. degree, having previously studied sculpture in Paris. From 1934 to 1936, he traveled and worked in Europe. When he returned to the United States, he worked for the Flint Institute of Planning, taught at Cranbrook Academy, and practiced architecture with his father, Eliel. His wartime duty was with the OSS in Washington, D.C. Upon his father's death in 1950, Eero formally started his own firm, where several now-prominent architects apprenticed. He also designed furniture and was the recipient of numerous awards and honorary degrees, including Doctor of Engineering, Technische Hochschule, Hanover, 1961. His first wife was Lilian Swann Saarinen, sculptor; his second, Aline B. Louchheim Saarinen was an art critic and news correspondent. He died in 1961.

Each of Saarinen's best buildings was an innovative, proud solution to the problems posed by the physical and spiritual requirements of the client. Each solution evolved through methodical analysis and continuous redesign and refinement.

The General Motors Technical Center, Warren, Michigan (1948–1956) was his first major commission. In keeping with the slick, high-technology image of an automobile manufacturer, Saarinen's office and the GM engineers perfected new products for the center, including the neoprene window gasket and the thin laminated window panel.

For two other corporate clients, the Bell Laboratories and Deere & Company, Saarinen's firm invented reflective, metalized glass façades. Although approximately 5000 people work at the Bell Laboratories, Holmdel, New Jersey (1957–1962), the interior respects the scale of the individual employee, while the exterior and the formal landscaping enhance the surroundings (Plate 21). The Deere & Company headquarters, Moline, Illinois (1957–1963), with its siting between two hills, horizontal massing, and earth-tone metal sunscreens, suggests fields being plowed by Deere farm machinery. For this project, oxidizing steel was used for the first time in architecture.

Although Saarinen had several corporate commissions, he designed only one skyscraper, the CBS Building, New York City (1960–1964). Its façades of dark granite triangular piers make an uncompromised, perhaps unequalled, vertical statement.

One of Saarinen's academic commissions, the Kresge Auditorium, Massachusetts Institute of Technology, Cambridge (1953–1956), was the first large-scale use of thin-shelled concrete in the United States.

Saarinen's first airport commission was the TWA Terminal at John F. Kennedy Airport, New York (1956–1962). Also built in concrete, the roof's four connected shells soar as though they are about to fly.

The terminal at Dulles International Airport, Chantilly, Virginia (1958–1962), however, better

---

1   Citation.

Eero Saarinen: Dulles Airport
Terminal, Chantilly, Virginia,
1958–1962, preliminary sketches.

Eero Saarinen: pedestal furniture
designs, 1958.

expresses the drama of flight and is a drastic refinement of the concept of the airport terminal. Through the introduction of the mobile lounge, the passenger's long walk between the airplane and terminal was eliminated. Unlike the buses used at European airports, the mobile lounges were intended to be luxuriant extensions of the terminal. With its slung roof and giant angled piers, Dulles is a monumental entrance for foreign visitors to the United States and a dignified symbol of the federal government, owner of the airport.

CONTRIBUTED BY WILLIAM LEBOVICH

GOLD MEDAL FOR 1963 **ALVAR AALTO**

AWARDED ON MAY 9, 1963
AT THE AMERICANA HOTEL
BAL HARBOUR, FLORIDA

Alvar Aalto.

In deep appreciation of all that he has contributed in developing the strong foundations and eloquent philosophy of contemporary architecture and in richly endowing its vocabulary of design with his own warm humanism, ready wit and perceptive use of materials, texture and color during more than three decades of creative achievement in his native Finland and the western world.[1]

Alvar Aalto was born in 1898 in the Ostro-Bothnian village of Kourtane. His father, J. H. Aalto, was a surveyor. After attending the Jyväskylä Classical Lyceum, Aalto entered the Helsinki Polytechnic in 1916. While a student, he was a member of Armas Lindgren's atelier and worked for Carolus Lindberg. Graduated in 1921, Aalto sought employment in Sweden: He entered the office of Arvid Bjerke, being unable to work for Gunnar Asplund. In 1924, after establishing his office in Jyväskylä, he married the architect Aino Marsio. Aalto moved his office to Turku in 1927, and finally to Helsinki in 1933. After the death of his first wife in 1949, he married the architect Elissa Mäkiniemi in 1952. Aalto died in 1976.

Representative of the rational classicism found throughout Scandinavia during the 1920s, Aalto's initial buildings were classical in inspiration, order, and execution. The Workers' Club and Civil Guards' building in Jyväskylä exemplify his work of this period. From the austere classicizing quality of his early works, Aalto readily mastered the formal and theoretical canons of the International Style, as witnessed in the Turun Sanomat Newspaper Building and the Paimio Tuberculosis Sanatorium. Although his was an ardent voice in the development of Finnish modernism, a more personal style began to emerge in Aalto's architecture by the late 1930s. The Viipuri Library, Villa Mairea, and the Finnish pavilions at the 1937 and 1939 world's fairs embody this change, with their romantic and picturesque imagery and composition.

By the 1950s, Aalto had developed a mature style,

which was often lauded as being uniquely Finnish. The Säynätsalo Town Hall, House of Culture, and Public Pensions Institute are representative works, characterized by the use of red brick, copper, and wood. The picturesque volumetric massing found in these buildings, their responsiveness to the particulars of context, and the juxtaposition of materials and textural effects seem reminiscent of the qualities found in Finland's turn-of-the-century national-romantic style. During his last fifteen years of practice—beginning with the Vuoksenniska Church and seen in the Seinäjoki, Wolfsburg, and Rovaniemi civic and cultural complexes, Finlandia Hall, and the Riola Church—Aalto's work became more complex, even mannered, in formal order and composition, expression, and material usage. These works reincorporate classical imagery and motifs while simultaneously maintaining the romantic and picturesque qualities found in Aalto's previous buildings.

Throughout his career Aalto constantly explored a series of specific architectonic concerns and elements which formed a thematic consistency that complimented the stylistic evolution in his architecture. Centralization as a primary ordering device in Aalto's compositions was realized through the use of exterior courtyard spaces and multileveled interior courtlike spaces. Representative examples include the Säynätsalo Town Hall, Viipuri Library, Rautatalo Building, and Seinäjoki civic complex. Within many of the centralized spatial constructs

---

1   Citation.

Aalto incorporated staircases, landings, and handrails as dynamic elements celebrating human action and movement. Beginning with the Viipuri Library he continually explored the architectonic possibilities found in the sinuous, or undulating, line and surface; this can also be seen in the 1939 Finnish Pavilion, House of Culture, and Vuoksenniska Church. Aalto developed unique, highly expressive architectural forms to manipulate the natural light within his buildings. To achieve a romantic and picturesque imagery Aalto used fragmented and incomplete building forms and geometries, differentiated building masses and volumes, and broken and rugged building profiles and added planting to the building's wall surfaces. The Säynätsalo Town Hall and the Vuoksenniska Church in Rovaniemi demonstrate these qualities. While these are merely a selective sample of the concerns or themes found in Aalto's buildings, many of these same ideas recur in his furniture and other applied designs.

Alvar Aalto believed architecture to be an affirmative act practiced through responsive and responsible design. His significance as an architect resulted from the highly creative architectural language he developed. This language, which explored and examined the full range of expressive means available to the architect, results in an architecture of unique richness and variety in form and meaning. Aalto's buildings are extremely humane, yet profoundly corporeal in their presence.

CONTRIBUTED BY WILLIAM C. MILLER

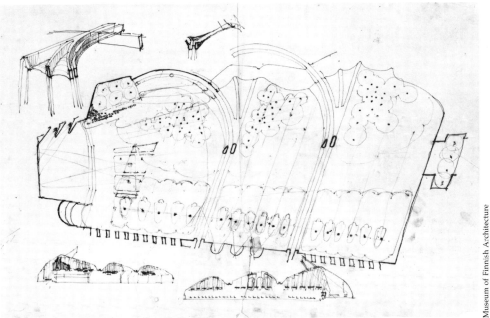

Alvar Aalto: Vuoksenniska Church, Imatra, Finland, 1956–1958, development drawing.

Vuoksenniska Church, exterior.

PIER LUIGI NERVI

AWARDED ON JUNE 18, 1964
IN THE CHASE-PARK PLAZA
ST. LOUIS, MISSOURI

Pier Luigi Nervi.

Eighteen centuries ago in Rome, Hadrian and his builders gave the world one of its great landmarks, the Pantheon, its dome built of a brick-arched frame and pumice concrete, spanning 142 feet.

Only yesterday another great landmark came to Rome, the Sports Palace, its low dome spanning 312 feet, in which, with many other structures, Luigi Nervi carried the science and art over a tremendous leap of structural skill and daring.

New mass forms, possible with the plasticity of ferro-concrete, called for engineering imagination and formulae no longer based on the simple forces of gravity and wind, but visualized and checked by small-scale models.

Nervi's own vision of the primary requirements for the architect of today rings true: "Esthetic sensibility, a profound understanding of structural needs, and a precise knowledge of the methods, possibilities, and limitations of constructional techniques." The Master apparently thought it unnecessary to add "and if the known techniques will not serve, invent a new one"—a proceeding in which Nervi again and again conquered the impossible.

It has been said before that the role of the master builder should never have been subdivided. Luigi Nervi has proven that engineer, architect, and builder can be reassembled in one professional, but we might caution against forgetting the essential ingredient—Nervi's genius.[1]

Initiator of "ferro-cement." Master of prefabricated intricacies coupled with delicate soaring space and sunflower bursts of geometric patterns. Structural expressions laid bare and exposed by a creative spirit which dominates the design and construction process. Pure geometry utilized to define the essence of architectural genius.

Pier Luigi Nervi was born in Sondrio, northern Italy, in 1891. He graduated from the Civil Engineering School in Bologna in 1913. He was the recipient of many awards and honorary degrees from various countries. Since 1946 he lectured on structural engineering in the Faculty of Architecture at the University of Rome, where his classes were exceedingly popular with international audiences. He died in 1979.

Nervi firmly believed that the total design process contained three fundamental interrelated factors: architectural concept, structural analysis, and construction technologies. To achieve an appropriate design solution, it was necessary to seek a direct balance between these three factors, which influence visual impact, public safety, and long-term maintenance of all buildings. It became his approach to architecture almost as if it were a direct response to the principles of "firmness, commodity, and delight," first stated by Vitruvius in the first century B.C. and then restated by many architects and theorists. Nervi believed that structure and construction were not a constraint on the creative process, but rather served to reinforce design in a search for solutions to the client's requirements. He often indicated that the identification and development of the aesthetic harmony of form and program requirements served as guides to the final definition of alternate structural schemes.

Nervi was also one of the early proponents of the "design-build" approach to architecture. He strongly maintained that it was necessary for the architect to have direct control over the construction phase in order to deliver a finished quality product to the corporate client. Accordingly he formed a subsidiary construction firm to execute his designs. In many cases when dealing with important buildings, particularly in Italy, his firm was responsible

1 Citation.

for not only the design phase but also the actual construction. Many of the delicate prefabricated forms and intricate architectural details identified with his work were a direct result of his control over the construction process, where he utilized highly trained technicians under his direct supervision. The inspiring quality of each one of Nervi's structures illustrates a firm adherence to this philosophy. In this way the architectural details of his creative fervor, which produced simple, highly articulated structures, have become the most important part of his inventiveness. Nervi's resistance to focusing only on formal and aesthetic issues totally separated from structural and construction considerations led him toward the most brillant achievements in his career. Some of his works are probably among the best examples of clear interrelation between formal and technical parameters. Understanding this approach to the design process partially explains why in some of his work the usual high level of integration was not achieved; in most cases this happened when Nervi thought he could delegate the solution of formal aspects to others.

Whether Nervi was an architect or an engineer is academic. One only needs to perceive his buildings to realize that they are highly articulated architectural masterpieces. The sweep and scale of his structures are bold and imaginative, in many cases results of radical experimentation. The soaring quality of the airplane hangars designed in Orvieto (1935) and Orbetello (1939) stand out as inspiring structural solutions to utilitarian architecture. The outstanding exposition halls in Turin designed in 1949 (Salone B) and 1950 (Salone C) achieved international recognition and, both in their prefabricated form and execution, remain inspirational.

Nervi's creative genius reached a high point during 1958–1960, when he was commissioned to design several structures for the 1960 olympic games held in Rome. Of these, the small Palazzetto dello Sport is acknowledged to be a structure which exemplifies all of Nervi's design principles in one single building. It is an architectural gem, in which the structural theory of strength through form is embodied in design by the use of corrugated surfaces to transfer building loads to the foundation system. At the same time, Nervi designed the International Labor Exposition Hall in Turin (1961) which marked the celebration of the first centennial of the unification of Italy. The use of a prefabricated steel roof system was a departure from former reliance on reinforced concrete structures, but nonetheless represents another classic example of Nervi's ability to develop new forms and devise experimental technologies in the construction process.

Nervi has published extensively over the years. Two notable publications are *Arte o scienza del costruire?* (Rome, 1950) and *Costruire correttament* (Milan, 1954). Both present in detail his design theories and construction principles, which were developed over the years. Among the large number of architects who collaborated with Nervi over more than forty years of activity are M. Breur, B. Rehrfuss, G. Ponti, A. Vitellossi, M. Piacentri, A. Libera, and L. Moretti.

CONTRIBUTED BY HENRY J. LAGORIO
AND CARLO PELLICCIA

Pier Luigi Nervi: Hangar, Orvieto, Italy, 1939–1942

Pier Luigi Nervi: Salone B, Exposition Building, Turin, Italy, 1948–1949.

GOLD MEDAL FOR 1966 **KENZO TANGE**

AWARDED ON JULY 1, 1966
IN THE DENVER HILTON BALLROOM
DENVER, COLORADO

Kenzo Tange & Urtec

Kenzo Tange.

Architect, Philosopher, Teacher, Writer—who has through the poetry of his architecture brought a spirit of dignity, grace and integrity to his own land and to man everywhere. In his relentless search to understand and translate reality, he has welcomed the architect's responsibility to give visual and physical form to the unawakened desires of society. The eloquence of his thought and his design has given outstanding leadership in architecture and city planning to bridge the gap between advancing technology and human aspiration. Majestic in conception, his buildings beginning with the Peace Memorial at Hiroshima only seventeen years ago have proved him truly a first architect of the world.[1]

Kenzo Tange has been the most influential Japanese architect of the past thirty years, widely recognized at home and abroad. His honors are many and include the Gold Medals of the RIBA (1965), Italy (1970), and France (1973), Medal of Honor, Denmark (1968), the Thomas Jefferson Medal (1970), and many fellowships and awards.

The success and recognition of Tange's architecture parallels in many ways the story of Japan's economic miracle and cultural restructuring in the years since World War II. The astuteness of Japanese manufacturers and salespeople in adapting essentially western products, images, and practices and producing quality goods—from calculators to motorcycles and cameras—is evident throughout the world. Tange's architecture fits much the same mold. He was able to adapt western ideas of modernism and synthesize them with traditional Japanese concerns. The Japanese economic miracle has not been accomplished without some problems: The dislocation and resettlement of large segments of the population in urban conglomerations such as Tokyo has a further parallel with Tange, for he has become increasingly concerned with the development of large-scale urban-planning models as a response to the changing concerns of the city.

Tange was born in 1913 and received all his education at the University of Tokyo in 1935–1938 and 1942–1945. Subsequently, in 1959, he received a doctorate for his dissertation, entitled "Structure of Tokyo City." He taught at the university between 1946 and 1974, following the prototype of Walter Gropius in the integration of practice and instruction. Gropius is both a hero and collaborator of Tange; together they wrote *Katsura: Tradition and Creation in Japanese Architecture* (1960). For years Tange's class and office were the center of architectural ideas in Japan, and while he was never a member of the younger metabolist group, many of its ideas and personalities came from his office and class, and his work, from the theoretical to the actual, both influenced and reflected metabolist concerns.

Tange's architecture can be seen as developing through several distinct periods, from an earlier International-Style weightless box, as in the Hiroshima Peace Center (1949–1956), to the massive *beton brute* of neo-Corbusier, as in the Kurashiki Town Hall (1958–1960), to a later, more exploratory and indeterminate mode, as in the Yamanashi Press and Broadcasting Center (1966) (Plate 16) and the Shizuoka Newspaper and Broadcasting Building (1966–1969); still later he returned to the elegance of materials and formal design issues, as in the Minnesota Museum of Art Gallery and Schools (1970–1974). These shifts reflect both the general international architectural situation and, more importantly, Tange's increasing realization of the problems of urban architecture, the need for flexibility, expandability, and yet some formal architectural spatial order. All of his later work is (theoreti-

---

1   Citation.

cally) possible of expansion or contraction, of the addition or subtraction of parts, or "plug-ins." In spite of his urban concerns and the very important "Plan for Tokyo Bay," 1960, the only project on an urban scale to reach fruition was Expo 70, for which he was chief planner and architect.

On another level Tange's architecture can be interpreted as an attempt to mediate tradition and modernism, a subject that has extensively preoccupied him both in work and writings. In 1956 he wrote:

> The realities of present-day Japan, while part of an historically conditioned world-wide reality, are at the same time given their unique shape by the traditions of Japan. Living within this reality, yet also trying always to comprehend it afresh in a forward-looking spirit, these traditions force themselves insistently upon our attention. Were it otherwise, were the problems of today not so pressing, we might accept tradition calmly and unreflectingly as inherited custom, or something out of the past. Only those who adopt a forward-looking attitude realize that tradition exists and is alive.[2]

Tange's work has at times directly reflected traditional Japanese architecture, as in the sliding partitions of his own house, the extended beams of the Kurashiki Town Hall, or simply the feeling of status and quietude of the Hiroshima Peace Center. Yet they are never historical revivals, and as Tange indicates above, it is the modernist position that is the central reality of today. Herein lies Tange's real achievement: not in the usage of traditional forms or details or the forms of western modernism but in making Japanese architecture part of a world-wide development.

---

2   Quoted in Robin Boyd, *Kenzo Tange*, Braziller, New York, 1962.

Kenzo Tange: National Gymnasiums for Tokyo Olympics, 1961–1964.

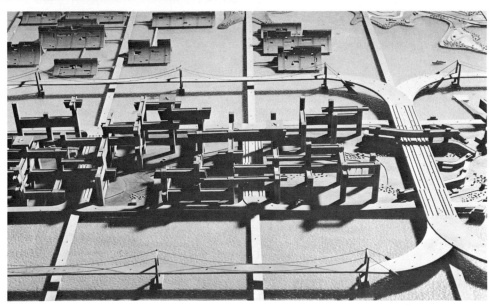

Kenzo Tange Team: "A Plan for Tokyo," project, 1959–1960.

GOLD MEDAL FOR 1967 WALLACE KIRKMAN HARRISON

AWARDED ON MAY 18, 1967
IN THE NEW YORK HILTON
NEW YORK, NEW YORK

Gil Amiaga, photographer; courtesy of Wallace K. Harrison

Wallace Kirkman Harrison.

To Wallace K. Harrison, FAIA, architect, who has shown the highest order of architectural statesmanship. He has led a team in producing significant architectural works of high quality over a period of more than thirty years. He has worked with the concept of urbanism, creating architecture as part of the fabric of the city, with great dedication and loyalty to the best interest of his own city, New York.[1]

Wallace K. Harrison gained a reputation as a pragmatist. He was involved in and led the design teams for several of the largest urban and institutional complexes of the twentieth century: Rockefeller Center, the United Nations, and Lincoln Center, all in New York City, and the Empire State Mall in Albany. He could speak the language of business executives and politicians, and he became known as an architect who could give the client a modern, yet safe, image. His statements on architecture reinforced the pragmaticism: "I never like fake stuff on buildings"; "Decoration is not architecture"; "Why add something when you don't need it?"; and "I've not time to worry about style when I'm working on a building."[2] He projected an earthy, no-nonsense quality: "Every damn thing is an accident"; and "You're lucky if you can come close."[3]

Yet there was another side to Harrison, a passionate romantic who painted wild, distorted, Picasso-like paintings and created sensational forms, such as the Trylon and Perisphere for the 1939 New York world's fair and the First Presbyterian Church in Stamford, Connecticut, 1953–1956 (Plate 17). The real Wallace K. Harrison was not a chameleon, but an architect caught between the tide of functionalism and radical-modern puritanism and his roots, which lay in the beaux-arts and romantic imagery.

Harrison was born in Worcester, Massachusetts, in 1895, the son of a foundry superintendent. He dropped out of high school to work for Norcross Brothers, a famous Worcester building firm, and then as a draftsman for Frost & Chamberlain, local architects. In 1916 he came to New York and got a position with the McKim, Mead & White firm. From 1917 to 1919 he was in the navy on a destroyer and visited Paris for the first time. He then studied in Paris in the atelier of Gustave Umbdenstock and in 1922 won the Rotch Travelling Scholarship and spent some time at the American Academy in Rome. In 1923 he married Ellen Hunt Milton, whose brother was married to Abby Rockefeller. From 1923 to 1924 he was in the office of Bertram Goodhue. He joined the firm of Helmle & Corbett — Harvey Wiley Corbett had taught Harrison in the McKim, Mead & White office — in 1927, and subsequently, he became a partner. From 1929 on he was involved in the design of Rockefeller Center, and in 1935 he formed a new partnership with Henri Fouilhoux. Max Abramovitz became a partner in 1941, and after the death of Fouilhoux the firm became Harrison & Abramovitz. He remained in partnership with Abramovitz until 1978 when, at the age of 83, he struck out on his own again. During World War II he was in the Office of Inter-American Affairs, first under Nelson Rockefeller and finally as director. He taught briefly at Columbia University in 1925 and 1926, and then from 1939 to 1942 he was at Yale and helped to transform the program from beaux-arts to modern. A tall, courtly gentleman, he greatly enjoyed good company. He died on December 2, 1981.

The Rockefeller connection has been used by some critics to explain Harrison's success, yet he

---

1 Citation.

2 Personal communication, January 8, 1981; "Fact Sheet on Wallace K. Harrison, FAIA," AIA, Washington, D.C., ca 1967.

3 Personal communication, January 8, 1981; "Profile," *The New Yorker,* November 20, 1954, p. 51.

had undeniable talent and charm. The Corbett firm was selected to work on Rockefeller Center because of their expertise in high-rise design. Harrison described the Rockefeller Center opportunity as "pure gain, . . . I was a kid."[4] Of the team of architects assembled for the project, Harrison was clearly subordinate to Raymond Hood. They argued over Hood's setbacks for the RCA Building, Harrison advocating a more purely modern, unadorned approach. Hood won, but after his death Harrison emerged as the leading force and designed the Eastern Airlines Building, a largely unadorned and unindented slab. One of his other responsibilities was to work with Nelson Rockefeller—who was assigned to the project by his father, John D. Rockefeller II—to obtain the services of "modern" artists to decorate the center.

The Rockefeller association would continue for the remainder of Harrison's life. For the site of the family's old New York City mansion, Harrison designed a flamboyant "streamlined-modern" apartment house in 1936. In 1938 he designed for Nelson Rockefeller a small glass-and-concrete hideaway pavilion for the family's Pocantico Hills estate; containing all the transparency and luminescence expected of radical modernism, Paul Goldberger claimed it is an "early modern gem."[5] Later he would be one of the leading figures on the Rockefeller-financed Lincoln Center in New York and the main designer for the large mall Nelson wanted in Albany. He was also the architect in charge of the expansion of Rockefeller Center across Sixth Avenue in the 1950s and 1960s, buildings which even Harrison acknowledged were not very good.[6] His involvement with the United Nations was intimate and long-lasting: He helped to secure the property rights for the site for the Rockefellers to give to the United Nations, and then he was appointed to be in charge of the design. With the memory of the unsuccessful League of Nations competition, Harrison insisted on a seventeen-member international advisory panel and the inclusion of superstars such as Le Corbusier, Oscar Niemeyer, and Sven Markelius, "an architectural pudding" which the British participant, Howard Robinson, claimed "threatened indi-

gestion." It was Harrison's tact and diplomacy that allowed them all to survive.[7] The basic scheme of the United Nations, a slab 544 feet tall and 72 feet wide with low-lying surrounding pavilions, was basically Le Corbusier's, though Harrison substantially modified them in form, purpose, and details. They were designed and constructed in the short period of eight years, and the cost came in substantially at budget.

Harrison was responsible for other than Rockefeller-controlled work, and some of it was epoch-making, such as the "waffle" aluminum-paneled Alcoa Building in Pittsburgh, the "new" La Guardia airport terminals and control tower, numerous residences, and other office buildings. The First Presbyterian Church in Stamford best represents Harrison's dramatic and romantic flair, though he always claimed that the building's structure was entirely rational and economical. The church's ancestry goes back to Auguste Perret's work, especially Le Raincy, which Harrison admired.[8] While having symbolic overtones—a great fish or whale—the form resulted from the structure (at least so Harrison claimed) of precast folded-concrete planes and the desire for free, unobstructed interior space. The stained-glass windows, really walls, were designed by Gabriel Loire, a Frenchman and disciple of Fernand Leger, and are filled with colored-glass nuggets. The result is a modern Ste. Chapelle. To writers of the late 1950s, the effect was "Piranesian," and it was seen as a significant break with the sterility of most modernism.[9] Clearly Harrison had a flair for the dramatic, while at the same time claiming a functional basis for the decision. The result was an architectural achievement of actual constructed designs, perhaps unmatched in the twentieth century.

4   Personal communication, March 16, 1981.

5   Paul Goldberger, "Architecture: Harrison Retrospective," *The New York Times*, January 2, 1980, p. C15.

6   Personal communication, March 16, 1981.

7   "Voices from Afar," *AIA Journal*, vol. 10, July 1948, p. 37.

8   Personal communication, March 16, May 5, 1981.

9   "A Piranesi for Today," *Architectural Forum*, vol. 99, December 1953, pp. 92–95; Arthur Drexler and Wilder Green, "Four New Buildings: Architecture and Imagery," *Museum of Modern Art Bulletin*, vol. 26, 1959; Wolf von Eckardt, "The Final Question," *AIA Journal*, vol. 31, June 1959, pp. 37–40.

Gil Amiaga, photographer; courtesy of Wallace K. Harrison

Harrison & Abramovitz: First Presbyterian Church, Stamford, Connecticut, 1953–1956.

GOLD MEDAL FOR 1968 MARCEL LAJOS BREUER

AWARDED ON JUNE 26, 1968
IN THE GRAND BALLROOM OF THE PORTLAND HILTON
PORTLAND, OREGON

Marcel Lajos Breuer.

As an architect, he has pioneered in diverse fields such as the design of private houses, the design of religious and education buildings, and the design of public buildings such as the Headquarters of UNESCO in Paris and departmental buildings of the United States Government in Washington; as a designer, especially of furniture, during the past half century he has been a most influential innovator in this country and Europe; as a teacher, he has inspired entire generations of architects who came under his influence at the Bauhaus in the 1920s and at Harvard in the 1930s and 1940s; as a planner, he has made outstanding contributions to the development of new communities in the United States during World War II, and in Europe and Latin America in more recent years.[1]

Perhaps more than any other single figure, the work and career of Marcel Breuer epitomizes the development and transformation of modern architecture in the twentieth century. Part of a generation younger than Mies, Gropius, and Le Corbusier, Breuer never acquired an academic and historically based design tradition. He was one of the first architects to be trained according to the new concepts of architectural education—function, technology, rejection of history, and abstract design—and then to rise to the stature of an international leader and in the process to alter significantly the original formulas. His contributions lie in several distinct areas: furniture design, the single-family house, concrete, the new façade, and education.

Marcel Breuer was born in Pécs, Hungary, and went to Vienna to study art. Balking at the traditional, historically oriented methodology still being taught at the academy and hearing of the new Bauhaus School at Weimar, Germany, he went there in 1920 to study. In 1923, Breuer was involved in the reorganization of the Bauhaus and the rejection of the expressionist, mystical, and craft orientation that had largely controlled it since the end of World War I. In 1924 he became master of the furniture and carpentry shops. The design and construction of furniture according to function had been a concern of the Bauhaus from the early 1920s, and Breuer had made some designs in wood. In 1925 the new orientation of the Bauhaus became evident with Breuer's Wassily chair (designed for his friend and colleague at the Bauhaus, Wassily Kandinsky), a tubular steel chair inspired by bicycle handlebars and intended for mass production. This

was followed in 1928 with the cantilevered tubular chromium steel chair, undoubtedly the most famous and most imitated modern chair. Subsequently Breuer designed a variety of other furniture, not all of it so rigidly technological and machine-oriented, as with the wooden free-form Iskoton chair of 1935.

In 1928, Breuer left the Bauhaus and set up practice as an architect and city planner in Berlin. In 1933 and 1934 in collaboration with Alfred and Emil Roth, he designed the Dolderthal Apartments in Zurich for Sigfried Giedion. Breuer left Germany in 1935 for England where he collaborated with F. R. S. Yorke on several projects. In 1937 he emigrated to the United States at the invitation of Walter Gropius to join him in practice as a partner and to teach at the School of Architecture at Harvard University. Around Boston, Breuer and Gropius designed a number of suburban houses that utilized wood sheathing and natural stone and tempered for the Americal palate the extreme reductivist and aesthetic International-Style white box. Breuer, being younger and less reserved became the hero of the Harvard students, influencing an entire generation of architects including Edward Larabee Barnes, Harry Siedler, Paul Rudolph, Philip Johnson, and John Johansen, among many.

Breuer and Gropius collaborated intermittently in the early 1940s, and he remained at Harvard until 1946, when he moved to New York and set up his own practice. The majority of his work until 1952 involved single-family suburban houses; his own

---

1   Citation.

206

houses, 1947 and 1951 at New Canaan, Connecticut, indicate the continuing transformation of the extremes of the International Style. His big breakthrough came in 1953 when the international commission headed by Gropius, entrusted with the selection of the architect for the new UNESCO headquarters in Paris chose Breuer, Pier Luigi Nervi, and Bernard Zehrfuss. Breuer seems to have dominated the collaboration. He produced a design that split into functional parts the secretariat and assembly hall and provided for each a different image; glass predominated in the former, and concrete in the latter. The monumental scale of the commission, the contact with Nervi and his use of concrete, and also undoubtedly the influence of Le Corbusier's later works at Marcelles Block and Ronchamp caused Breuer to rethink some of his architectural forms. Where previously he had gloried in "transparency"—open structure and light-filled interiors—he began to investigate new ways of handling the façade. Structure had previously meant

minimal pinpoint *pilotis* carrying flat slabs; now it returned as the actual enclosure. The "new façade" went through a series of experiments with fenestration and structure intertwined, until in the early 1960s, the "Faceted, Moulded Façade," full of "Depth, Sun and Shadow" emerged.[2] Breuer made a personal aesthetic of precast-concrete panels that combined structure, enclosure, sun protection, and utility conduit runs. At the same time the boldness of his massing as in St. John's Abbey and University, Collegeville, Minnesota, indicates his search for a new monumentality, free from history. In a sense Breuer's transformation of the modern image from the weightless box covered by a thin membrane to the sculptural depth and heaviness of a building such as the Whitney Museum, New York, is prefigured in his furniture design, the transition from the chrome-tube upright chair to the free-form lounge chair.

2   Marcel Breuer, "The Faceted, Moulded Façade: Depth, Sun and Shadow," *Architectural Record*, vol. 139, April 1966, pp. 171–186.

Knoll International

Marcel Breuer: Furniture. Left to right: "Cesca" arm chair, 1928; "Cesca" side chair, 1928; "Laccio" table, 1925; "Wassily" lounge chair, 1925; "Iosokon" reclining chair, originally designed 1936, redesigned 1969.

Marcel Breuer, Pier Luigi Nervi, and Bernard Zehrfuss: UNESCO Headquarters, Paris, 1953–1958.

Marcel Breuer and Hamilton P. Smith: St. John's Abbey Church, Collegeville, Minnesota, 1953–1961.

Marcel Breuer Associates

Hedrich-Blessing, photographer; Marcel Breuer Associates

GOLD MEDAL FOR 1969   **WILLIAM WILSON WURSTER**

AWARDED ON JUNE 26, 1969
IN THE PALMER HOUSE BALLROOM
CHICAGO, ILLINOIS

William Wilson Wurster.

As an architect, he contributed to the liberation of architecture in the United States with a free and creative approach to design—undogmatic, non-doctrinaire, forthright in its response to local and regional conditions—demonstrated in his own work through buildings which, confident today, will in the future seem inevitable.

As an educator, he changed the course of architectural education through his vision, leadership and determination, expanding its scope to include concern for all the visual environment, thus providing the prototype for professional education today.

In all his endeavors, he has directed creative ability, professional achievement, influence and leadership to assert and preserve the universal values, individual freedoms and humanism which are essential to architecture.[1]

William Wilson Wurster was born on October 20, 1895, in Stockton, California. Family legend preserved one of his childhood inquiries: "How do chimneys stay on a roof?" Wurster attended Stockton High School and during summer vacations received his earliest architectural training in the office of E. B. Brown, a noted architect of the San Joaquin Valley. Wurster enrolled in the School of Architecture at the University of California in Berkeley in 1913, then directed by the famous architect John Galen Howard. After serving in the Merchant Marine during World War I, he graduated with honors in 1919. Wurster apprenticed with John Reid Jr. of San Francisco and Charles Dean in Sacramento, receiving his license to practice architecture in California in 1922. From 1922 to 1923 he traveled in Europe, and upon his return worked in the prominent New York office of Delano & Aldrich. In 1925 he returned to the Bay area and began his own practice, primarily doing houses. One of these early houses was the now-famous Warren Gregory Farmhouse, 1927–1929, whose simple forms, generous, open quality, and handling of local materials won the House Beautiful Award in 1931 and brought national recognition to Wurster. From 1930 to 1943 the Wurster office designed over 200 houses, and he was recognized as the leader of a group of San Francisco Bay area architects whose work was important in the development of mid-twentieth-century American domestic architecture. In 1937, Wurster traveled to Scandinavia and Eu-

rope with his close friend Thomas Church, the acclaimed west coast landscape architect, visiting the works of Gunnar Asplund, Kay Fisker, Le Corbusier, and, most importantly, Alvar Aalto. In 1940, Wurster married Catherine Bauer, noted planner and author of *Modern Housing,* and they had a daughter, Sarah. In 1943, Wurster attended the Graduate School of Design at Harvard University and studied regional planning, and in 1944 he was appointed dean of the School of Architecture and Planning at the Massachusetts Institute of Technology, where he remained until 1950. Wurster brought Aalto to MIT as a visiting professor and arranged for him to design his first American building, the Baker House Dormitories, for the institute. During this time President Truman appointed Wurster chairman of the National Park and Planning Commission. In 1951 he returned to California to become dean of architecture at the University of California, Berkeley, which he reorganized in 1957 into the College of Environmental Design. He remained as dean until 1963.

Internationally recognized as the "great American regionalist," Wurster's architecture respected the social and economic conditions suitable to the region and responded to the climatic variances, materials and methods of building, and the architectural heritage of the area. His buildings, whether rural, suburban, or urban, are consistently personal in expression, and he fitted each design to its pur-

1   Citation.

pose, its occupants, and its site. In 1946, Wurster formed a partnership with his long-time associates Theodore Bernardi and Donn Emmons, and this distinguished firm, whose work continued the Wurster tradition, received the AIA Firm Award in 1965 for significant architectural achievements in residential, educational, and commercial designs. Thus from such noted early houses—which include the Voss House, Big Sur, the Church House, Pasatiempo, the Clark House, Aptos Beach, and the Grover Townhouse, San Francisco—to the later great country and city houses—the Pope Ranch, Modesto, the Heller House, Lake Tahoe, the Henderson House, Hillsborough, the Salz House, San Francisco, and his own house at Stinson Beach—Wurster's ideas of simplicity, practicality, and beauty without pretentiousness remain an indelible trademark.

In addition to milestone Wurster buildings such as the Stern Dormitories, University of California, Berkeley (1939) and the Schuckl Canning Office Building, Sunnyvale (1942), the works of Wurster, Bernardi & Emmons include such notable contributions as the Center for Advanced Study of Behavioral Science, Palo Alto (1954), Golden Gateway Housing, San Francisco (1965), Cowell College, University of California Santa Cruz (1965), Ghirardelli Square, San Francisco (1967), and the World Headquarters of the Bank of America, San Francisco (1970).

As a person Wurster was a great humanitarian. As an architect, planner, and educator, his vision, leadership, and deep concern for human values in architecture remained with him until his death from Parkinson's disease in 1973; Catherine had died in 1964. What made Wurster unique was his dedication to the belief that architecture "must be measured by its meaning for people" and must be concerned with the everyday things which shape their physical and psychological needs. He believed that architects must be concerned with the total environment, and that the importance of architecture was not the isolated building but its relation to the people, the community, and all other buildings.

William Wilson Wurster's philosophy of simplicity, directness, and honesty of expression was reflected in his buildings. His was an architecture of understatement, not dogma.

CONTRIBUTED BY RICHARD PETERS

William Wilson Wurster: Gregory Farmhouse, Santa Cruz, California, 1927–1959.

William W. Wurster: Schuckl Canning Company Office, Sunnyvale, California, 1942.

RICHARD BUCKMINSTER FULLER

AWARDED ON JUNE 25, 1970
AT THE SHERATON HOTEL
BOSTON, MASSACHUSETTS

Richard Buckminster Fuller.

Hans Wild, photographer; courtesy of Buckminster Fuller

Engineer, inventor, mathematician, educator, cartographer, philosopher, poet, author, cosmogonist, industrial designer and architect, whose ideas, once considered visionary, have now received national and international acceptance.

A man responsible for the design of the strongest, lightest and most efficient means of enclosing space yet devised by man. A man who has used himself as a laboratory of human response, who has at all times concerned himself with the social implication of his discoveries, who has understood that real wealth is energy, and a man whose objective was humanity's comprehensive success in the universe.[1]

"Bucky" Fuller ranks as one of the popular and best-known architectural figures of the midtwentieth century. His influence has been both far-reaching and enigmatic. He has been "discovered" and "rediscovered" by both architects and the general public numerous times in the past fifty years, and yet his ultimate impact is difficult to assess. Measured in terms of built form, Fuller is a major success. There are over 100,000 geodesic domes in the world, all in some way related to his work and publicity of the building system. Yet he has gone further, proposing not simply a world-wide building system but a universal system of the utilization of resources, an imperative if Earth is to survive. He is, in a way, the ultimate conclusion of the architect-savior myth; Fuller's thoughts have touched on practically every aspect of human and natural world existence. He would define himself as not just an architect but also a universal philosopher, who has acted in roles as diverse as cartographer, mathematician, engineer, futurist, poet, teacher, environmentalist, machinist (he belongs to the International Association of Machinists), sailor (he is Lieutenant, U.S.N. Retired), industrial designer, and architect.

While to many he is "the man with the dome-house bug," the essence of Fuller's ideas goes far beyond. He has claimed: "I did not set out to design a house that hung from a pole, or to manufacture a new type of automobile, invent a new system of map projection, develop geodesic domes or Ener-

getic Geometry. I started with the Universe—as an organization of regenerative principles frequently manifest as energy systems of which all our experiences, and possible experiences, are only local instances. I could have ended up with a pair of flying slippers."[2]

Richard Buckminster Fuller was born in Milton, Massachusetts, in 1895 into an old New England family with a tradition for unconventional and nonconformist thought. One of his best known forebears, Margaret Fuller, was an early feminist and a leader of transcendentalism. Fuller's youth was rather wild, and he attempted Harvard College briefly and unsuccessfully. After a period of odd jobs, he landed in the Navy during World War I and spent a brief period at the Naval Academy at Annapolis. The naval experience was crucial for Fuller. Many of his later ideas of energy conservation, utilization, and self-sufficiency, along with actual forms, come from ships, rigging, and naval engineering. The concept of fitness of form leading to beauty, enunciated by Horatio Greenough in the 1840s with relation to sailing ships, became in a sense the foundation of Fuller's credo. In 1917 he married Anne Hewlett, the daughter of James Monroe Hewlett, a successful New York beaux-

1   Citation.

2   R. Buckminster Fuller and Robert Marks, *The Dymaxion World of Buckminster Fuller*, Doubleday, New York, 1973, p. 2.

arts-oriented architect and vice president of the AIA. While Fuller never had a conventional architectural education, and therein undoubtedly lies one of his strengths, he certainly knew traditional architecture.

After the war Fuller again passed through a series of jobs; perhaps most importantly he founded with his father-in-law a building-block company and acquired firsthand experience in both building and manufacturing. The death of a daughter in 1922 brought a prolonged depression and ultimately a profound moral commitment to improve the world. Throughout the remainder of the 1920s, Fuller experimented with a variety of ideas regarding shelter and transportation and attempted to maximize the most advanced technology available. Nondoctrinaire in comparison to European International-Style architects such as Le Corbusier and Mies, Fuller attempted to design a house completely determined by prefabrication, function, and portability. The result, the 4D Dymaxion House, 1927–1928, was one of the most electrifying images of the day, though never built. This was followed by a host of other Dymaxion designs, such as the car, 1930–1934, and the bathroom, 1937. During the 1930s, Fuller's horizons expanded. The idea of technological determinism was applied by him to a variety of concerns, from resource management to world-wide energy systems.

The consummation of Fuller's architectural career came in 1948 when the first geodesic dome was constructed and subsequently patented. Over the years a number of different structural trusses and grids have been developed for the dome; however, the basic principle of the dome has always remained the same: to use minimal structural elements, to be lightweight (hence energy efficient) and flexible, and to encompass practically any volume. For Fuller, the geodesic dome became the ultimate building system, being applicable to almost any situation, from the smallest domestic shelter to the entire city. The former has been accomplished many times; the latter still remains. The principle of the dome has been used in a variety of situations, from U.S. defense outposts to theaters, banks, and factories. The dome ultimately became a symbol of American ingenuity. One was used for the United States Pavilion at Expo 67 in Montreal.

Fuller's success has been compounded by a strong moral purpose and an ability to seize publicity. Practically every movement and utterance of the man is recorded in the press. He has authored over twenty books, countless articles, and many patents. And yet Fuller has not been simply a "paper" architect—a science-fiction designer up in the stratosphere—but a man of action, who has seen many of his ideas come to fruition through his own promotion, and also a man who has at least awakened some people to the problems of modern technology.

Buckminster Fuller: Dymaxion Dwelling Machine, prototype, Wichita, Kansas, 1944–1945.

Buckminster Fuller: "Big Geodesic Dome over Mid-Manhattan," project, 1950.

GOLD MEDAL FOR 1971 **LOUIS ISIDORE KAHN**

AWARDED ON JUNE 24, 1971
IN THE GRAND BALLROOM OF COBO HALL
DETROIT, MICHIGAN

Courtesy of Joan Ruggles, photographer

Louis Isidore Kahn.

Architect, educator, "form-giver" in the highest tradition of his profession — through his design and his teaching, he has influenced architects of the current generation as much as Corbu, Mies, and Gropius influenced those of an earlier period.

He has always strived to incorporate in his work the essential nature of the purpose which the finished building will serve — to capture in architecture the essence of the life which will take place within. . . .

We honor a man whose architectural genius is equalled only by his tireless generosity in sharing his wealth of ideas with colleagues and students.[1]

Louis Isidore Kahn was born on the Baltic island of Saaremaa, Estonia, in 1902 and emigrated with his parents, Leopold and Bertha Kahn, to Philadelphia as a young boy in 1905. His upbringing was traditional Jewish, and his later pursuit of knowledge had a Talmudic, questioning quality. He studied architecture at the University of Pennsylvania (then following the beaux-arts tradition under the leadership of Paul Philippe Cret) from 1920 to 1924.

After graduating, Kahn worked for several architects, including Cret, and traveled in Europe. He was a consultant to various housing authorities and planning commissions, and was associated with George Howe and Oscar Stonorov from 1941 to 1948. In 1930 he married Esther Virginia Israeli. Noted as a teacher and philosopher as well as a designer, Kahn taught at Yale from 1948 to 1957 and at the University of Pennsylvania from 1957 to 1974. He died in 1974. He was concerned with ultimate being, which he called "Order," using the metaphor of silence and light.

Kahn related three directions in modern architecture: the beaux-arts, from which he took a sense of hierarchy; European modernism, represented by Mies and Le Corbusier, from whom he took the austerity of an unornamented architecture, a reverence for materials, and a sense of structure as a source of order; and the organic architecture of Sullivan and Wright, who went beyond material functionalism to express the inner essence of the building. Kahn would begin design with the question, What does this building want to be? implying an inner essence.

Owing to the depression and World War II, and to his creative struggles, Kahn's first significant com-

mission did not come until he was fifty: the Yale University Art Gallery in New Haven (1951–1953), which had the seeds of his first ideas — the separation of served and servant spaces, the integration of mechanical systems, the use of structure to define space, and a clear use of materials. These ideas received full expression in the Richards Medical Research Building and Biology Building in Philadelphia (1957–1961), which quickly brought him international recognition.

In the Salk Institute in La Jolla, California (1959–1965), Kahn used the sculptural richness of poured-in-place concrete and created a contemplative space in the center court. In the National Assembly Hall in Dacca, Bangladesh (1962–1974), Kahn revived the use of the central space. In the Phillips Academy Library at Exeter, New Hampshire (1967–1972), he responded to how a person comes together with the book in light (Plate 22). In the Kimbell Art Museum, Fort Worth, Texas (1966–1972), and in the Yale Center for British Art and Studies, New Haven (1969–1974), Kahn combined a sensitive use of materials with a strong organizing structural grid to create spaces to present paintings in natural light.

Vincent Scully said: "Nobody ever gave off so much light. It was a physical light that came from the activity of his imagination and the aliveness of his intellect."[2]

CONTRIBUTED BY JOHN LOBELL

---

1   Citation.

2   Quoted in John Lobell, *Between Silence and Light: Spirit in the Architecture of Louis I. Kahn*, Shambhala, Boulder, Colorado, 1979, p. 4, from "Unpublished transcripts of memorials for Louis Kahn held in Philadelphia and New York in 1974."

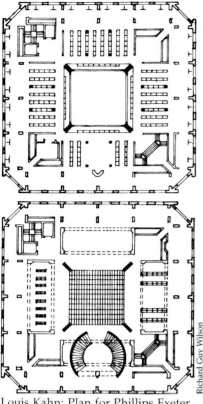

Louis Kahn: Plan for Phillips Exeter Academy Library, Exeter, New Hampshire, 1967–1972.

Phillips Exeter Academy Library, exterior. (See Plate 20.)

GOLD MEDAL FOR 1972 **PIETRO BELLUSCHI**

AWARDED ON MAY 10, 1972
IN THE RICE HOTEL BALLROOM
HOUSTON, TEXAS

Pietro Belluschi.

His buildings evoke the essence of place, respect the demands of function and the disciplines of structure and material, and respond with eloquent simplicity to all aspects of human need and aspiration. His creative counsel, both as educator and as consultant, has quickened the architectural comprehension of his students and his colleagues alike, and stimulated them to new heights of architectural achievement. His pioneering service as architectural adviser to public agencies has significantly advanced the cause of public architecture and notably contributed to the elevation of environmental quality. His vision of architecture transcends dogma, whether old or new; exalts integrity of purpose in the service of society, unites the wisdom of feeling with the discipline of knowledge, and exemplifies the renaissance of the architect as "interpreter of the new order" and "prophet of his age."[1]

Pietro Belluschi's career has been one of seemingly separate and distinct stages, each complete unto itself. Yet overall there is a certain symmetry and a tendency toward a particular type of design approach. He has been at the forefront of the American architectural profession since the late 1930s, first as a designer, later as an educator and spokesman, and finally as a design collaborator. The buildings Belluschi has been involved with number well over 1000 and include some of the most important designs of the past fifty years, along with some of the most controversial.

Belluschi was born in Ancona, Italy, in 1899, served in the Italian army during World War I, and then studied architectural engineering at the University of Rome, obtaining a degree in 1922. He came to the United States in 1923 as an exchange graduate fellow to study civil engineering at Cornell University. The United States awoke him: "Coming to America changed my life to a greater extent than I thought possible. From a dreamy, lazy boy I became almost overnight an aggressive and determined man—determined to succeed at all costs as a student, as a person and as an architect."[2] After obtaining a degree, he worked for a brief period with a mining company in Idaho and then secured a position in 1925 with an old and respected Portland, Oregon, firm, A. E. Doyle & Associates. The origins of the Doyle firm went back to McKim, Mead & White's work in the northwest in the 1880s, and their work was in the romantic-eclectic beaux-arts

vein. Belluschi quickly became Doyle's chief designer and in 1943 purchased the firm, renaming it Pietro Belluschi & Associates. In 1950 the firm was acquired as the Portland office of Skidmore, Owings & Merrill. From 1951 to 1965 Belluschi was the dean of architecture at MIT, helping the school to maintain its national prestige as a center for modern architectural thought and experimentation. Belluschi also developed a career as a national spokesman for architecture, traveling almost continuously and serving on panels, juries, and advisory commissions, including the National Fine Arts Commission, the Foreign Buildings program for new embassies for the Department of State, and the Air Force Academy at Colorado Springs. Concurrently he developed a career as a design associate and consultant, working either as the primary concept designer or an adjudicator on projects as varied as the Pan American Building in New York (with Walter Gropius and Emery Roth & Sons) and the Bank of America World Headquarters, San Francisco (with Wurster, Bernardi & Emmons and Skidmore, Owings & Merrill). He continues to act in this capacity after retirement from MIT, first with offices in Boston and, since 1973 in Portland, where he lives in a house he designed in 1939.

Belluschi's architecture has included many seem-

---

1   Citation.

2   Jo Stubblebine (ed.), *The Northwest Architecture of Pietro Belluschi*, F. W. Dodge, New York, 1953, p. 1–2.

ingly different design approaches, from canonical International-Style abstraction to a woodsy vernacular. What he has maintained is a spirit of independence which allowed him to explore new approaches and images. The Bank of America Headquarters in San Francisco, 1965–1970, the design concept of which was his, broke completely with the commonly accepted Miesian notions of the high-rise building. The design prefigured many of the 1970s experiments in skyscraper design.

Belluschi's architecture attempts to speak about its function and also its location, not through historical references but through a process of abstraction that leads to either simplification or elaboration of elements that recall traditional forms. Belluschi first appeared on the national architectural scene in the later 1930s as a modern regionalist, utilizing forms, shapes, and materials that recalled barns, farmhouses, and cabins of the northwest. With low-pitched roofs, wood siding, exposed timber beams, his houses fit into the landscape, and yet they had some of the angular geometry, open plans, and object fixation of more radical-modern architecture. His church designs also followed much the same approach, retaining vestiges of bell towers and steeples. The Equitable Building in Portland, 1943–1948, exploded in the national architectural consciousness as an early International-Style high-rise. It contained all of the radical-modernist trademarks: a glistening aluminum skin, green glass, structure emphatically revealed, and a sealed environment. Certainly Belluschi drew upon radical-modernist thought for the Equitable design, though in restrospect, the design can also be seen as an abstraction and simplification of the essential nature of office buildings. Some critics have labeled his earlier architecture "soft" modernism, indicating his interest in texture, color, and freedom for the extremes of machine-age geometry and polemics.

Belluschi's later work, such as the Bank of America in San Francisco, generally escaped from the extremes of radical modernism. The First Lutheran Church in Boston's Back Bay, 1957, is typical of Belluschi's extreme "understatement," as he described it.[3] Located on a busy intersection, the "stern" exterior calmly reflects on the more agitated movements of its surroundings, especially the flamboyant high-Victorian Gothic First Church by Ware & Van Brunt across the street (since remodeled by Paul Rudolph after a fire). The building indicates his role as a conciliator and a temporizer, attempting to create a new synthesis that fits more easily into the city and the natural landscape.

---

3 "Four Houses of Worship," *Progressive Architecture*, vol. 40, June 1959, p. 114.

Pietro Belluschi: First Lutheran Church, Boston, Massachusetts, 1953–1957.

Pietro Belluschi: Kerr House, Geaghart, Oregon, 1941.

GOLD MEDAL FOR 1977 **RICHARD JOSEF NEUTRA**

AWARDED ON JUNE 5, 1977
AT SPRECKELS THEATRE
SAN DIEGO, CALIFORNIA
ACCEPTED BY DIONE NEUTRA

Courtesy of Dione Neutra

Richard Josef Neutra.

Richard Joseph Neutra, FAIA, whose work has profoundly influenced the architectural thought of this century and whose timeless buildings testify to the lasting significance of his achievement. With keen and original insight, he brought forth an architectural style that belonged uniquely to the Southern California landscape and way of life.

He was among the first architects to explore the relationship between biology and behavior, and the design of optimal environments for human activity. Form-giver, teacher, mentor, communicator, he exemplified all that he felt an architect should be: "a coordinator, an applied physiologist, a biological realist, full of sympathy for man."[1]

Richard Neutra is a seminal figure in the development of radical modernism in the United States. His career is archetypal in his passionate belief in the need for a new architecture, the struggle for acceptance, the role of the architect as writer and polemicist, the concern with social and physiological benefits, the problem of architecture as art, and the concept of serving mass society and establishing a new order. Stylistically, Neutra was most closely allied with the International Style, and he helped to introduce it to the United States in the 1920s. Later he would transform this predominately European expression into a particularly regional, southern California idiom. He advocated the designer's involvement with all aspects of life, from the most intimate to regional planning, and he was one of the first American members of CIAM.

Neutra was born in Vienna, Austria, in 1892 and grew up in the sophisticated cultural milieu of secessionist art and architecture, atonal music, and Freudian psychology. He came under the influence of Adolf Loos while attending the Technische Hochschule in Vienna, and after a period in the Austrian army and in Switzerland, he secured a position in Berlin with Erich Mendelsohn during the early 1920s. He was in Germany at the critical point when the new European modern architecture took form, and he worked with Mendelsohn on several projects. America and the work of Frank Lloyd Wright and Louis Sullivan had long remained an

attraction to Neutra, and in 1923 he emigrated to the United States with his new wife, Dione. He met Sullivan who was practically on his deathbed, worked briefly with Holabird & Roche (later Holabrid & Root), and for a few months with Frank Lloyd Wright at Taliesin.

Neutra's goal, however, remained Los Angeles, where an old acquaintance from Vienna, Rudolph Schindler—who had formerly been with Wright—had established an architectural practice. Between 1926 and 1930, Neutra and Schindler collaborated on a number of projects including the League of Nations competition. Their entry—with only Neutra's name attached—was circulated in Europe along with the projects of Le Corbusier and Hannes Meyer. In 1926, Neutra published *Wie Baut Amerika*, a book devoted to advanced American structural systems. In 1927, Neutra's designs for the Jardinette Apartments in Los Angeles were erected, notable for their usage of reinforced-concrete frame construction, horizontal fenestration, and lack of ornament, all features of the yet-unnamed International Style. At the same time he gathered about him a group of students—notably Harwell Hamilton Harris and Gregory Ain, who would become well-known architects in their own right—and worked on a continuing project, "Rush City Reformed," a speculative city of the future that would serve as a

---

1 Citation.

216

generator of designs throughout his life.

In 1929 came the Dr. Philip Lovell "Health House," which remains perhaps his best-known work. Sited on a steep hillside in Los Angeles, the building appears as a series of floating white trays, abstract, and machine-crafted. The steel frame was erected in forty work-hours, and the enclosing white panels were sprayed gunite (concrete), shot from hoses. The technological features of construction and the health equipment, swimming pool, gymnasium, playground, Jacuzzi, and so forth were adroitly publicized by Neutra. Harwell Hamilton Harris summed up Neutra's attitude at this time: "for Neutra, Sweet's Catalogue was the Holy Bible and Henry Ford the holy virgin."[2] A Ford headlight rim was used in the Lovell house as a stair light.

By 1930, Neutra was a leading American radical modernist, a position confirmed by his inclusion in the 1932 Museum of Modern Art International-Style exhibit. Notable projects that expanded upon European functionalist principles came forth, and at the same time, he began to investigate, more seriously than most other modernists, the biological and environmental possibilities of the new architecture. This concern emerged in a series of articles and books, the most notable of which were *Architecture of Social Concern in Regions of Mild Climate* (1948) and *Survival Through Design* (1954). The Corona School in the Bell area of Los Angeles, 1935, dem-

onstrated the possibilities of minimal enclosure, with the low, one-story configuration, outdoor corridors, and entire walls of sliding-glass doors. The 1942 Channel Heights Public Housing Development in San Pedro, consisting of 600 units, was a notable demonstration of his social consciousness in providing decent housing at minimal cost.

In the 1950s and 1960s Neutra's practice expanded considerably, with commissions throughout the United States and abroad. He was associated in the Robert E. Alexander firm of Los Angeles from 1949 to 1958 and from 1965 onward with his son Dion Neutra. While much of this later work was at a larger scale and more institutional, his best and most characteristic work remained the single-family house. The James D. Moore house, 1950–1952, Ojai, California, is an elegantly crafted minimal pavilion of thin planes and glass which integrates interior and exterior space as a single continuum. Lush vegetation surrounds the pool and the house, typifying in many people's minds the paradigm of the modern house. In 1954 it won the AIA First Honor Award.

An imposing figure, tall, and at times arrogant, Neutra could be a demanding architect for clients to work with. He made himself a mythic persona, larger than life, and then lived up to it, establishing himself as a leading figure of modernism. He made the localized response to the southern California climate an almost universal radical-modernist expression. Heavily honored with awards, doctorates, and medals, Neutra died in 1970.

2   Esther McCoy, *Vienna to Los Angeles: Two Journeys*, Arts and Architecture Press, Santa Monica, 1979, p. 8.

Richard Neutra: Mr. and Mrs. James D. Moore House, Ojai, California, 1950–1952.

Courtesy of Dione Neutra

GOLD MEDAL FOR 1978 **PHILIP CORTELYOU JOHNSON**

AWARDED ON MAY 24, 1978
IN THE FAIRMONT HOTEL
DALLAS, TEXAS

Philip Cortelyou Johnson.

Johnson/Burgee

A distinguished career dedicated to the creation of masterworks of architecture. He has articulated and demonstrated for us the concept that architecture exists in time as well as space. He has given us a new definition of "monumentality" at every scale, from the personal residence to the commercial complex and the contemporary cathedral. Above all, he has given the world a body of distinguished work which exemplifies his belief that architecture is, first and foremost, art.[1]

By virtue of his buildings, writings, and encouragement of young architects and students Philip Johnson has occupied a position at the forefront of architectural theory, historiography, and design for nearly fifty years. In addition, Johnson's social grace, and his highly articulate, even commanding, platform presence affords him a unique influence over the public's interpretation of architecture.

Born to affluence in Cleveland, Ohio, in 1906, Johnson studied philosophy and classics at Harvard College. After traveling in Europe, he collaborated in 1932 with Henry-Russell Hitchcock and Alfred Barr on "Modern Architects," the inaugural architectural exhibition at the Museum of Modern Art in New York. In the same year, again with Hitchcock, he published *The International Style*. Together, the book and the exhibition offered to Americans their first systematic introduction to the forms and some of the ideals of Europeran modernism and significantly affected its course in American architecture for the following twenty-five years or more. The authors' prescriptive style emphasized an aesthetic, rather than utopian, viewpoint. In the early 1930s, Johnson continued to propagandize on behalf of modernism at the MOMA, through exhibitions and special events such as Le Corbusier's first stormy visit to the United States in 1935.

In 1941, after a foray into politics and political journalism, Johnson returned to Harvard to study architecture. The comparative lateness with which he came to the field and the breadth of his previous experience as a critic and museum director com-

bined to give Johnson a particular clarity of perception about his own work and that of others. Since the late 1920s Johnson's chosen mentor was Mies van der Rohe rather than Walter Gropius or Marcel Breuer, then principal design critics at Harvard. Thus Johnson frequently found himself at odds with his teachers, designing two solutions for many projects, one to please them, one in the manner of Mies to please himself. In 1942, Johnson built for his own use a house on Ash Street in Cambridge, based on Mies's courtyard houses of a decade earlier. In the Ash Street house Johnson established the principal direction for his work over the next fifteen years. His association with Mies deepened when, after serving in the Army, he returned to the MOMA as director of its Department of Architecture. In 1947, Johnson organized the first major exhibition of Mies's work and wrote a monograph which remains the standard text.

The development of Johnson's highly personal estate in New Canaan, Connecticut, began in 1949 with his Glass House which has become one of the few widely known and admired icons of American modernism. Given contemporary architecture's functionalist and antihistorical pretensions, his frank publication in the *Architectural Review* in the following year of the Glass House's derivative nature (drawing upon Greek planning, Schinkel, Ledoux, and others) was a daringly inconoclastic act and heralded his later self-description as a "functional eclectic."

1 Citation.

218

Johnson's association with Mies was to climax with their collaboration on the Seagram Building (1956–1958), which effectively codified the typology of the modernist skyscraper and led to a revision of zoning laws across the country. Although the Munson-Williams-Proctor Institute of 1960 continued his use of a Miesian vocabulary, it combined with a statically classicizing plan and a character distinctly indebted to that of Ledoux, thereby heralding a new, more explicitly historicizing phase in Johnson's work.

In the late 1950s and early 1960s Johnson, then in partnership with Richard Foster, carried out a series of public commissions, among them the Amon Carter Museum, the Sheldon Memorial Art Gallery, and the New York State Theater at Lincoln Center. The neoclassicism evoked in these works coincides with what some critics see as Johnson's most problematic phase, in which his attempts to make more expressive the already-codified Miesian vocabulary through an exploration of themes derived from historical examples were not always well integrated.

For a short time after Foster's resignation from the firm Johnson practiced on his own, but since 1967 he has been in partnership with John Burgee, a collaboration which has resulted in some of Johnson's most provocative and satisfying work since the early 1950s. Among the works of his partnership, the IDS Center in Minneapolis and the Crystal Cathedral continue to historicize Mies, harking back now to the 1920s experiments in their dependence for effect on the qualities of glass in reflection; yet each brings with it a positive sense of interior space at a public scale eschewed by Mies. Penzoil Place in Houston epitomizes the modernist skyscraper's tendency towards minimal sculpture, although it also recalls the drawings of Hugh Ferriss, in which the analogy between buildings and crystalline forms was poetically posited. More recently, the AT&T Building, New York, (Plate 5) and the PPG Tower, Pittsburgh, as well as the façade of 1001 Fifth Avenue, New York, and a small office building for the Gerald Hines Interests at Sugarland, Texas, display a new depth of commitment to the specific forms of the past, and demonstrate that the course of architectural history before the modernist revolution is no more finite than it has been since. This sudden flowering of historical contextualism and recovery of issues and possibilities deliberately ignored in the work of so many of Johnson's contemporaries testify to Johnson's continuing ability to refresh himself. For Johnson, more than any other architect of his time, has understood a key characteristic of our moment in history; for Johnson, change is the only constant.

CONTRIBUTED BY ROBERT A. M. STERN

Johnson/Burgee and Edward F. Baker Associates: IDS Center, Minneapolis, Minnesota, 1969–1973.

IDS Center, Crystal Court.

GOLD MEDAL FOR 1979 IEOH MING PEI

AWARDED ON JUNE 6, 1979
AT MUSIC HALL CONVENTION CENTER
KANSAS CITY, MISSOURI

Ieoh Ming Pei.

Jack Mitchell, photographer; I. M. Pei & Partners

In recognition of a career devoted to the creation of outstanding architecture. His buildings—whether dedicated to living, learning, science, commerce, or the enjoyment of art—are themselves works of art to be enjoyed. The body of his work speaks eloquently of its architect's creative genius, his intellect, his urbanity, and above all his humanity.[1]

The career and work of I. M. Pei transcends a number of issues which have preoccupied architects around the world in recent years. He is the head of a large office with several design partners and several hundred employees, a "General Motors-Type firm," according to one critic.[2] He is well-known for his involvement with developers as the architect of large superblock buildings, and yet he and his firm have demonstrated an ability to produce quality architecture, urban in nature. His designs, whether the hooded towers of the National Center for Atmospheric Research, Boulder, Colorado, 1961–1967, or the knife-edge-sharp corners of the east extension of the National Gallery, Washington, D.C., 1969–1978, are elegant, their forms and details superbly refined (Plate 4). His buildings are immensely popular with both the general public and architects. He has succeeded in domesticating radical modernism, in making it acceptable both as a monument and in the urban context. While not given to theory or long-winded pronouncements, Pei has subtly questioned and transformed radical modernism, showing a concern for image and creating abstract and yet vital buildings. He has been one of the more highly honored architects of recent years: Medal of Honor, AIA New York chapter, 1963; Thomas Jefferson Memorial Medal, University of Virginia, 1976; D.F.A., University of Pennsylvania, 1970; Rennsselaer Polytechnic Institute, Troy, New York, 1978; LL.D., Chinese University of Hong Kong, 1970; Honorary Fellow, Royal Institute of British Architects; and member, Ameri-

can Academy of Arts and Sciences, National Academy of Design, and American Academy and Institute of Arts and Letters.

I. M. Pei was born in Canton, China, in 1917. Through travels with his father, a banker, Pei became interested in architecture, and in 1935 came to the United States, intending to enter the School of Architecture at the University of Pennsylvania. The beaux-arts emphasis on drawing at Pennsylvania daunted him, and he later enrolled at MIT in architectural engineering. Subsequently, though, through the initiative of Dean W. Emerson, a former student of Laloux, Pei became reconciled to the beaux-arts system—still in control at MIT in the later 1930s—and graduated with a degree in architecture. Pei stayed on in Cambridge, working for a number of firms, marrying Eileen Loo, who was a student in landscape architecture at Harvard, and through her, making the acquaintance of Gropius and Breuer and other Harvard students. From 1943 to 1945 he worked with the National Defense Research Committee and subsequently received a masters degree in architecture from Harvard, teaching there until 1948. In 1948, William Zeckendorf of Webb & Knapp, Inc., one of the largest developers in the United States, hired Pei as the director of architecture and research and plunged him into the boiler-hot world of urban redevelopment. The con-

---

1   Citation.

2   Peter Blake, "I. M. Pei & Partners," *Architecture Plus*, vol. 1, February 1973, p. 52.

tact with Zeckendorf was frowned on by the professional ethics of the AIA at the time; subsequently, it has been changed. Pei worked for Zeckendorf full-time until 1955 and then more intermittently until 1962. Their work included Mile High Center in Denver, Place Ville-Marie in Montreal, Society Hill in Philadelphia, and Kips Bay Plaza in New York. Pei remembers the time with Zeckendorf as an awakening: "I learned . . . the big picture, the flow of economic, political and civic decision, the importance of seeing land as a precious raw material to be carefully used, since urban land was worth millions. . . . I see a lot more than most architects because of the Zeckendorf education."[3] The consequence is that Pei became a favorite of corporations and developers looking for an architect who would both speak their language of economics and give them a quality architectural image. The disaster of the John Hancock Tower in Boston of the mid-1970s with windows falling out appeared to be the end of the Pei involvement with developers. Yet ultimately the problem appeared to have been caused by material failure, and Pei returned stronger than ever as the architect of large-scale, income-producing urban projects.

Pei's big breakthrough came in the early 1960s when he received the commission for the Everson Art Museum at Syracuse University, a commission he describes as having been turned down by all the big-name architects—Bunshaft and Johnson—since it had a small budget and art collection. He, however, "saw it as a chance to do something," and the result was a minimalist creation of interlocking geometries. At the same time he received the National Center for Atmospheric Research commission. These two buildings, indebted as Pei openly

3 I. M. Pei, "The Sowing and Reaping of Shape," *The Christian Science Monitor*, March 16, 1978, p. 33. See also William Zeckendorf and Edward McCreary, *Zeckendorf*, Holt, Reinhardt Winston, New York, 1970.

admits to Le Corbusier's concrete work, moved beyond him and incorporated some of the ideas of Louis Kahn, another hero of Pei's. Yet influences do not explain the drama, the quiet, brooding hoods, the almost archaic quality of the National Center for Atmospheric Research. Pei in a sense rediscovered architecture as an art, design as the ultimate act, a heritage of his beaux-arts training, subluminated under the neo-Bauhaus orthodoxy of Harvard in the 1940s. As a consequence of the success of these buildings he was chosen as the architect of the John F. Kennedy Library in 1964, a project of long delays and interminable political wrangles, which finally opened in 1979, as well as of east-wing extension to the National Gallery in Washington, D.C., in 1969. While there are many other works of major importance that can be pointed to, such as the Dallas City Hall, 1971–1978, the National Gallery extension ranks as the most important. A large courtyard building, the galleries are sublimated to the major event of the building, the large 16,000-square-foot atrium, covered by a tetrahedral space-frame skylight. The form of the building is really a trapezoid cut into two triangles and then further subdivided. The plan has all the qualities of a radical de stijl painting by Theo von Doesburg. The severity of the geometry is subdued by texture, color, and on the interior, the suspended bridges, vistas to the exterior, and lighting. It is clearly a building of procession. On the exterior, the color and scale make it a continuation of the main building of the National Gallery, designed by John Russell Pope in 1936, in the classical beaux-arts style. Pei's extension is profoundly beaux-arts inspired, not in style but in geometry and the processional urban nature. His architecture is classical at its base, a language of abstract geometry that he transforms into building programs and human purposes and ultimately transcends to become an inspiring force.

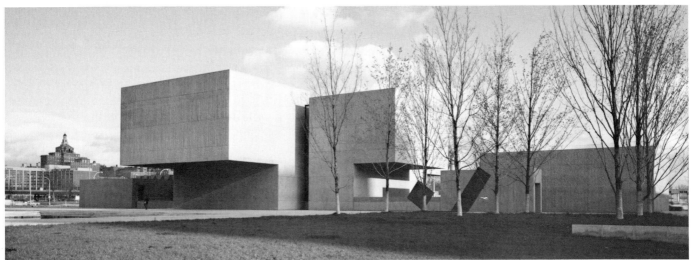

I. M. Pei & Partners: Everson Museum of Art, Syracuse University, Syracuse, New York, 1968.

Ezra Stoller © ESTO, photographer: I. M. Pei & Partners

GOLD MEDAL FOR 1981 JOSEP LLUIS SERT

AWARDED ON MAY 20, 1981
AT THE MINNEAPOLIS CONVENTION CENTER
MINNEAPOLIS, MINNESOTA

F. Catala-Roca, photographer; courtesy of Josep L. Sert

Josep Lluis Sert.

Dedicated to enriching the quality of life. Through his example, he has taught both architects and laymen to view individual buildings in the context of the entire urban fabric and the necessity for creative solutions to housing, working and leisure environments that will help to unite, rather than divide, the human family.[1]

Josep Lluis Sert has stood for several of the fundamental tenets of radical modernism: the need for a new expression, the vitality of the unconscious vernacular, and the belief of the total integration of art, architecture, and city planning. According to Sigfried Giedion, "Sert's talents are closely bound up with the organization of the city, with an architecture that has its roots in Mediterranean culture and, inseparable from these, with an intensive relationship with art."[2] For over fifty years Sert has been at the forefront of modern architecture, occupying a succession of important positions and producing seminal buildings that illustrate the changing concerns from the early reductivist puritanism to the later vocabulary of plastic forms, luminescent expanding space, and a sense of connection with the surrounding environment. Sert continues to view himself as a modernist and to claim: "No. Modern Architecture is not dead. It has not yet followed its full course. If you have a sense of history and compare it with other great changes in different periods, you will find it is still young and very much alive."[3]

He was born in Barcelona, Spain, in 1902 and trained first as a painter before attending the Escuela Superior de Arquitectura from which he graduated in 1929. During a trip to Paris in 1926, Sert discovered the writing of Le Corbusier and returned to Barcelona to organize an informal student avant-garde group. In 1929, Sert secured a position in the office of Le Corbusier and Pierre Jeanneret in Paris and remained there until 1931. He worked on the second League of Nations de-

signs and the plan for Rio de Janeiro, the Mundaneum, and the house for Mme de Mandrot. Sert and Le Corbusier maintained a close connection throughout the latter's life, and owing to Sert's influence, Le Corbusier received his only American commission, the Carpenter Center for the Visual Arts at Harvard University, Cambridge, Massachusetts, 1961–1964. (Sert acted as the supervising architect on the building, and his hand is directly observable in the refined details.)

In Barcelona between 1931 and 1937, Sert's designs indicate the influence of the International-Style manner of Le Corbusier, along with interests in local vernacular. This latter was also probably partially inspired by Corbusier's renewed vernacular interests, as in the de Mandrot house. Yet, Sert introduced a particularly Spanish mediterranean aspect of harsh contrasts of light and shade, solid and void, sunswept patios, and the building as a sequence of interconnected units. In 1981 he said, "Light has always been a constant concern."[4]

Sert attended the second CIAM congress in 1929, and in Spain he founded a branch, GATEPAC, which designed several projects for the Barcelona area. He helped draft the Charter of Athens in 1933

1   Citation.

2   Quoted in Knud Bastlund, *José Luis Sert*, Editions d'Architecture, Zurich, 1967.

3   Josep Lluis Sert, "Gold Medal Speech," Minneapolis, Minnesota, May 20, 1981.

4   Personal communication, June 18, 1981.

222

and edited CIAM's *Can Our Cities Survive?* (1942). From 1947 to 1956 and the dispersal of CIAM, Sert served as president. The urban-planning studies Sert did in the 1930s served as the basis of his career in the United States from 1939 to the late 1950s when he was associated in New York with Paul Lester Wiener and Paul Schulz as the Town Planning Associates. A series of major city plans and assorted buildings were produced for Brazil, Peru, Colombia, Cuba, and Venezuela. While few of these were carried out, the urban designs in particular were very influential with the continuous lineal park spaces, tight clustering of housing units, and at the same time, the solitary object fixation of the major public and commercial buildings.

From 1953 to 1969 Sert served as dean of the School of Design at Harvard University. Also in 1953 he began a design practice in Cambridge, and in 1958 formed Sert, Jackson & Gourley Associates, which became Sert, Jackson & Associates in 1963. He has received many awards and honors including the Thomas Jefferson Medal in Architecture, 1970, and the Gold Medal of the Académie d'Architecture, Paris, 1975.

Since the late 1950s his architecture has reflected Le Corbusier's later more plastic and sensual manner, as in Ronchamp, but also Sert's increased interest in the vernacular and the work of Gaudi and his close friendship with the painter Joan Miró. Sert's buildings become more extensive structures that are not unique objects located apart from their surroundings, but an element of the cityscape. An exhibit and book he helped prepare on the Barcelona architect Antoni Gaudí in 1960 reintroduced him to a figure he had "hated" in his youth.[5] Similarly, Miró, who Sert had known since the 1930s, can be seen as increasing in influence through the almost surrealistic bulges, hoods, and details that come to occupy Sert's formal vocabulary. In the United States, Sert's most notable buildings were large complexes, such as the Peabody Terrace Married Student Housing, 1963–1965, and the Undergraduate Science Center, 1970–1973, at Harvard, in Cambridge. These buildings, with their eccentric fenestration and revelation of function, are entirely rational, scientific, and functional. Yet they also project a feeling of collision of forces, or eccentric and unfathomed dreamlike expressions. Certainly this is the impression one receives with Sert's two major museums for the Maeght Foundation in Saint-Paul-de-Vence, France, 1959–1964, and the Miró Center in Barcelona, 1972–1975. In both cases, modern and largely surrealistic art fills the buildings. Underneath they are entirely rational and functional structures, and many of the features such as the light hoods are entirely sensible, yet the expression has a sense of dissonance, of age and newness, of rough against smooth, of flat walls contrasting with bulging sensuous forms. Sert's rich, plastic language is one of the few serious modern architectural expressions which has drawn upon and has an affinity with surrealism. He died in March 1983.

5   Ibid.

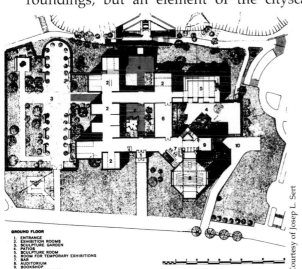

GROUND FLOOR
1. ENTRANCE
2. EXHIBITION ROOMS
3. SCULPTURE GARDEN
4. PATIOS
5. SCULPTURE ROOM
6. ROOM FOR TEMPORARY EXHIBITIONS
7. BAR
8. AUDITORIUM
9. BOOKSHOP
10. SERVICE ENTRANCE

Miro Foundation, plans.

Courtesy of Josep L. Sert

Sert, Jackson & Associates: Miro Foundation, Barcelona, Spain, 1972–1975.

F. Catala-Roca, photographer; courtesy of Josep L. Sert

GOLD MEDAL FOR 1982 **ROMALDO GIURGOLA**

AWARDED ON JUNE 9, 1982
AT THE ROYAL HAWAIIAN HOTEL
HONOLULU, HAWAII

Romaldo Giurgola.

A brilliant designer whose work has earned him worldwide recognition, he is also a gifted teacher and administrator, a talented writer, superlative draftsman and a selfless contributor to the advancement of the profession. In the man and his work are combined a profound respect for the past and a confident vision of the future.[1]

The Gold Medal award to Romaldo Giurgola came shortly after the announcement that his design had won the competition for the new national Parliament House of Australia in Canberra. Giurgola's design, a graceful reflection upon the abstract 1911 "City Beautiful" plan of Canberra by an earlier American architect, Walter Burley Griffin, has classical elements while at the same time displaying a sensitive response to the landscape. The building does not posture on top of the hill but sits below it, both completing the land axis and opening up the landscape beyond. The design is monumental. A sequence of particulated spaces recalls the beaux-arts, and the imagery, while abstract, contains hints of broken pediments, triumphal arches, and other remembered fragments of history. Giurgola combines the gifts of a teacher, a conceptual theorist, and a designer.

Romaldo Giurgola was born in 1920 in Rome; his father was a well-known architect. He graduated from the University of Rome in 1948 and came to the United States in 1949 as a Fulbright Fellow at Columbia University where he remained to receive a M.S. in architecture in 1951. Between 1952 and 1957 he worked as an editor of the magazines *Interiors* and *Industrial Design*. In 1954 he began teaching at the University of Pennsylvania, remaining there until 1967 when he transferred to Columbia University, first as chairman, and subsequently as Ware Professor of Architecture. In 1958, with Ehr-

man B. Mitchell, Jr., he formed the firm of Mitchell/Giurgola with an office in Philadelphia, and from 1967 onward, a second office in New York City. Between 1962 and 1966 Giurgola was on the Philadelphia City Planning Commission as a design consultant. The firm's buildings have received numerous architectural awards, and in 1976 they received the AIA Architectural Firm Award. Giurgola has written numerous articles and coauthored one book, *Louis I. Kahn* (1975). Individual distinctions have included the National Institute of Arts and Letters, Arnold Brunner Award, "Commendatore" of the Republic of Italy, and member of the American Academy and the Accademia Nazionale di San Luca.

For Giurgola two seminal influences can be defined: his Italian background and Louis I. Kahn. His youth in Italy left Giurgola with a view of architecture as an intensely urban art form. The building, whether in the city or the country, is not a definable, autonomous entity but a complex overlapping of the site, experience, and history. About Rome of his youth he has written:

> The real molder was the atmosphere, working with those flying forms, shaping the profile of buildings and streets into precise pieces of sky. There was a huge door, I remember, the door of a church—shades and half shades, a long way

---

1   Citation.

to it. Turns, ramps, long steps (so long for a child), bollards, chains, then a heavy mat at the entrance, and now a memory of a big effort to lift the mat to enter. Across the threshold, there was silence within the darkness, then suddenly, the silent stream of a sun ray from the lantern above into the round space, brushing the molding and sculptures—a sun ray, like Quasimodo said, waiting to be climbed.[2]

In Philadelphia in the 1950s he became an intimate friend of Louis Kahn's. Kahn's and Giurgola's architectural leanings and predominantly beauxarts proclivities were mutual, though Kahn as elder statesman of American architecture—though separate from the radical-modernist mainstream of the period—was undoubtedly the leader. Through a series of buildings and projects of the late 1950s and 1960s Giurgola developed a position that became independent of Kahn, though they both became known leaders of the Philadelphia school. The process of forming a building through deep introspection and references to context and history is common to both. For Giurgola the primary act is to make a place, to create feeling and space as identifiable, though at the same time part of the surrounding fabric. Giurgola's buildings stand out, but never aggressively so. The strategies to handle this have been refined by Mitchell/Giurgola over the years and include clearly marked but changeable paths through the building, inflected façades, and strong

geometry that picks up and then refines and comments upon its neighbors. Certain trademarks of radical modernism, from exposed structure and glass walls to pipe railings, do make an appearance—never as dogma, but rather as a specific solution to the problem.

The Sherman Fairchild Center at Columbia University is basically an insertion of a large, bulky building into the original McKim-designed campus that over the years had been overbuilt and altered by insensitive buildings (Plate 23). The Giurgola structure restates the varying modular grid of the campus and buildings through its double wall, while at the same time indicating the varying programmatic changes on its own interior. The hung-tile outer skin does not attempt to exactly replicate the surrounding materials which vary from brick to granite; rather it is a subtle comment on the varying materials. Giurgola's fear of "slickness' is evident; the tile panels outlined by white-enameled aluminum trim add verticle texture and interest in much the same way as the older McKim-designed buildings do, but it is purely a modern interpretation. And what appears in daytime to be a flat surface with voids reverses itself at night when the building is fully lighted to become a positive space overlaid by an anonymous skin. His architecture is a deflected classicism, strongly geometrical and ordered and yet sensitive to its users and the surroundings.

The 1982 Gold Medal to Giurgola reflects the continued reorientation of American architecture away from radical modernism and toward a new synthesis of environment and history.

---

2   Romaldo Giurgola, "Architecture, the Impetus to Build," *The Christian Science Monitor*, April 21, 1977.

Mitchell/Giurgola: Sherman Fairchild Center for the Life Sciences, Columbia University. New York, 1977.

Mitchell/Giurgola/Thorp: Parliament House Competition, Canberra, Australia, House of Representatives, 1979–1980.

NATHANIEL ALEXANDER OWINGS

AWARDED ON MAY 25, 1983
AT THE HILTON HOTEL
NEW ORLEANS, LOUISIANA

Nathaniel Alexander Owings.

His drive, imagination and sense of mission inspired many of America's most brilliant designers; his professional skill and social commitment have enriched major urban design projects from San Francisco's Market Street to Washington's Pennsylvania Avenue; his love of nature and wildlife and his insistence on their preservation have made him a friend of all who value this nation's precious natural heritage.[1]

The forty-fourth Gold Medal awarded in 1983 to Nathaniel Owings confirms earlier directions and also recognizes some of the substantive changes that have occurred in architecture in the past fifteen years. His Gold Medal is the second to go to one of the founders of Skidmore, Owings & Merrill, and as such it is the first to recognize the multiple personalities necessary in any successful architectural practice. At Skidmore, Owings & Merrill he guided the firm to a preeminence unequaled as creator of buildings such as Lever House, the United States Air Force Academy, Inland Steel, and Chase Manhattan Bank, structures that have been seminal landmarks of radical modernism. Yet Owings has come to question some of the dogmas of radical modernism and to express the need for conserving both the natural and the manmade environment. His accomplishments include different areas, as he has claimed: conservation; historic preservation; Skidmore, Owings & Merrill; and Pennsylvania Avenue in Washington, D.C.[2]

Nathaniel Owings was born in Indianapolis, Indiana, in 1903. His midwestern upbringing imbued him with a respect for the land and hard work and a suspicion of the destructive capacities of large cities. In 1920 he won a Rotary Club trip to Europe, and through visits to Chartres, Notre Dame, and Mont-Saint-Michel he discovered architecture. He entered architecture school at the University of Illinois, and after a sickness caused him to withdraw, he completed his training at Cornell University in 1927. In New York City he worked for York & Sawyer; he recalls that, "At that time architect Bertram Gros-

venor Goodhue was my hero."[3]

In 1929, Owings met Louis Skidmore and their life-long partnership began. They became involved in the Century of Progress Exposition in Chicago and subsequently, in 1936, set up a partnership with offices in Chicago and New York. In 1939, John Merrill, an engineer, joined them. They wanted to create a "modern 'Gothic Builders Guild'"—an architectural practice in which individual talents would give way to the goal of a full-service office that could "influence social and environmental conditions."[4]

The firm began to prosper especially during World War II and the great public, military, and commercial building boom that followed. Owings has said, "I as an individual cannot point to any major building for which I am solely responsible."[5] Indeed he was not the designer, but a facilitator. As Gordon Bunshaft points out: "He's very good at—I hate to use the word, he hates it, too—selling." Another partner, Bruce Graham, has said: "He was a new breed of architect in that he created opportunities for architecture out of nothing."[6] With both Skidmore and Owings on the road as salesmen, and John Merrill handling the engineering end, the firm

1 Citation.

2 Personal communication, June 1, 1983.

3 Nathaniel Owings, *The Spaces In Between,* Houghton Mifflin, Boston, 1973, p. 37.

4 Ibid. p. 66.

5 Ibid. p. viii.

6 "Owings Selected as AIA's 44th Gold Medalist," *AIA Journal,* vol. 72, January 1983, pp. 13, 15.

was able to hire a group of talented designers. Key to the firm's success were the devotion to modern planning and design—at first the International Style—and the office organization that involved a partner, a project manager, and a designer as a unified team.

In retrospect, while designs such as Lever House were very significant in an image-making sense, the large-scale projects such as Oak Ridge, Tennessee, 1942–1946, and the United States Air Force Academy, 1954–1962, were the most significant. These projects, along with a term as chairman of the Chicago Plan Commission, 1948–1951, ultimately led Owings to question and then renounce certain aspects of modern architecture. Owings described his views in 1971: "I feel like a reformed hunter. We should create a non-building program for all of our cities, and open up our spaces, get rid of the automobile in our downtown centers and encourage human activities."[7]

After his second marriage, to Margaret Wentworth, in the late 1950s Owings began a spiritual regenesis. He moved to Big Sur, California, and became involved in a fight against the placement of a four-lane highway down the coast. At the same time he also worked for the restoration of Las Trampas Chruch, an adobie structure in New Mexico, and was appointed by President John F. Kennedy as chairman of the Advisory Council on Pennsylvania Avenue in Washington, D.C. The result was a new career as a spokesman and activist for conservation and historic preservation, at a time when the nation was appallingly unconcerned. Indeed, Owings was the first major architectural figure to take such a strong stand and to admit "the

fallacies of our existing way of life."[8] His *The American Aesthetic* (1969) can be regarded as a seminal statement of the environmentalist movement.

In 1964, Owings presented President Lyndon B. Johnson with a set of recommendations for Pennsylvania Avenue, and then in 1965 he became chairman of the newly created Pennsylvania Avenue Commission. In 1972 the Pennslvania Avenue Development Commission was established; Owings served as a board member until 1978. He was largely responsible for the underground placement of the superhighway in front of the Capitol and the design of the Capitol Reflecting Pool and Constitution Gardens. He conceived of returning the Mall to pedestrians and closing roads used mainly as parking lots. Over time some of Owings's original grand schemes for Pennsylvania Avenue have been modified, yet without his initial drive and belief in the importance of the project nothing would have ever happened.

Owings's involvement in the problem of superhighways and their capacity to destroy cities caused him to lead a long fight to keep the Interstate Highway out of downtown Baltimore. For Owings such activities are the special providence of the architect, and typically he used his Gold Medal acceptance speech to call for the AIA to lead the fight against "the accelerating corruption of our habitat. An abyss has been created between . . . the recognized environmentalist movements and the public enterprises which often are unwisely blind to anything but the dollar. This abyss must be bridged. And it can be bridged best through the leadership of a trained architect-planner."[9]

For Owings architecture is far more than style or buildings, but the relationship of humanity to its planet. Of the Gold Medal award he said: "I am very happy to have received this honor. I consider myself a member of the kind of common man department. I'm not an I. M. Pei, not an Alvar Aalto, not a Frank Lloyd Wright. My field has been the conceptual field, the broad scope."[10]

7   Benjamin Forgey, "Owings Gets AIA Award," *The Washington Post*, December 3, 1982, p. E6.

8   Nathaniel Owings, *The American Aesthetic*, Harper & Row, New York, 1969, p. 16.

9   Nathaniel Owings, Gold Medal acceptance speech, May 25, 1983, p. 4.

10   Forgey, op. cit., p. E6.

President's Advisory Council on Pennsylvania Avenue, 1964, drawings of "National Square," Washington, D. C.

Source Material

In addition to the references already cited in the footnotes, the following materials are important biographical sources.

Sir Aston Webb

Basic biographical information is rare; information was gleaned from:
Creswell, H. B.: "Seventy Years Back," *Architectural Review*, vol. 124, December 1958, pp. 403–405.

"Sir Aston Webb, R.A., FRIBA, F.S.A.," handwritten résumé, AIA Archives, Washington, D.C., ca 1906.

Charles Follen McKim

A Monograph of the Works of McKim, Mead & White, Architectural Book Publishing, New York, 1915, reprinted 1973.

Baldwin, Charles: *Stanford White*, Dodd, Mead, New York, 1931.

Moore, Charles: *The Life and Times of Charles Follen McKim*, Houghton Mifflin, Boston, 1929.

Reilly, Charles H.: *McKim, Mead & White*, Ernest Benn, London, 1924.

Roth, Leland: "The Urban Architecture of McKim, Mead & White," Ph.D. thesis, Yale University, New Haven, 1973.

Wilson, Richard Guy: "Charles F. McKim and the Rise of the Renaissance in America," Ph.D. thesis, University of Michigan, Ann Arbor, 1972.

George Browne Post

Sturgis, Russell: "Great American Architects Series: George B. Post," *Architectural Record*, Supplement, May 1895, pp. 1–111.

Weisman, Winston: "The Commercial Architecture of George B. Post," *Journal of the Society of Architectural Historians*, vol. 31, October 1972, pp. 176–203.

Jean Louis Pascal

Cook, Walter F.: "Jean Louis Pascal—Institute Gold Medalist, 1913," *Journal of the AIA*, vol. 3, January 1915, pp. 19–26.

Curinier, C. E. (ed.): *Dictionnaire national des contemporains*, Office general d'édition, Paris, n.d. [1899], pp. 197–198.

Drexler, Arthur (ed.): *The Architecture of the École des Beaux-Arts*, Museum of Modern Art, New York, 1977, pp. 236–237.

"Jean-Louis Pascal: An Appreciation," and "Sir John Burnet's Memories of Pascal," *The Architect's Journal*, vol. 51, June 2, 1920, pp. 693, 709–710.

"The Royal Gold Medalist, 1914," *Journal of the Royal Institute of British Architects*, ser. 3, vol. 31, June 27, 1914, pp. 533–543.

Victor Laloux

Cox, H. Bartle: "M. Victor Laloux: The Man and His Work," *The Architect's Journal*, vol. 51, April, May, June 1920, pp. 555–557, 609–611, 639–640, 731–732.

Curinier, C. E. (ed.): *Dictionnaire*, op. cit., vol. 2, n.d. [1907], pp. 36–37.

Delaire, E.: *Les Architectes élèves de l'École des Beaux-Arts, 1793–1907*, Librairie de la Construction Moderne, Paris, 1907.

Drexler, Arthur (ed.): *The Architecture*, op. cit., pp. 459–463, 501.

Hautecoeur, Louis: *Histoire de l'architecture classique en France, 1848–1900*, vol. 7, A. Picard, Paris, 1957, pp. 438–442.

"Homage à Laloux de ses élèves américains," *Pencil Points*, vol. 18, October 1937, pp. 621–630.

The American Architect, vol. 28, May 31, 1890, p. 126, and vol. 151, September 1937, pp. 138, 140.

Henry Bacon

Conklin, Edward: *The Lincoln Memorial, Washington*, U.S. Government Printing Office, Washington, D.C., 1927.

Cram, Ralph Adams: "The Lincoln Memorial, Washington, D.C., Henry Bacon, Architect," *Architectural Record*, vol. 53, June 1923, pp. 479–508.

Selden, Ruth Ryley: "Henry Bacon and His Work at Wesleyan University," Master's thesis, University of Virginia, Charlottesville, 1974.

Swales, Francis S.: "Henry Bacon as a Draftsman," *Pencil Points*, vol. 5, May 1924, pp. 42–62.

Sir Edwin Landseer Lutyens

Butler, A. S. G.: *The Architecture of Sir Edwin Lutyens*, 3 vols., Country Life, London, 1950.

Hussey, Christopher: *The Life of Sir Edwin Lutyens*, Country Life, London, 1950.

Greenberg, Allan: "Lutyens's Architecture Restudied," *Perspecta*, vol. 12, 1969, pp. 129–152.

Inskip, Peter: *Edwin Lutyens*, Architectural Monographs 6, London, 1979.

Irving, Robert Grant: *Indian Summer: Lutyens, Baker and Imperial Delhi*, Yale University Press, New Haven, 1981.

Lutyens, Mary, *Edwin Lutyens, a Memoir by His Daughter*, John Murray, London, 1980.

Lutyens: The Work of the English Architect Sir Edwin Lutyens (1869–1944), Arts Council of Great Britain, London, 1981.

Weaver, Lawrence: *Houses and Gardens by Sir Edwin Lutyens*, Country Life, London, 1913.

Bertram Grosvenor Goodhue

Cram, Ralph Adams: *My Life in Architecture*, Little, Brown, Boston, 1936.

Goodhue, Bertram Grosvenor: *A Book of Architectural and Decorative Drawings*, Architectural Book Co., New York, 1914.

Whitaker, Charles Harris (ed.): *Bertram Grosvenor Goodhue—Architect and Master of Many Arts*, Architectural Book Co., New York, 1925.

Howard Van Doren Shaw

Dart, Susan: *Evelyn Shaw McCutcheon and Ragdale*, Lake Bluff Historical Society, Lake Forest, 1980.

Eaton, Leonard K.: *Two Chicago Architects and Their Clients: Frank Lloyd Wright and Howard Van Doren Shaw*, MIT Press, Cambridge, 1969.

Talmadge, Thomas: "Howard Van Doren Shaw," *Architectural Record*, vol. 60, July 1926, p. 73.

Milton Bennett Medary

Bright, John Irwin: "Milton Bennett Medary—Memorial Section," *T-Square Club Yearbook*, Philadelphia, 1929.

Eley, Jeff: "The Architecture of Milton B. Medary," Master's thesis, University of Virginia, Charlottesville, 1982.

"Milton B. Medary, F.A.I.A. 1874–1929," *The American Architect*, vol. 136, September 1929, p. 218.

Ragnar Östberg

Cornell, Elias: *Ragnar Östberg*, Byggmastarens Forlag, Stockholm, 1965.

Wilson, Richard Guy: "Ragnar Östberg," *AIA Journal*, vol. 71, August 1982, pp. 52–57.

Paul Philippe Cret

Grossman, Elizabeth: "The Architecture of Paul Cret," Ph.D. thesis, Brown University, Providence, R.I., 1980.

McDonald, Travis C.: "Modernized Classicism: The Architecture of Paul Philippe Cret in Washington, D.C.," Master's thesis, University of Virginia, Charlottesville, 1980.

"Paul Cret," *Federal Architect*, vol. 14, Final Number, 1946, entire issue.

Reid, Kenneth: "Paul Philippe Cret, Master of Design," *Pencil Points,* vol. 19, October 1938, pp. 608–638.

Swales, F. S.: "Draftsmanship and Architecture as Exemplified by the Work of Paul Philippe Cret" *Pencil Points,* vol. 9, November 1928, pp. 688–704.

White, Theo B.: *Paul Philippe Cret: Architect and Teacher,* Art Alliance, Philadelphia, 1973.

Louis Henry Sullivan

Bush-Brown, Albert: *Louis Sullivan,* Brazillier, New York, 1960.

Morrison, Hugh: *Louis Sullivan: Prophet of Modern Architecture,* W. W. Norton, New York, 1935.

Wright, Frank Lloyd: *Genius and the Mobocracy,* Horizon, New York, 1949.

Eliel Saarinen

Christ-Janer, Albert: *Eliel Saarinen: Finnish-American and Educator,* University of Chicago Press, Chicago, 1979.

Pound, Arthur: *The Only Thing Worth Finding: The Life and Legacies of George Gough Booth,* Wayne State University Press, Detroit, 1964.

Saarinen, Eliel, *Munksnas-Haga,* Lilius & Hertzberg, Helsinki, 1915.

————: *Search for Form,* Reinhold, New York, 1948.

————: *The City: Its Growth, Its Decay, Its Future,* Reinhold, New York, 1943.

Tilghman, Donnell: "Eliel Saarinen," *Architectural Record,* vol. 63, May 1928, pp. 393–408, 413–427.

Charles Donagh Maginnis

Adams, Rayen: "Maginnis and Walsh," *Architecture,* vol. 63, April 1931, pp. 199–204.

Baxter, Sylvester: "A Selection from the Works of Maginnis & Walsh, Architects," *Architectural Record,* vol. 53, February 1923, pp. 93–115.

Byrne, Barry: "An Appreciation," *Liturgical Arts,* vol. 5, March 1936, pp. 90–104.

"Charles Donagh Maginnis, 1867–1955," *Liturgical Arts,* vol 23, August 1955, pp. 152–155.

Frank Lloyd Wright

Hitchcock, H.-R.: *In the Nature of Materials,* Dwell, Sloan & Pearce, New York, 1942.

Manson, Grant C.: *Frank Lloyd Wright to 1910,* Reinhold, New York, 1958.

Smith, Norris Kelley: *Frank Lloyd Wright, A Study in Architectural Content,* American Life Foundation, Watkins Glen, N.Y., 1979.

Twombly, Robert C.: *Frank Lloyd Wright,* Harper & Row, New York, 1979.

Wright, Frank Lloyd: *Autobiography,* Longman & Greens, London, 1932.

————: *The Future of Architecture,* Horizon, New York, 1953.

————: *The Natural House,* Horizon, New York, 1954.

————: *A Testament,* Horizon, New York, 1957.

————: *The Living City,* Horizon, New York, 1958.

Sir Patrick Abercrombie

Dix, Gerald: "Little Plans and Noble Diagrams," *Town Planning Review,* vol. 49, July 1978, pp. 329–352.

————: "Patrick Abercrombie: Pioneer of Planning," *Architectural Review,* vol. 166, August 1979, pp. 130–132.

Bernard Ralph Maybeck

Cardwell, Kenneth H.: *Bernard Maybeck, Artisan, Architect, Artist,* Peregrine Smith, Santa Barbara, 1977.

Jordy, William H., *American Building and Their Architects: Progressive and Academic Ideals at the Turn of the 20th Century,* Doubleday, New York, 1972.

Maybeck, Bernard Ralph: *Palace of Fine Arts and Lagoon,* P. Elder, San Francisco, 1915.

McCoy, Esther: *Five California Architects,* Reinhold, New York, 1960.

Sargeant, Winthrop: *Geniuses, Goddesses and People,* E. P. Dutton, New York, 1949.

Auguste Perret

Champigneulle, Bernard: *Perret,* Arts et Métiers Graphiqes, Paris, 1959.

Collins, Peter: *Concrete: The Vision of a New Architecture; A Study of Auguste Perret and His Precursors,* Faber & Faber, London 1959.

William Adams Delano

Bottomley, W. L.: "A Selection for the Works of Delano and Aldrich Drawings by Chester B. Price," *Architectural Record,* vol. 54, July 1923, pp. 3–71.

Delano, William Adams: "Memoirs of Centurian Architects," *Journal of the AIA,* vol. 10, July 1948, pp. 81–87; August 1948, pp. 3–9; September 1948, 130–136; October 1948, pp. 180–184.

Portraits of Ten Country Houses Designed by Delano and Arldrich, Drawn by Chester Price, W. Heldorn, New York, 1924.

Willem Marinus Dudok

Cramer, Max, Hans van Grieken, and Heleen Prone: *W. M. Dudok 1884–1972,* Stichting Architectuur Museum, Amsterdam, 1981.

Wilson, Richard Guy: "Willem Dudok," *AIA Journal,* vol. 71, August 1982, pp. 44–51.

Clarence Samuel Stein

"Clarence Stein Remembered," *AIA Journal,* vol. 65, December 1976, with articles by Lewis Mumford (pp. 19–28), Marjie Baughman (pp. 30–31), and Douglas Haskell (pp. 32–33).

Dal Co, Francesco: "From Parks to the Region: Progressive Ideology and the Reform of the American City," in G. Ciucci (ed.), *The American City,* MIT Press, Cambridge, 1980.

Lubove, Roy: *Community Planning in the 1930s,* University of Pittsburg Press, Pittsburg, 1963.

Sussman, Carl (ed.): *Planning the Fourth Migration: The Neglected Vision of the Regional Planning Association of America,* MIT Press, Cambridge, 1976.

Ralph Walker

Bosserman, Joseph Norwood: *Ralph Walker Bibliography,* Publication 17, American Association of Architectural Bibliographers, Charlottesville, Va., 1960.

Walker, Ralph: *Ralph Walker, Architect,* Henahan House, New York, 1957.

75th Anniversary, Voorhees, Walker, Smith, Smith & Haires, New York, 1960.

Louis Skidmore

Danz, Ernest: *Architecture of Skidmore, Owings & Merrill, 1950–1962,* introduction by H.-R. Hitchcock, Praeger, New York, 1963.

Owings, Nathaniel, *The Spaces Between,* Houghton Mifflin, Boston, 1973.

Skidmore Papers, Library of Congress.

Woodward, Christopher: *The Architecture of Skidmore, Owings & Merrill,* Simon & Schuster, New York, 1971.

John Wellborn Root II

Breugmann, Robert: "Holabird & Roche and Holabird & Root: The First Two Generations," *Chicago History,* vol. 9, Fall 1980, pp. 130–165.

"Holabird & Root," *Inland Architect,* vol. 20, July 1976, entire issue.

Laine, Christian K.: "Holabird and Root: A Heritage of Drawing," *Inland Architect,* vol. 24, December 1980, pp. 6–15.

Reed, Earl H. Jr.: "Some Recent Work of Holabird and Root, Architects" *Architecture,* vol. 61, January 1930, pp. 1–38.

Whitehead, Russell F.: "Holabird and Root: Masters of Design," *Pencil Points,* vol. 19, February 1938, pp. 67–95.

Wilson, Richard Guy: "Holabird & Root: Century of (Intermittent) Progress," *AIA Journal,* vol. 72, February 1983, pp. 43–51.

Walter Adolph Gropius

The Architects' Collaborative, 1945–1965, Gustavo Gili, Barcelona, 1966.

Fitch, James Marston: *Walter Gropius,* Braziller, New York, 1960.

Franciscono, Marcel: *Walter Gropius and the Creation of the Bauhaus in Weimar,* University of Illinois Press, Urbana, 1971.

Giedion, Sigfried: *Walter Gropius, Work and Team Work,* Reinhold, New York, 1954.

Winger, Hans: *Bauhaus,* MIT Press, Cambridge, 1972.

Ludwig Mies van der Rohe

Carter, Peter: *Mies van der Rohe at Work,* Praeger, New York, 1974.

Glaeser, Ludwig: *Ludwig Mies van der Rohe: Drawings in the Collection of the Museum of Modern Art,* Museum of Modern Art, New York, 1969.

Hilberseimer, Ludwig: *Mies van der Rohe,* Paul Theobald, Chicago, 1956.

Johnson, Philip: *Mies van der Rohe,* 3d ed., Museum of Modern Art, New York, 1978.

Spaeth, David: *Ludwig Mies van der Rohe: An Annotated Bibliography and Chronology,* Garland, New York, 1979.

Le Corbusier

In addition to Le Corbusier's own writings, see:

Blake, Peter: *Le Corbusier: Architecture and Form,* Penguin, Baltimore, 1963.

Choay, Françoise: *Le Corbusier,* Braziller, New York, 1960.

Jencks, Charles: *Le Corbusier and the Tragic View of Architecture,* Harvard University Press, Cambridge, 1971.

Serenyi, Peter (ed.): *Le Corbusier in Perspective,* Prentice-Hall, Englewood Cliffs, N.J., 1975.

Eero Saarinen

Dean, Andrea O.: "Eero Saarinen in Perspective," *AIA Journal,* vol. 70, November 1981, pp. 36–51.

Halik, Nancy Lickerman: "The Eero Saarinen Spawn," *Inland Architect,* vol. 25, May 1981, pp. 15–52.

McQuade, Walter: "Eero Saarinen, A Complete Architect," *Architectural Forum,* vol. 116, April 1962, pp. 102–119.

Saarinen, Aline B. (ed.): *Eero Saarinen on His Work: A Selection of Buildings Dating from 1947 to 1964 with Statements by the Architect,* Yale University Press, New Haven, 1968.

Spade, Rupert: *Eero Saarinen,* Simon & Schuster, New York, 1971.

Temko, Allan: *Eero Saarinen,* Braziller, New York, 1962.

Alvar Aalto

"Alvar Aalto," *Arkkitehti,* vol. 73, July/August 1976, pp. 18–79.

Fleig, Karl (ed.): *Alvar Aalto,* 3 vols., Verlag fur Architektur, Zurich, 1963, 1971, 1978.

Hoesli, Bernhard (ed.): *Alvar Aalto Synopsis: Painting, Architecture, Sculpture,* Birkhauser, Basel, 1970.

Ruusuvuori, Aarno (ed.): *Alvar Aalto 1898–1976,* Museum of Finnish Architecture, Helsinki, 1978.

Schildt, Goran (ed.): *Alvar Aalto: Sketches,* Stuart Wrede, trans., MIT Press, Cambridge, 1978.

Pier Luigi Nervi

Desideri, Paolo, Pier Luigi Nervi, Jr., and Giuseppe Positano: *Pier Luigi Nervi,* Serie di Architettura no. 5, Zanichelli Editore, Bologna, 1979.

Huxtable, Ada Louis: *Pier Luigi Nervi,* Braziller, New York, 1960.

Joedicke, Jurgen, and Ernesto Rogers: *The Works of Pier Luigi Nervi,* Praeger, New York, 1957.

Lagorio, Henry J.: *Pier Luigi Nervi: Space, Structure and Integrity,* San Francisco Museum of Art, San Francisco, 1961.

Kenzo Tange

Boyd, Robin, *Kenzo Tange,* Braziller, New York, 1962.

"Kenzo Tange & Urtec," *Space Design: SD,* no, 184, January 1980, entire issue.

Wallace Kirkman Harrison

Much of this bibliography is based on personal communication. Other sources include:

"Art, Cheops' Architect," *Time,* September 22, 1952.

Goldberger, Paul: "Wallace K. Harrison Obituary," *The New York Times,* December 3, 1981, p. 1, D20.

Thomsen, Charles: "Professional Spokesman for a Complex Society," *AIA Journal,* vol. 47, May 1967, 121–124.

———: "The Making of an Architect," *AIA Journal,* vol. 48, August 1967, pp. 73–78.

Wind, Herbert Warren: "Profile," *The New Yorker,* November 20, November 27, and December 4, 1954.

Marcel Lajos Breuer

Blake, Peter, (ed.): *Marcel Breuer, Sun and Shadow,* Dodd, Mead, New York, 1946.

Marcel Breuer Buildings and Projects, 1921–1961, introduction by Cranston Jones, Praeger, New York, 1962.

Papchristou, Tician: *Marcel Breuer: New Buildings and Projects, 1960–1970,* Praeger, New York, 1970.

Wilk, Christopher: *Marcel Breuer: Furniture and Interiors,* Museum of Modern Art, New York, 1981.

William Wilson Wurster

Grotz, Paul: "William Wurster Portfolio," *Architectural Forum,* vol. 19, August 1958, pp. 45–65.

"Meet William Wurster," *House Beautiful,* vol. 87, June 1945, pp. 68–89.

Peters, Richard C.: "The Integrity Is Implicit: The Sincerity Intense," *AIA Journal,* vol. 51, May 1969, pp. 72–78.

———: "William Wilson Wurster: An Architecture of Houses," in Sally Woodbridge (ed.), *Bay Area Houses,* Oxford University Press, New York, 1976.

Richard Buckminster Fuller

"The Dymaxion American," *Time,* January 10, 1964.

Fuller, F. Buckminster, and Robert Marks: *The Dymaxion World of Buckminster Fuller,* Doubleday, New York, 1973.

Kenner, Hugh: *Bucky: A Guided Tour of Buckminster Fuller,* Wm. Morrow, New York, 1973.

McHale, John: "Buckminster Fuller," *Architectural Review,* vol. 120, July 1956, pp. 12–20.

———: *R. Buckminster Fuller,* Braziller, New York, 1962.

Tomkins, Calvin: "Profile," *The New Yorker,* January 8, 1966.

"The World of Buckminster Fuller," *Architectural Forum,* vol. 136, January/February 1972, pp. 49–96.

Louis Isidore Kahn

Chang, Ching-Yu (ed.): "Louis I. Kahn: Memorial Issue," *Architecture and Urbanism,* A & U Publishing, Tokyo, 1975.

Giurgola, Romaldo, and Maimini Mehta: *Louis I. Kahn,* Westview Press, Boulder, 1975.

Ronner, Heinz, Sharad Jhaveri, and Alessandro Vasella (eds.): *Louis I Kahn: Complete Works, 1935–1974,* Westview Press, Boulder, 1977.

Pietro Belluschi

Gubitosi, Camillo, and Alberto Izzo: *Pietro Belluschi, Buildings and Plans, 1932–1973,* Officina Edizioni, Rome, 1974.

Chenoweth, Art: "Pietro Belluschi: The Architect as Prophet," *Northwest Magazine,* December 5, 1976, pp. 14–18.

Griffin, Rachael (ed.): *Oregon Chruches by Pietro Belluschi,* Contemporary Crafts Association, Portland, 1979.

Kay, Jane Holtz: "Architect Pietro Belluschi: Broker between Budgets and Beauty," *The Boston Globe Sunday Magazine,* May 14, 1972, pp. 6–7, 26–29.

Stubblebine, Jo (ed.): *The Northwest Architecture of Pietro Belluschi,* F. W. Dodge, New York, 1953.

Richard Josef Neutra

"Architect Richard Neutra," *Time,* August 15, 1949, pp. 58–66.

Boesiger, Willy, (ed.): *Richard Neutra: Buildings and Projects,* 3 vols., Praeger, New York, 1951, 1959, 1966.

Drexler, Arthur, and Thomas S. Hines: *The Architecture of Richard Neutra: From International Style to California Modern,* Museum of Modern Art, New York, 1982.

Harris, Harwell Hamilton: "AIA Gold Medal, First in Five Years, Awarded to Neutra," *North Carolina Architect,* vol. 15, May/June 1977, pp. 8–11.

Hines, Thomas S., *Richard Neutra and the Search for Modern Architecture,* Oxford University Press, New York, 1982.

McCoy, Esther: *Richard Neutra,* Braziller, New York, 1960.

———: *Vienna to Los Angeles: Two Journeys,* Arts and Architecture Press, Santa Monica, 1979.

Neutra, Richard: *Life and Shape,* Appleton-Century-Crofts, New York, 1962.

Philip Cortelyou Johnson

Goldberger, Paul: "Philip Johnson: A Controversial New Vision for Architecture," *The New York Times Magazine,* May 14, 1978, pp. 26–27, 65–73.

Hitchcock, H.-R.: *Philip Johnson Architecture, 1949–1965,* Holt, Rinehart & Winston, New York, 1966.

Jacobus, John: *Philip Johnson,* Braziller, New York, 1962.

Johnson, Philip: "House at New Canaan, Connecticut," *Architectural Review,* vol. 108, September 1950, pp. 152–159.

———: *Writings,* Oxford University Press, New York, 1979.

Miller, Nory: *Johnson/Burgee Architecture,* Random House, New York, 1979.

Tomkins, Calvin: "Profiles: Forms under Light," *The New Yorker,* May 23, 1977, pp. 45–79.

Ieoh Ming Pei

The biography was prepared with information supplied by I. M. Pei and his office. Additional source material includes:

Blake, Peter: "I. M. Pei & Partners," *Architecture Plus,* vol. 1, March 1973, pp. 20–78.

Goldberger, Paul: "Winning Ways of I. M. Pei," *The New York Times Magazine,* May 20, 1979, pp. 24–27, 116–124.

Josep Lluis Sert

Borras, Maria Llusia (ed.): *Sert: Mediterranean Architecture,* New York Graphic Society, Boston, 1974.

Freita, Jamie: *Josep L. Sert,* Gustavo Gili, Barcelona, 1979.

Zevi, Bruno: *Sert's Architecture in the Miro Foundation,* Ediciones Poligrafa, Barcelona, 1976.

Romaldo Giurgola

In addition supplied by Giurgola in personal interviews, see:

"Mitchell/Giurgola Architects," *Process: Architecture,* 2, October 1977, pp. 1–267.

Nathaniel Alexander Owings

In addition to information supplied by Owings and the firm of Skidmore, Owings & Merrill, see:

"The Architects from 'Skid's Row,' " *Fortune,* January 1958, pp. 3–10.

Drexler, Authur, and Menges, Axel: *Architecture of Skidmore, Owings & Merrill, 1963–1973,* Architectural Book Publishing Co., New York, 1974.

"To Cherish rather than Destroy," *Time,* August 2, 1968, pp. 39–43.

Danz, Ernest: *Architecture of Skidmore, Owings & Merrill, 1950–1962,* introduction by H.-R. Hitchcock, Praeger, New York, 1963.

Owings, Nathaniel: *The Spaces In Between,* Houghton Mifflin, Boston, 1973.

Woodward, Christopher: *The Architecture of Skidmore, Owings & Merrill,* Simon & Schuster, New York, 1971.

Gold Medal presentation to Sir
Patrick Abercrombie, Mayflower
Hotel, Washington, D.C., May 12,
1950. On right, Ralph Walker, AIA
president.

Haines, Lundberg & Waehler

THE GOLD MEDAL AT SEVENTY-FIVE

The seventy-fifth anniversary of the AIA Gold Medal marks not the end of an architectural epoch or the date of a momentous reorientation, but a time for stocktaking. This volume has attempted to explicate the reasons why the Gold Medal was awarded. As indicated, the honor has been for many types of accomplishment: education, theory, organization, service, and design. While there have been many peripheral issues, all of the Gold Medalists have been involved in the real world of architecture, of getting commissions and seeing them completed. Naturally such a study does raise the expectation of an assessment: What does the Gold Medal mean?

The Gold Medal has never been awarded by the board of directors of the AIA with the notion of stylistic or architectural consistency. The award has fluctuated between men as diverse as Charles Donagh Maginnis in 1948, Frank Lloyd Wright in 1949, and Sir Patrick Abercrombie in 1950. Still as this volume indicates, there are certain patterns and affinities that emerge. The shifts in taste and the identification of new trends become increasingly problematical the closer one comes to the present. A future historian may well see very different patterns, especially for the last two decades, for the Gold Medal goes to individuals and not to movements or styles. The closest the medal has come to recognizing an office rather than an individual came with Louis Skidmore's 1957 Gold Medal. Yet Skidmore was very responsible, not as a designer, but as an organizer and promoter, for the seminal Lever House and Connecticut General Life Insurance Company.

Certainly the Gold Medal—as any award—is open to charges of arbitrariness or caprice. The posthumous award appears at times rather dubious. If these individuals were so important, why not honor them while alive? Actually, of the forty-three medals, only six have been posthumous: McKim's and Shaw's were voted upon before their deaths, and Goodhue's and Eero Saarinen's within a year of their passing. More problematical were the awards to Louis Sullivan and Richard Neutra, twenty and seven years, respectively, after their deaths. They were important architects, who significantly challenged traditional perceptions of how architecture was conceived. While the belatedness of Sullivan's and Neutra's recognition can be bemoaned, the awards stand and indicate the conservative nature of the medal.

There are other Gold Medals that might appear dubious. Who remembers Jean-Louis Pascal? Milton B. Medary? Charles Maginnis? or John W. Root II? Certainly, in all cases there can be questions that arise, and the perspective of history might indicate others who fit more clearly our notions of who is important. But therein lies the value of the Gold Medal, for it shows who at the time was considered so important that they should receive the highest honor in American architecture. Fickleness might be applied to some of the Gold Medal awards, but equally fickle is our sense of architectural history, of who is important and why. Our perceptions of importance do change. Charles McKim, after years of being condemned to the dustbins of "unimaginative historical revivals," is all of a sudden being recognized as an imaginative architect who created memorable buildings. Edwin Lutyens, Paul Cret, and Bertram Goodhue were forgotten for years, not even mentioned in supposedly reputable histories of twentieth-century architecture. Today, they are being seriously reexamined and studied, not just by historians but by architects. Awards that might be seen as cautious, such as those to Maginnis or Delano, might with time be seen as remarkably prescient.

The Gold Medal indicates that architecture does not develop in a straight line of evolution, but that there has always been a variety of approaches, some more dominant than others. The idea of a "mainstream" which historians use—and I have used—is at best a tenuous myth and is only a viable concept if it is seen in relation to alternatives and other approaches. Architecture has a certain cyclical nature; it does not proceed by violent revolution, but slow change, though those changes tend to emphasize one idea or approach at the expense of another: structure over history, or axial alignment over asymmetry. Such is the oscillating nature of architecture: What is currently despised will soon again rise in esteem.

While the Gold Medal recognizes individual accomplishments, there is a correlative to that recognition, and that is the issue of promotion and the role of critics, historians, writers, and editors. This study has tried to indicate the major role publications had in shaping the various ideas of modernism from the 1930s to the 1970s. The rise of architectural publications in the nineteenth century, and especially the changes that took place in the 1920s when they began to assume—in concert with certain architects—the arbitration of architectural taste, has had a major impact upon architectural recognition and assumptions of who is important. For no matter how great a building is, if it is not known and made available to a wide audience—wider than that which sees the actual building — it will be unrecognized. The number of buildings that have become recognized landmarks through word of mouth in the period since the advent of mass architectural photojournalism is infinitesimal. In a sense the opposite is the truth — nonbuildings become well known through publicity. Mies van der Rohe's Barcelona Pavilion is a prime example: A small ceremonial pavilion that stood for only a few months in the summer of 1929, it is one of the best-known buildings of the twentieth century, not through experience but through photographs.[1] Another example is the 1893 Chicago world's fair, a plaster-of-paris stage set that became through photographs a model for urban planning. The fact of publication helps to create importance and leads, whether intended or not, to the creation of movements, styles, and groups.

This question of taste, or how it is formed, brings up the issue of the Gold Medal and the idea of architectural popularity or celebrity. Throughout this volume, polls of most-admired buildings have been cited to indicate constants and shifts in architectural taste. A recent 1980 poll of 371 architectural students and 201 practitioners from across the United States indicates the validity of the Gold Medal as an indicator of architectural taste.[2] The groups were asked to name their five favorite architects. The student result was:

1. Frank Lloyd Wright
2. Le Corbusier
3. Alvar Aalto
4. Louis Kahn
5. Ieoh Ming Pei

The practitioners listed:

1. Frank Lloyd Wright
2. Ieoh Ming Pei
3. Philip Johnson
4. Alvar Aalto
5. Louis Kahn

Both groups were also asked to name their favorite buildings, both in the United States and in the world; most interpreted the latter to mean "outside the United States." The overwhelming favorite for both students and practitioners outside the United States was Le Corbusier's Ronchamp. Inside the United States, the student top five were:

1. Falling Water
2. National Gallery, East Building
3. Chrysler Building
4. Kimball Art Museum
5. Philips Exeter Academy Library

The practitioners cited:

1. The National Gallery, East Building
2. Falling Water
3. Seagram Building
4. Dulles International Airport

All of the architects (including those responsible for the buildings, except for the Chrysler) are Gold Medalists, which indicates, in one sense,

Gold Medal presentation to Wallace K. Harrison, New York Hilton, May 18, 1967. On right, Charles M. Nes, Jr., AIA president.

the accuracy of the Gold Medal. But significantly, neither of the two most recent Gold Medalists, Sert and Giurgola, makes an appearance. The Gold Medal is more than a popularity poll; it is an attempt by the AIA to recognize accomplishment and significance.

Who wins the Gold Medal? The first chapter gave a breakdown as to origin, place or practice, and average age of the Gold Medalists. The study has revealed that certain educational backgrounds seem to be of importance, with the École des Beaux-Arts far and away the most important. Similarly there has been a certain lineage between many of the Gold Medalists. George B. Post was trained by and worked briefly for Richard Morris Hunt, the first American to receive the Royal Institute of British Architect's Gold Medal. From McKim's office came Henry Bacon, and later — after McKim's death — Wallace K. Harrison. From Louis Sullivan's office came Frank Lloyd Wright. Richard Neutra worked briefly with Wright. Louis Kahn studied under and worked briefly with Paul Cret, and Romaldo Giurgola was associated informally with Kahn in Philadelphia for a time. Eero Saarinen, of course, worked closely with his father, Eliel, for a number of years. Louis Skidmore worked for Charles Donagh Maginnis in the 1920s. Le Corbusier spent several crucial years in the office of Auguste Perret. Marcel Breuer studied at the Bauhaus under Walter Gropius and later became his partner. I. M. Pei and Philip Johnson studied at Harvard under Breuer and Gropius. And from the office of Bertram Goodhue came Ralph Walker, Clarence Stein, and Wallace K. Harrison.[3] What this indicates is not some incestuous lineage, since in most cases, the "master" and the "pupil" differed widely in what became their predominant architectural expressions, but that talent attracts talent.

The winners of the Gold Medal have been by definition, successes in one form or another. Success can, of course, be measured differently. Some of the Gold Medalists have made handsome livings: Charles F. McKim, George B. Post, Ralph Walker, Wallace K. Harrison, and I. M. Pei, among many. A few brought some inherited wealth with them: Howard Van Doren Shaw, William Adams Delano, and Philip Johnson. And for several, money proved to be a problem: Sullivan died in poverty; Wright was always short

Gold Medal presentation to Romaldo Giurgola, Royal Hawaiian Hotel, June 9, 1982. On left, AIA president Robert Lawrence.

of money and sometimes in court over debts and taxes; and Kahn ran a money-losing office. Yet money is not necessarily a measure of success; there is personal happiness. Of choice, this study has not concentrated upon the personal and intimate lives of the Gold Medalists, yet enough has emerged to make an observation. All of the Gold Medalists were totally dedicated to architecture; that is one of the critical measures of their achievements and successes. Whether they have experienced, as a result of this dedication, more personal anguish with families, broken homes, and unhappiness than the average architect or the average twentieth-century man—whoever that may be—is impossible to tell. Yet success does generally entail singlemindedness to task, a willingness to give up nights at home for the drawing board or airport waiting rooms. Success, as all the Gold Medalists show, is not something easy, but involves dedication, work, and belief in oneself. The reward is frequently the knowledge of success.

The Gold Medal is a record of accomplishment; it is the recognition of forty-three individuals, and by extension, their collaborators, partners, builders, clients, and supporters. The accomplishment varies from theory to education and from structural systems to service to the profession. But above all, the Gold Medal recognizes a dedication to the activity of architecture, of making memorable buildings and spaces and environments wherein human activities not only take place, but are enhanced. The Gold Medalists are remarkable individuals who believed in their vision, and most importantly, accomplished it. They succeeded in uniting art and life as architecture.

Notes

1   Juan Pablo Bonta, *Architecture and its interpretation*, Rizzoli, New York, 1979.

2   Walter F. Wagner, Jr., "Profile of the 1981 Graduates: Conservative, On-track, Main-line Modernists," *Architectural Record*, vol. 169, January 1981, pp. 84–89. A recent poll of American architectural school deans rated I. M. Pei as the "nation's best designer." The remaining top five were: Romaldo Giurgola, Cesar Pelli, Kevin Roche, and Philip Johnson. See *AIA Journal*, vol. 71, June 1982, p. 12.

3   For another interesting study, see Roxanne Williamson, "An Architectural Family Tree That Traces the Paths to Fame," *AIA Journal*, vol. 67, January 1978, pp. 46–48.

INDEX

About the Author

Richard Guy Wilson has lectured at schools and institutions throughout the United States and abroad, and has written numerous articles and reviews for such publications as *Architectural Record, Progressive Architecture*, the *AIA Journal*, and *Winterthur Portfolio*. Mr. Wilson was co-curator of the major museum exhibition "The American Renaissance 1876–1917," seen in New York, Washington, D.C., San Francisco, and Denver in 1979 and 1980. He is the author of the book *McKim, Mead & White, Architects* and co-author of the books *The American Renaissance* and *The Prairie School in Iowa*, and he is currently working on a new exhibition book, *Machine-Age America, 1920–1941*. Currently, Mr. Wilson is Associate Professor of Architecture at Iowa State University and at the University of Virginia.